# JOYFUL misfits

# JOYFUL
## misfits

building a beautiful life in difficult times

# TODD CANTELON

**LIFT INK** publishing
Guelph, Ontario

Follow the author on social @toddcantelon or
at gracecommunity.ca/listen

**LIFT INK** is an imprint of LIFTINC.

Joyful Misfits: *living a beautiful life in difficult times*.

Author Photograph by Michael Dyment.
Designed by Becky Goodwin and Wordzworth Books.
Edited by Lindsay Irvine.
Proofed by Susan Wilks.

ISBN: 978-1-7772425-0-3

To Jesus, who gives this misfit *joy*.

To Niki, who's been waiting patiently for me to finish one of these for *twenty* years.

To Jordan, Sarah, Sam, and Zoë who are the *reason* I do what I do.

To my parents, Jim and Kathy, who told me I *could*.

To Grace, who let me work it out *with them*, in community.

*I love you.*

# CONTENTS

# CHAPTER BREAKDOWN

## 1   Never Enough

In a World where no one ever seems to be satisfied, the message that Jesus is *enough* is more than just counter-cultural, it will place you at odds with the way most people build their lives, turning you into a misfit. So, in a culture that is the victim of an insatiable appetite, let's show you how to find joy; at the Supermarket.

## 2   A Recipe for Livin' Clean

You're going to have to decide whether the Universe is Godless or not. If it's not, then you're going to need to figure out how to *relate* to the God who is the heart of the Universe; and for that, you're going to need holiness. The key to understanding holiness lies in seeing it not as a duty, but as an opportunity. Kind of like a basketball game.

## 3   Love Actually

How will I know if I'm really in love? What about belonging to Jesus; how do I know if it's for real? When purity, obedience, and self-giving love start showing up in your life as a *reflex*. Because the love of God has *reached* to you, you need to learn to do the same and, in so doing, you'll discover the key to finding your way to holiness, and out of the lingerie store in one piece.

## 4   Under Construction

Please forgive the mess, but our beautiful screwed-up lives are *meant* to be a work in progress. As Jesus works on you, and in you, you're going to find yourself sticking out more and more from the people in the World around you. Don't sweat it though because you're also going to find that you're starting to *holy-ize* the World as you submit to Jesus, who *is* the Cornerstone that this new life of yours is being built on.

## 5    Live Different

What does it look like to live different, and if living different is going to make my life difficult, why would I do it? Because, as you do, you're going to learn that you're loved, that you're free and that— contrary to what you've been told—you're *not* the center of the Universe, Jesus is; and He's about to teach you how to change the World, one snowstorm at a time.

## 6    Some Counter-Cultural Advice for Husbands and Wives

The problem at the root of your existence is that you're a rebel. Seeing as that's true (you know it is) how far would you be willing to go to make a change? Would you change your ethics? Your priorities? How about your marriage; would you change that? If your answer is 'Yes!' then get ready to learn how to do the exact *opposite* of what every movie, television show and piece of conventional wisdom you ever got from your peers about staying married told you to do. Big boy and big girl pants are *definitely* needed for this one.

## 7    The Good Life

Surrender is the key to winning because, when you surrender to Jesus, you're surrendering to the Winner. Turns out you're pretty lucky to be His friend so stop trying to get even with everyone who's ever wronged you, and focus on cultivating tenderness instead. Let Him lead, and watch as He makes something beautiful out of your ordinary life.

## 8    Victory Lap

If the story about Jesus is really true, you can *really* build your life on it. The key to Jesus' story is the resurrection, which promises new life and ultimate victory to you because you belong to Him. So, hop on into His backseat, and let Him drive you home, to Glory.

## 9    God's Future is My Future Now

Jesus is the key to changing your mindset so that you can get the most out of life. 'Not my will but Yours be done' is basically what it all comes down to. The moment you adopt a 'God First' mindset is the moment you will find yourself on the way to *really* living because, life is hard, but God is good. Find your satisfaction in God and His beauty will eclipse all lesser beauties in your life and, because His future is your future now, you'll find yourself truly alive.

## 10   Playing for Keeps

Nothing lasts forever, which means, ultimately, you can't win; but you *can* play for keeps. The key is learning to live like you're on borrowed time, like you're the tide, continuously giving and receiving love, from the God Who is a *diamond* (which I'm told, last forever).

## 11   God's Neighbourhood

Suffering is the key to becoming someplace good; particularly learning to suffer *well*. This impossible task is made possible because of Jesus' love for you, because He's made you His friend. The extent to which you *really* believe the story about Jesus is the extent to which you're going to be able to deal with suffering without it stealing your joy.

## 12  Finding Freedom

Everyone wants to be free. Want to know how? Live with urgency; like there are no diminishing returns in God's Kingdom. Live like you don't come first, but have been made by God to do a specific thing as part of His Family, and that's *enough*. Realize that He's got you in the palm of His hand and let that beautiful truth change your perspective so that you no longer live with a 'Me First' mentality but like Humility is your favorite thing to wear. Know your part. Be only who God made you to be and start defining your place in this World by what Jesus has done for you. Remember, you're never alone. You're free.

## 13  The Greatest Do-It-Yourself-Er of All Time

Some things in life you can handle yourself. Others, you're going to need a little help with. Fortunately God, the 'Greatest Do-it-Yourself-er of All Time', has got you by the scruff of your neck and He's never going to leave you alone. You're on His heart, on His mind, and are even being spoken on His lips. Jesus would pick you every time, because He likes misfits, He's in the restoration business, and you, are His *favorite* project.

This is a book about Jesus,
and *your* beautiful, screwed-up life.

# ONE

# Nev**e**r Enough

*It's never enough.*

Do you ever feel that way? No matter how much you get, it's never enough. No matter what you achieve, it's never enough. You buy something new, like the new dress clothes my wife made me buy recently, and hope it will break the cycle. I put them on for the first time, and I still didn't look as good as Brad Pitt.

*It's never enough.*

Chances are this feeling of deep inadequacy is one you experience often. In fact, if our culture is any indication, most of us feel this way *most* of the time.

I took my littlest daughter Zoë to the supermarket to prove it to you.

Turns out even the supermarket is working very hard at convincing you that it's never enough.

*Take the broccoli for example.*

As you enter the produce section at our local supermarket, you're greeted by the broccoli – two kinds of it. On the left is the "organic" broccoli and, on the right, you'll find the pedestrian kind. It's the broccoli that gave me the idea. See, the thing about the broccoli is that the pedestrian kind costs ninety-nine cents a bunch whereas the organic version will set you back $3.99.

*Four times the price.*

Because, as you know deep in your bones, pedestrian broccoli is never enough. We have two types of broccoli, one for the poor folk, the other for those who are "making something" of their lives.

Next the apples.

*Twelve different kinds.*

That's right, *twelve* different kinds of apples. Me? I only buy one kind of apple. Have you ever gone home with a "mix and match," choose-your-own-adventure bag of apples?

"Hey kids, we're going on a World Tour of apples this week!"

Ridiculous.

Yet there they were, twelve different kinds of apples and, when Zoë and I did this experiment, apples weren't even in season! Shiny, wax-covered, *imported* apples, sprayed to keep them spot free, and arranged strategically with the perfect overhead light making them glisten so I'd be tempted to buy them to make my sad excuse for a life just that little bit better.

*Thirty-seven different kinds of bread.*

I'm not making this up.

You'll notice, as we go, that it gets progressively more absurd. Literally every section of the store we explored was worse than the one before. That's when I knew that Jesus had something to teach us that day.

"Who *needs* thirty-seven different kinds of bread (not counting the bagels or English muffins)?"

*Nobody.*

Forty-five toothpastes. Apparently, we all have very stinky breath. There's the extra shiny kind, the "Maxx Fresh" kind (yes, with two x's), and you can even buy one with little "bits of freshness" mixed into it. What exactly *is* a little "bit of freshness"? It's also funny how similar brands all have different nuances to the promises printed on their packaging. Some promise whiteness quicker, some say theirs will last longer; *all* promise you the vibrant love life of a Hollywood starlet if you'll just fork over the cash and get on with it.

*Because it's never enough.*

One hundred and ninety-three different kinds of shampoo.

This is where it started to get a little silly. Because me, when I go to the gym, I just use a bar of soap for everything: hair, body, whatever. Clean is clean.

There are two hundred and four different kinds of chips. It's at this point that I began feeling like we've failed as a culture. Any group of people who will allow and endorse the creation of more than two hundred varieties of chips has clearly lost its way.

At first blush, you'd think the ice-cream makers were working against trend because there are only twenty-three different ice creams, but on closer examination, you lose all hope because there are twenty-three *brands* of ice cream. I especially liked the look of a very fussy progressive type that cost $12.99 for 500ml, and that's when I realized they'd sucked me in.

You see, each brand had between six to ten different types on offer, so we ended up with about two hundred and twenty different kinds of ice cream to choose from.

Broccoli, apples, bread, toothpaste, shampoo, chips and ice cream: proof that everybody's always looking for more, because it's never enough.

*We are the prisoners of an insatiable appetite.*

And don't start thinking you're the exception. You shop at a grocery store just like mine and you've probably thought to yourself, once upon a time, "You know, it *would* be nice to have shinier locks..."

*Enter the Christian Genius.*

The "Way of Jesus" (Christianity) looks at all of us running around buying all of this stuff to fill the emptiness of our souls and says, "You don't need all that ice cream or toothpaste. *All you need is Jesus.*" And that's the point a man who would one day be called "The Bishop of Rome" was trying to make in his book of 1 Peter. You'll see what I mean as we work our way through it.

*All you need is Jesus.*

Keep that in mind.

> *"Peter, an apostle of JESUS Christ, to those who are elect exiles of the Dispersion in Pontus, Galatia, Cappadocia, Asia, and Bithynia, according to the foreknowledge of God the Father, in the sanctification of the Spirit, for obedience to Jesus Christ and for sprinkling with his blood: May grace and peace be multiplied to you. Blessed be the God and Father of our Lord Jesus Christ! According to his great mercy, he has caused us to be born again to a living hope through the resurrection of Jesus Christ from the dead, to an inheritance that is imperishable, undefiled, and unfading, kept in heaven for you, who by God's power are being guarded through faith for a salvation ready to be revealed in the last time. In this you rejoice, though now for a little while, if necessary, you have been grieved by various trials, so that the tested genuineness of your faith—more precious than gold that perishes though it is tested by fire—may be found to result in praise and glory and honor at the revelation of Jesus Christ. Though you have not seen him, you love him. Though you do not now see him, you*

*believe in him and rejoice with joy that is inexpressible and filled with glory, obtaining the outcome of your faith, the salvation of your souls. Concerning this salvation, the prophets who prophesied about the grace that was to be yours searched and inquired carefully, inquiring what person or time the Spirit of Christ in them was indicating when he predicted the sufferings of Christ and the subsequent glories. It was revealed to them that they were serving not themselves but you, in the things that have now been announced to you through those who preached the good news to you by the Holy Spirit sent from heaven, things into which ANGELS long to look..."*

—1 PETER 1:1-12 ESV

"Things into which *angels* long to look..."

I come from a long line of preachers. My dad loves that last verse: "Into which *angels* long to look..." He always told me that he believed that when a preacher preaches well, the angels listen. He told me that we ought to aspire to be the kind of preachers who cause long lines in Heaven, like the angels can't wait to pull up a seat and listen to us. My father clearly suffered from the same conviction that Peter suffered from. He believed that the Story of Jesus (the Gospel) was a pretty big deal, a deal so big that even *angels* long to look into it.

And what is the heart of the Gospel?

*All you need is Jesus.*

Since we're going to be spending a whole book exploring its text, let me give you a little background on 1 Peter.

It was written by Peter.

"Uh, yeah..." you're thinking, but not so fast. There are a few books in our Bible whose authorship is unknown or in dispute; more than you'd expect, actually. 1 Peter is not one of those. There are virtually no scholars who doubt that what is stated right off the top of 1 Peter isn't in fact the case.

*"Peter, an Apostle of Jesus Christ..."*

Peter is writing here.

If Peter, one of Jesus' twelve original disciples, wrote the book himself, he probably wrote it between 62-63 AD in the City of Rome. Why Rome? Well, that's where Peter was living near the end of his life. We know that he was martyred in Rome during the reign of the Emperor Nero sometime in 64-65 AD; obviously, he wrote it before he was killed.

Now, there are some scholars who challenge whether Peter wrote it himself or if he had the assistance of a trained scribe because, they say, the Greek it was written in is far too refined for what we'd expect from a Galilean fisherman. I don't see this as a matter worth fighting over because, as you'll see at the end of the book, Peter actually credits his scribe with his closing words. I expect that Peter probably spoke, or dictated, his thoughts while his scribe scribbled feverishly in the "King's Greek."

If that was the case (working with a scribe), then it's possible that Peter wrote the book somewhere in the mid-60s AD.

Some scholars suggest that it was written at a later date, somewhere between 70 and 90 AD. Either way, if Jesus was crucified somewhere between 30 and 35 AD (as most scholars agree He was), the *point* is that 1 Peter was written very shortly after the events of Jesus' actual life. These events gave rise to a huge movement (Christianity) that, by the time Peter was writing the book we're going to use as the basis for our journey, had swept across most of the Roman world.

1 Peter was written to five "districts," in what is today the northern part of modern-day Turkey. These districts weren't self-govern-ing (which is why we call them districts, not provinces) but were

distinctly located *geographically* within Turkey; most of the scholars I studied believe that each of these districts was made up of ethnic groups whose roots in their respective regions went back centuries.

Here's why that matters.

*Christianity was a very new thing there.*

And, as the people of the regions Peter was writing to began to hear about and then to follow Jesus, this new "way," this following of Jesus, started really messing with their way of life – a way of life that had been their tradition, and that of those around them, for a *very* long time. So, 1 Peter is essentially an encouragement to new Christians from those five districts to *persevere* in following Jesus even while being discriminated against by their friends, family, and peers, because of the ways in which their newfound allegiance to Jesus was putting them at odds with the everyday culture around them.

*They were becoming misfits, and Peter is writing to help them not lose hope because of it.*

This is why 1 Peter resonates very strongly for *us* today.

As I was writing this book, I heard a Christian teacher (Jon Thompson from Sanctus Church outside Toronto) make a very good point. He said that "true" Christians are inhabiting this very weird space in culture right now where the radically secular world sees us as right-wing, judgmental, archaic bigots because of our faithfulness to Jesus and the Bible, while *truly* right-wing people see us as liberal, compromised, vacillators who won't stand on principle.

We're caught in the middle.

*We're misfits.*

Some of the Roman writers who were contemporaries of Peter referred to Christians as "pig-headedly obstinate" troublemakers who would no longer toe the line in terms of normal, everyday Roman life. Sound familiar? Has anyone ever accused you of being a "killjoy" or, flipping the coin a bit, harassed you for not being more rigid in how you apply the way of Jesus to your life? If that's *you*, then Peter is writing to you. He's writing to encourage those of us who find ourselves out of step with culture because of our ongoing allegiance to Jesus, and Peter is saying *this* to us: "Endure suffering. *Keep your eyes on the prize*, and be encouraged."

*"So, what's the prize?"* you should be asking.

> *"BLESSED be the God and Father of our Lord Jesus Christ! According to his great mercy, he has caused us to be born again to a living hope through the resurrection of Jesus Christ from the dead, to an inheritance that is imperishable, undefiled, and unfading, kept in heaven for you..."*
>
> —1 PETER 1:3-4 ESV

God is the prize.

You are not the prize; you are not the point. God is the One who is blessed.

"Blessed be the Lord..." Peter says.

God is blessed. God is the center of the Universe, not us. Take that one point and apply it to your life and your whole life will change.

*Life is not about you.*

See, most of the time, most of us spend most of our energy trying endlessly to put ourselves at the center of our story. When you do that, you're living out of sync with the way things truly are, because God is the prize, He is blessed, He is, and is at, the center of the

Universe. What you really need to do in light of this is remember *your place* in the story, the place of a child.

> *"Blessed be the God and FATHER of our Lord Jesus Christ!"*
>
> —1 PETER 1:3 ESV

God is "Father"; you are "Child." He's your Father and He's a good one. Now, it's certainly true that some of you will have had nasty fathers, so the thought of God as father isn't exactly a pleasant one. The key, if that's the case, is to accept that fact –you can't change it, after all – and move *through* the brokenness of that past reality (keeping in mind that it's in the past) to look upon our great and glorious "Heavenly Father" who is good in everything He does.

*We know He's good because He's shown us mercy.*

The actual word in the original language here for "great mercy" is "VAST mercy."

> *"According to his VAST mercy, he has caused us to be born again to a living hope through the resurrection of Jesus Christ from the dead..."*
>
> —1 PETER 1:3B ESV

You see, God is blessed, He's your Father, and He has shown you *vast* mercy by giving you, in Jesus, the second chance of all second chances. In raising Jesus Christ from the dead, God has given you a whole new opportunity at life. He has shown in Christ a whole new way to be human, showing us how to be restored to the relationship with God that we were originally designed to enjoy forever; the really big idea here is that *He* is the One who has *caused* all of this.

Don't miss this.

God is the *active* one here. God is the One who has done this.

Now, in emphasizing so strongly what God has done, you may find yourself feeling like you have nothing to do, and when it comes to achieving salvation, that's true. But, having read that, you may find yourself thinking, "Well then, what *does* the story of Jesus have to do with me, if I don't have to *do* anything?" And I wouldn't want you to miss a very important point we can learn from a woman named Mary.

> *"Now on the first day of the week Mary Magdalene came to the tomb early, while it was still dark, and saw that the stone had been taken away from the tomb. So she ran and went to Simon Peter and the other disciple, the one whom Jesus loved, and said to them, 'They have taken the Lord out of the tomb, and we do not know where they have laid him.' So Peter went out with the other disciple, and they were going toward the tomb. Both of them were running together, but the other disciple outran Peter and reached the tomb first. And stooping to look in, he saw the linen cloths lying there, but he did not go in. Then Simon Peter came, following him, and went into the tomb. He saw the linen cloths lying there, and the face cloth, which had been on Jesus' head, not lying with the linen cloths but folded up in a place by itself. Then the other disciple, who had reached the tomb first, also went in, and he saw and believed; for as yet they did not understand the Scripture, that he must rise from the dead. Then the disciples went back to their homes. But Mary stood weeping outside the tomb, and as she wept she stooped to look into the tomb. And she saw two angels in white, sitting where the body of Jesus had lain, one at the head and one at the feet. They said to her, 'Woman, why are you weeping?' She said to them, 'They have taken away my Lord, and I do not know where they have laid him.' Having said this, she turned around and saw Jesus standing, but she did not know that it*

*was Jesus. Jesus said to her, 'Woman, why are you weeping? Whom are you seeking?' Supposing him to be the gardener, she said to him, 'Sir, if you have carried him away, tell me where you have laid him, and I will take him away.' Jesus said to her, 'Mary.' She turned and said to him in Aramaic, 'Rabboni!' (which means Teacher). Jesus said to her, 'Do not cling to me, for I have not yet ascended to the Father; but go to my brothers and say to them, "I am ascending to my Father and your Father, to my God and your God."' Mary Magdalene went and announced to the disciples, 'I have seen the Lord'— and that he had said these things to her..."*

—JOHN 20:1-18 ESV

In John's account of the resurrection, Mary Magdalene is the first person to see Jesus after He wakes up from death. Mary has been called a "prostitute" for many years in Christian tradition, though some scholars are now questioning whether that was actually the case. Either way, considering the way in which men and women interacted in that time, it is noteworthy that John records in his Gospel that it is a woman who first sees Jesus after He exits His tomb that first Easter Sunday morning.

*A woman.*

Let's imagine for a moment that the traditional title of "prostitute" was accurate in terms of how Mary earned her living. Can you imagine? A prostitute is first to see the resurrected Jesus? Whether she was a whore or just a marginalized female, if Jesus made room for Mary that first Sunday morning, you should never again allow yourself to be disqualified from coming to Jesus, as if there's no room at His feet for *you* too. I'm sure Mary would have been quite happy to squeeze on over for you if you'd been there and Jesus would have called you by name too.

*You see, Jesus did it for you.*

He became a man, lived a sinless life, perfectly fulfilled His Father's will, went to the cross to suffer and die in your place for your sins, and rose again victorious the third day, for you! As you are in Jesus, His victory is your victory as well. In Jesus, you've been born again to a living hope; you've been welcomed into a whole new way of being human.

Don't miss this.

As you follow Jesus, you don't have to follow the ways of our sick and twisted culture anymore, a culture that would seek to sell you one hundred and ninety-three different kinds of shampoo in a vain effort to "cleanse yourself." You don't need to keep trying to go from high to high anymore because, in Jesus, you've been born again into something completely new! In the original language here you're being born into a *living expectation*.

A *living* expectation.

That means that the expectation of Jesus' ultimate victory, which will be revealed at the Last Day when He comes again in glory, should be enough to keep you going in the meantime. It should be enough to get you up, and out the door, in the morning. You shouldn't need to get high anymore because you have unbroken access to the "Most High." The "High King of Heaven" is your dearest Friend.

This is the *genius* of the way of Jesus.

You don't need a new purchase to make yourself feel better. You don't need to keep rushing from new experience to new experience anymore in an endless quest to find a thrill, because you have been born again, in Jesus, to a *living expectation*. And that living expectation of Jesus' ultimate victory is *yours*, as you are *in* him.

And here's what that victory looks like.

> *"According to his great mercy, he has caused us to be born again to a living hope through the resurrection of Jesus Christ from the dead, to an INHERITANCE that is imperishable, undefiled, and unfading, kept in heaven for you, who by God's power are being guarded through faith for a salvation ready to be revealed in the last time..."*
>
> —1 PETER 1:3B-5 ESV

*Simply put, you're "Old Money" now.*

In Jesus, you've been born again to an inheritance – except that "Old Money Allotment" (the term used here in the original language) you've been born into is the kind that will never perish or run out. Apparently, at one point in recent history, one of my ancestors was the wealthiest man in the world. I often find myself lamenting the fact that none of his Old Money found its way down through the years into my wallet. Unlike my silly ancestors (who frittered the money away), the allotment we get from Jesus will never run out, never perish, and never become filthy. There's no such thing as "filthy rich" in Jesus. The inheritance that comes from Jesus is not the sort of thing that ever *turns* on you; it never becomes a chain around your neck, never destroys your life, and it will never pass away.

*"How's that?"*

*Because it's guarded in Heaven by God Himself.*

You could wonder, "Why is God guarding it?" And then you'd see, from the text, that He's guarding it for a salvation *so* great that He's waiting to reveal it, at the Last Day, as the great culminating act of history.

If you've ever wondered why you don't experience the fullness of "Biblical Christianity" all the time in the here and now, it's because God is reserving some if it for the "Eschaton," the "End of Days." He's *holding back* some of the ultimate goodness He has planned for His people for that great and glorious day when Jesus Christ will return in glory to judge the living and dead and to inaugurate His Kingdom which will have no end – a Kingdom in which *you* have a place!

He's holding back the full revelation of your salvation and its benefits for the "Big Finish," the final curtain at the end of the Age. And this glorious salvation is so important that He's guarding it *Himself* until it's ready to take its bow.

There are some very exciting implications from this.

First, the fact that you're Old Money now, that's pretty awesome. Haven't you always secretly wanted to be an heir or heiress? I sometimes find myself daydreaming about a letter arriving in the mail linking me to some long-lost industrialist family and giving me a share, as a member of their clan, in their earth-shattering wealth. If that happened to you, I'm pretty sure you'd lead a *slightly* more relaxed life. You'd go from worrying about bills and work to wondering which causes you'd most like to support with your wealth: a *total* paradigm shift.

*That's how it is (or should be) with you now.*

In Jesus, you're taken care of. In Jesus, you're free. You're Old Money now; so, you should be able to do what you do in your everyday life with the kind of *joy* that comes from *security,* knowing that everything, ultimately, is going to be fine because Jesus is on His throne. You can start living like you're an heir to all things, in Christ, which should be a much more fun way of living than the day-to-day grind you've gotten used to.

You also don't have to *worry* the way you used to. You can trust the process. Every time doubt starts trying to creep its way into your heart you can remind yourself that "God's got this..." In fact, He's "got it" so good, He's holding some of it *back* for the Last Day. He doesn't need to spend all of His goodness all at once.

*He's got this, so I'm good.*

Also, because you're an heir now, you can stop striving. You're the heir of all things so, in light of that, you might as well spend your days doing what God *made* you to do, rather than just trading away the hours of your life for money.

Think about that for a second.

Would a wealthy person trade away the hours of their life for money? Absolutely not. The more money you possess the more you realize money is just a construct and the only truly precious commodity is *time*. Rich people do what they *want* to do, what's in their heart. You should *act* like a rich person *now*, because of Jesus. Decide today (even if it's just a few baby steps at first) to start doing what God has uniquely made you to do and to stop wasting your life chasing the almighty dollar.

"Money *follows* vision," my dad always said. So, get a new vision of yourself in light of who Jesus is and what He's done for you; start living it out, and watch the money follow. Start treating your entire *life* like it's a passion project. Be who God made you to be and do *that* thing with all the power and passion of your soul, because He is the One who placed the seeds of that passion in your heart in the first place.

*You're Old Money now.*

Second, the fact that your inheritance, in Jesus, is *imperishable* should make you very *excited*. "Imperishable" means that what you've been given in Christ will *last*. That means that you can stop being insecure, because nobody can take away what's been given to you in Jesus; your inheritance is going to last. Nobody can ruin it, it won't grow old or out of style, and it's not going to spoil. And because your inheritance in Jesus is *guaranteed* to last, you can stop filling your life with *perishable* goods.

What a waste of a life that would be – constantly striving to get more and more things to fill your life with when, deep down inside, you know that nothing material is going to last. Friend, you already *have* an inheritance that is imperishable, so stop wasting your time, energy, and treasure on things that *aren't*.

As you begin maturing into deep friendship with God, you'll begin noticing that you need (or even want) less and less. You will discover, as you walk with Jesus, that more and more contentment begins showing up over time and, as a direct result of this infilling, you'll need (and have space for) fewer and fewer things in the aisles of your heart. This is because you will have begun participating in the undefiled inheritance that God is already *guarding* in Heaven for you.

You see, when you walk with Jesus, you are not participating in a thought experiment or buying into a very powerful idea; you are taking part in something *real,* and the realness of it is proved by the way in which it impacts your *actual* life. It brings contentment where there used to be dissatisfaction, peace where there used to be turmoil, and joy where there used to be despair. Your destiny in Jesus is to wake up one day (perhaps very soon) and say, "You know, I don't really need *anything.* I've got Jesus!"

I've noticed this particularly around Christmas and my birthday. I remember, as a young boy then man, always having *things* burning in my mind that I wanted desperately as gifts. A new stereo (back before smart phones), a set of skis or an epic Lego set. Later it was cool clothes or a motorcycle.

*Things.*

These days, other than the sailboat I lost a couple years back as part of a career cataclysm, there's literally *nothing* I want or need other than to see God continue to show Himself strong in the lives of my wife and kids, in our friends and peers, at our church and in our work.

That's it. I don't want anything else anymore, just His Kingdom to come and His will to be done. And if I can somehow be a small part of that? That's good enough for me. I think that's what they call *contentment*.

Third, the fact that you've been given an imperishable inheritance, that's guarded in Heaven by God, means that you don't have to *fight* to defend yourself. Accepting, believing, and acting on this deep truth is how we can become a peaceable, winsome, lovely people: the planting of the Lord. See, you don't have to fight anymore, because God is *guarding* your inheritance. No one can snatch it from His hand, so you might as well calm down, and go out there and love people as best you can. Nobody can do *anything* that will steal your inheritance because they've got God to deal with, and He's going to win.

This is why you can walk in peace.

*"Why's that again?"*

Well, because God is completely in control, and He's holding you in His heart for a very big finish, and if that doesn't make you happy, I don't know what will.

> *"In this you REJOICE, though now for a little while, if necessary, you have been grieved by various trials, so that the tested genuineness of your faith—more precious than gold that perishes though it is tested by fire—may be found to result in praise and glory and honor at the revelation of Jesus Christ..."*
>
> —I PETER 1:6-7 ESV

Why should you be *rejoicing*?

Because God, the Blessed Center of the Universe, is your Father. He's shown you *vast* mercy by giving you the second chance of all second chances in raising Jesus from the dead, causing you to be able to live with constant hope and expectation of Jesus' ultimate victory. This means an imperishable, undefiled, and unfading inheritance for you, which God Himself is keeping safe until the last great act of history where He will rule and reign in Righteousness forever, and you *with* Him as kings and priests to our God (Rev 1:5).

Because that epic paragraph is your day-to-day reality, as a Christian, *suffering* is endurable.

That's the thesis of 1 Peter right there; you don't really need to read the rest of this book, though I sure hope you do.

*Because Jesus lives, we can live.*

*Because Jesus has been victorious, we will be.*

This is the root and foundation of all Christian hope.

You can look at life, no matter how difficult it may get from time to time, and say to yourself, utterly sure in your conviction, that you're going to be alright. You can live a completely unphased life, no matter what comes, as you walk with Jesus in what He has accomplished in His life, death, and resurrection. That 'unphasability', that unflappable demeanor, is what people *really* notice about *real* Christians.

Do you remember meeting someone like this before you were a Christian? No matter what happened to them, nothing every seemed to *truly* bother them. You could take their health but you couldn't take their hope. You could take their job but you couldn't steal their joy. They could lose a family member, but never fall into despair because they knew they'd see them again, in Jesus.

*This is the genius of life with Jesus.*

When you're His friend, it doesn't mean that you won't have trials anymore; it means that trials won't crush you like they used to. It doesn't mean that everything will always be *easy*, but it *does* mean that His yoke will *always* be easy and His burden light, and He's ever willing to trade His yoke for yours.

Yes, we weep, but not like those who have no hope! Yes, we get knocked down, but –in the strength that God supplies – we get back up! And that kind of tenacious and joy-filled lifestyle comes only from Jesus.

> *"...so that the tested genuineness of your faith—more precious than gold that perishes though it is tested by fire—may be FOUND to result in praise and glory and honor at the revelation of Jesus Christ..."*
>
> —1 PETER 1:7 ESV

In Jesus, you are becoming *exceptional* people.

People will *see* how you live and, at the End of Days, when all is said and done and Jesus returns to set all things right, they will put two and two together. It'll be the "aha moment" of all "aha moments." They will see the glory of Jesus in that day and, all of a sudden, the glory they'd seen flashes of in *you* down through the years will find its perfect reflection and they will finally *understand,* and give Him praise.

Until that day, your belief confounds the world.

People don't understand why you do what you do and why you don't do what you don't. When you're truly following Jesus, people won't understand why you give your time so freely to serve in your city. They will find it incomprehensible that you give ten percent (and beyond) of everything you earn to help your church fulfill its mission in your city. They won't know why you turn the other cheek or why sorrow never seems to crush you in the same way it does them. They won't get why you don't worship wealth or why you think one hundred and ninety-three shampoos is crazy.

It *confounds* them.

Here's why.

See, they know you're normal. Maybe they work with you, live next to you, or serve on a corporate board with you. Maybe you're their doctor or their investment advisor and you always get them the best return while being scrupulously honest. Maybe you coach their kids' football team and their kids keep telling them you're the best coach they've *ever* had. Whatever it might be, they *know* you're not some wing nut from another planet; you're a person just like them.

*Except you're not.*

While seeming in many ways to be just like them, you live your life according to a faith that they believe to be completely crazy, and yet you're not crazy; they find it very hard to reconcile those two. They don't understand how or why you rejoice in Jesus, a mythic figure they don't believe really *exists*.

> *"Though you have not seen him, you love him. Though you do not now see him, you believe in him and REJOICE with joy that is inexpressible and filled with glory..."*
>
> —1 PETER 1:8 ESV

This is where the Christian proves to the non-Christian, and to those who are on their way to tasting and seeing that the Lord is good, that the Lord *is* good, that He *is* real. The joy that inhabits the life of every true Christian is absolutely incredible, to the point that it cannot be expressed in words; you have to *see* it to believe it.

I find myself feeling this way sometimes when I pray. I get so overwhelmed by the kindness of Jesus that I know, that, if I even think about trying to pray out loud, I'll collapse into a blubbering mess. I'll sometimes just nod at my wife in these moments, and she knows what to do.

You see, God has been so good to me in Christ that I'm filled with joy unspeakable and full of glory, to the point that I'm just cut to the heart with the beauty and goodness of Jesus. So, all of that thankfulness just wells up in my heart and tries to escape through my eyes as tears.

And the thing is, that kind of heart-stopping, chest-constricting, tear-shedding joy isn't found in *my* heart only, but in the heart of every *true* follower of Jesus; the beauty of that (countless millions falling deeper and deeper in love with Jesus) is so glorious that no one can contain, or even explain it. It's heavy, and that's what "glory" means. *Heavy*.

All true Christianity ultimately works itself out as *joy*.

*"Why's that?"*

Because you're blessed. Why? Because *God* is blessed and He's your Father. You've been shown vast mercy in Jesus and you are being worked on by someone else, which means – of course – that you no longer have to keep trying to save yourself. You've been born again, given the second chance of all second chances, and have been raised up, with Jesus, to a living hope and expectation. You're the ultimate "Old Money" heir or heiress now, and you enjoy an allotment (with the saints) that will never perish, never become filthy, and which will never pass away, because it is guarded in Heaven by God Himself, through faith, for a salvation so great that He is waiting to reveal it as the *climax* of history itself.

In light of this you are *exultant* and full of joy and, because of that, your suffering *feels* temporary and is turning your faith into something more awesome than gold. That's why people will look at you at the end of time and glorify God, because of how incredibly kind He has so clearly been to you! You are, and will be, the *evidence* of God's goodness, which is why you love Him, even though you can't presently *see* Him, and which is why your joy is beyond expression and so *filled* with the life of God Himself, that it feels as if it weighs a glorious ton, because, my friend, for you?

Jesus *is*, actually, *enough*.

# TWO

# A Recipe for Livin' Clean

When it comes to the "How-To of Holiness," I've realized that it all turns on the *"therefore."*

Let me show you what I mean.

> *"THEREFORE, preparing your minds for action, and being sober-minded, set your hope fully on the grace that will be brought to you at the revelation of Jesus Christ. As obedient children, do not be conformed to the passions of your former ignorance, but as he who called you is holy, you also be holy in all your conduct, since it is written, 'You shall be holy, for I am holy.' And if you call on him as Father who judges impartially according to each one's deeds, conduct yourselves with fear throughout the time of your exile, knowing that you were ransomed from the futile ways inherited from your forefathers, not with perishable things such as silver or gold, but with the precious blood of Christ, like that of a lamb without blemish or spot. He was foreknown before the foundation of the world but was made manifest in the last times for the sake of you who through him are believers in God, who raised him from the dead and gave him glory, so that your faith and hope are in God..."*
>
> —1 PETER 1:13-21 ESV

It all *turns* on the "therefore."

What we have here is the *"How-To of Holiness"* or, put another way, a recipe for "living clean." It's kind of my standard answer, when people greet me.

"So, how you doin'?" they ask, and I usually reply, "You know me, I'm livin' *clean,* baby!" I often get a blank stare. Especially when I greet someone and I ask them, "Yo', baby, you livin' clean?"

(Yes, I was a teen in the Nineties, a product of the first non-urban generation hugely influenced by urban culture; nothing I can do about it.)

People don't know how to answer.

I assume they either haven't thought about it that much, or they don't know what to say because, even in the split second after I've asked it, they realize that their answer is going to be somewhat difficult.

"Umm, not really, come to think of it..."

Or, maybe you had a really awesome week. Even under those "best of times" circumstances, you'd probably answer: "Umm, yeah, alright..." if you were truth-telling. Because none of us are every truly living clean. Which makes this chapter perfect for you (and me) because it contains within it, dear reader, a recipe – yeah, I said it – for living clean! Heck, you could call this chapter "HOW TO BE HOLY," but that would sound a little too Fifties for this Nineties kid.

But before we get to the recipe, we need to ask ourselves a question.

Why bother?

Why bother living clean? Why bother with all the heavy lifting required to learn how to be holy? The "Why bother?" question begs two further questions. Either you're a random evolutionary accident, in which case – if that's true – look, do whatever you want or need to do, in order to survive. If you're just a random accident, a "do whatever it takes" ethic makes a lot of sense.

But, as I think most of us would readily acknowledge, there's at least a *chance* that we were *designed* to a live a certain way.

Humor me here for a second. Say you don't really believe any of this "Jesus stuff" just yet; you just picked up this book because the cover looked cool and the byline intrigued you with its whimsy. Either way, you're not fully on team Jesus yet. Let me say I'm super glad you picked this book up. I had you in mind when I was writing it. I'm impressed that you're diving into something like this, even while you're working the whole God thing out. Very cool. So right here in this moment (the first of many like it to come), cut me a little slack; give me a little rope with which to hang myself or possibly pull you in, ok?

Let's imagine for a moment that you *were* designed to live a certain way. If that was true, the more closely aligned your life was with the way you were designed to live, the happier you'd be, right?

Makes sense.

Like, if you were a cog in a wheel, the closer to being part of a car you were the happier you'd be right? Because you'd be living in connection to your *purpose*.

Or, say you were designed to be a basketball player, and you played a lot of basketball. You'd be a lot happier that way than if you'd never picked up a ball and stepped onto the court, right? Because you were *designed* to do a thing, and if you *do* that thing that you were designed to do, there's a chance you'll be happier than you would be if you never did it at all.

*See, at its heart, holiness is pragmatic.*

Ultimately, holiness is a common-sense kind of thing that will actually deliver you a happier, more fulfilled life, if you will but do the hard work of learning to walk *in* it.

Maybe a few examples will help.

We all know intuitively that it's better to be drug-free than drug-addicted, right? Maybe you know someone who's struggled with addiction and you know it's ugly. You might know someone who has gone through the addiction journey and come out the other side, and you can literally *see* that they're better off now than they were while enslaved to drugs, and you can also see that they'll always walk with a limp, even now that they're free.

Maybe that's your story.

Take another tack.

We all know it's better to be fit and strong than gluttonous and obese, right? Nobody wakes up one day and says; "Hey, you know what I'm going to do? I'm going to eat my way to 600 lbs!" Nobody sets out to become the 500-lb man who Emergency Services had to cut out of his home that one time on Nat Geo TV. Nobody wants to end up trapped in their own body.

Most of us like the idea of pizza and the football game on the couch once in a while; most of us also know that if we did that sort of thing as much as we wanted to – if we let our appetites run unrestrained – we would become gluttons (we would be practicing gluttony) and we all know what would happen to our lives as a result: hoisted out of our house by a crane on national TV.

Fit and strong > gluttonous and obese. Everybody knows this.

*Fit and strong, like a seventeen-year-old.*

Don't you wish you were seventeen again? Everybody wishes this so much that they made a mediocre movie about it. Do you remember what it felt like to be seventeen? Maybe you're seventeen and reading this: good for you. Enjoy it while you can!

When I was seventeen I could run like the wind, for hours, and I could run *fast*. All these years later I can still run fast, for very short bursts, and I'd better stretch first or my hamstrings are gonna go see Jesus at some point during the sprint. Also, no matter how hard I stretch, if I run as fast as I can (and I can still keep up with the Varsity linebackers I coach in a sideline-to-sideline sprint in a tackling drill; okay, maybe for *one* sprint) my left groin (an old injury spot from a University game back in the day) is going to make me pay the price for the rest of the week.

Because I'm not seventeen anymore.

Now I have to work at it. Like at our local YMCA. I go in there and try not to look too hard at all the young folk running laps around me hardly breaking a sweat. I try not to let the young bucks make me feel depressed with their four plates to my two. I try not to take my farmer's walk up a notch just to keep up with my fourteen-year-old son. I just kind of toddle along, doing what I can to stay fit – and I really have to work at it.

Because I'm not seventeen anymore.

Let me take you back to Jesus real quick.

See, we all know that, if God exists – and I mean *exists* in even some semblance to how we see Him portrayed in the Bible, as this awesome, all-powerful, glorious, beautiful, wonderful, amazing God who spoke everything that is into being by the power of His Word – and if He's really like the picture we see in the Bible, then it would be better to be His *friend* than it would be to be His *enemy*, right?

Exactly.

Now, look, I acknowledge the fact that God may not exist. I'm comfortable living with that reasonable doubt. I've asked the question at the root of that doubt many times myself throughout my life: "If

God exists, why is life so hard?" I get it. I'm comfortable with my doubt and, certainly, with yours.

Welcome to the human story.

But (and oh, but there's always a "but") if there's a *chance*, even just a chance, that God is real? I will do *whatever* it takes to be His friend; there ain't no way in heck (if you know what I mean) that I'm missing *that* train, baby.

You see, ultimately, you've got to decide if you believe the Universe is Godless or if it's not. If you end up thinking the Universe is Godless, then good luck to you; do whatever you want to do with your life, and I hope it works out for you. Invite me over for pizza and football sometime; I'd love to watch my 49ers whup your Bengals (told you I was a Nineties kid). There's a long way we can go in relationship together even if we believe categorically opposite things about the nature and purpose of life.

But, look, if the Universe is *not* Godless, then you better dang well figure out who God is and what it's going to look like for you to live in relationship with said deity right quick, or else it's not just the Bengals who are going to get whupped.

Make sense?

And, if we're going to learn to live in relationship with the deity who is not just at the heart of the Universe, but who *is* the heart of the Universe, we're going to need holiness.

Here's why.

Think of God as a Father. Think of Him as getting up this morning and He's going out to play golf. He's going to a very swanky country club – in fact He owns the club – and He's dressed in fine whites, like tennis whites. He's not wearing short shorts, not this God I'm thinking of. No, He's in proper, manly, knee-length shorts and a perfectly pressed shirt. He looks like a million bucks. Not a hair out of place, His eyes shine like the stars, and His face like the Sun. His young toddler gets wind that Daddy is leaving to play a round. Toddler's been playing by himself, in the backyard, with the garden hose, naked. He rushes out from around the house, covered head to toe in garden mud and dog poop (because what toddler knows the difference?) ,grinning ear to ear like the wildman he is, and wants to join Dad on His trip to the club.

He even puts his arms up for Daddy to lift him up.

Problem.

*Can Dad lift his son without making Himself dirty?*

Remember, Dad is pristine, flawless, perfect. He loves the crazed toddler at His feet; He made him Himself. Dad looks down at His toddler from his glorious height and smiles. Toddler, already forgetting what he came out front to ask, has turned his back on Dad and is peeing in the front garden, because you can never have too much mud.

That's kind of how we are with God.

God loves us, sure. But something has to be done about our filthiness before we're fit to join him for a round.

*We're the toddler in the yard.*

If you start thinking of yourself that way (like, hold that image in your mind, week to week) you're going to find it much easier to not be as impressed with yourself as you're in the habit of being. You'll also fight with people less, right? You've never seen anyone come to a schoolyard fight, or to an argument with their spouse, naked and covered in dog poop.

I sometimes think that's why God made us naked in the Garden. One, and I know this from personal experience, it's sort of hard for your typical husband to stay mad at his wife when she's always wandering around naked. Sooner or later the urge to take her in his arms is going to overwhelm his grumpiness. Two, most wives don't stay mad at their husbands once they see that look in his eyes.

The world would be a friendlier place if we remembered we're all just the naked kid in the backyard; I mean, could you fight someone who was grinning goofily and was covered in mud and dog poop? You'd be too busy laughing and would probably help show the kid how to turn the hose on himself.

We're all going to need a little help. So, what do we do?

> *"THEREFORE, preparing your minds for action, and being sober-minded, set your hope fully on the grace that will be brought to you at the revelation of Jesus Christ..."*
>
> —1 PETER 1:13 ESV

I told you, the whole thing turns on the *therefore*.

Anytime you see a "therefore" (my youth pastor taught me this) you need to check what it's there, *for*. The "therefore" at the top of verse thirteen is pointing back to the big idea from the previous chapter of this book, wherein the great, glorious, beautiful, precious, magnificent, awesome, amazing, life-changing *salvation* that we've been given in Jesus, through His resurrection, is lauded to the high heavens. The "therefore" is saying, "In light of that beautiful salvation that you've been given in Jesus, prepare your minds to *get busy*." And, being sober-minded (keeping your brain in gear), set your hope fully on the good things, which you do not deserve, that will be *brought* to you, when Jesus shows up.

All because of the beautiful salvation you've been *given* in Christ.

Peter is trying to remind us here that we've been gloriously saved in Jesus, so we ought to learn to *live* like it. This is the path of holiness: not cleaning *yourself* up so you can try and go play golf with the Father ('cause, let's face it, even without the dog poop, you aren't big enough to hold a club, let alone swing it), but recognizing that in Jesus you've been cleaned up, made *fit* for God's presence. So now you are enabled (because He is able) to go out and *play* the game of life like the Champion that He is: just a smaller, less talented, version.

*You're not trying to become holy in order to be saved. You learn the way of holiness because you've been saved.*

Many Christians flip that one, some consciously, others just beneath the surface of their awareness; but they do it. They think (and sometimes *we* think) that they (and, by extension, others) need a good cleanup before they're fit for polite society. People who think and act this way are annoying. How do you think it's going to work if you go to a world lost in sin and darkness with an ethic that suggests to them (even if you won't fully admit it) that they need to clean up their act *before* they come in for a hug? It's not going to go well. That kind of attitude is totally off-putting.

*"What, you're saying I have to qualify first?"*

Maybe, this week, spend some time carefully considering the way you live to see whether or not you are saying, with your actions, that your peers need to clean themselves up first, instead of declaring by what you say, how you act and carry yourself that we don't clean ourselves up to be saved; because we have *been* saved, we begin *learning* what it means to live clean.

Think of holiness this way: it's like you've been given the DNA of a six-foot-eight physical specimen with great agility, balance, and hand-eye coordination who can jump. You have "future NBA All-Star" written all over you. You've been *made* to play basketball, but now you need to go out and *learn* to play basketball. Imagine you'd been given all that natural physical ability; you're a genetic freak, something special. You're tall, strong, and able to jump out of the gym but you never pick up a basketball.

*What a shame. What a waste.*

Imagine standing before your Creator one day and He looks at you, and smiles, then spins a basketball in His palm. "Missed something?" He might ask. What an awful moment that would be. That's how it is with holiness.

So many Christians think of holiness as a duty, when they should be thinking of it as an *opportunity*.

> *"Therefore, (gird up the LOINS) of your mind for action..."*
>
> —1 PETER 1:13 ESV

That's what it says in the original language. "Tie up the *nut sack* of your mind for action..." And before you go thinking that this image is not applicable to us because we're not going into battle like our ancient Near-Eastern forebears – wearing what amounted to short skirts, so it behooved them to tie their jiggly bits up with a long piece of fabric – allow me to drop two words on you.

*Jock strap.*

Or, maybe this, if you're of the fairer persuasion: sports bra.

"Jock up, and let's go!" is what Peter is saying. He's saying that this adventure we're about to embark upon is going to be like a war, like a race, like a basketball game, so we're going to need to *prepare* ourselves to play the game at the highest level. We think of holiness as a duty, when really, it's a *sport*.

> *"Therefore, (gird up the loins) of your (COMPREHENSION) for action..."*
>
> —1 PETER 1:13 ESV

Get your mind right, and get training, so that you can maturely be ready to go all in on grace.

> *"...SET your hope fully on the grace that will be brought to you at the revelation of Jesus Christ..."*
>
> —1 PETER 1:13B ESV

There are a few things that I want you to be aware of that are happening here. First, you have *agency*. You're not a helpless bystander; you're being told to *"set* your hope..." as if hope is something you can lay hold of and put somewhere! Set your hope! You have agency. That's good news; you *can* do something about your screwed-up life. And you can do it all out.

"Set your hope...*fully.*"

I love this.

Here we have Peter reminding us to live our lives *full out*! Take your hope and set it *fully*. Go all in!

You know what happens in your life when you go all in on something, right? It bleeds; it has a cascading effect. You know what I mean? Say you decide to go all in in your devotions. Pretty simple, you're going to do it every morning, just one chapter in the Old Testament, one in the New Testament, and one Psalm or Proverb. You're just going to work your way through your Bible front to back, front to back like that (using three bookmarks, restarting each section – OT/NT/Psalms and Proverbs) for the rest of your life – all in. Then you decide maybe you should get back into the gym. Guess what? You figure, since you're all in on your devotions, you might as well push a little harder at the gym too. Then you figure, heck I'm starting to lose all this weight, maybe I'll go all in with my meals, start eating more veggies and fewer starches and limit empty calories, like those from chips and beer, to one special day on the weekend instead of every night of the week. Since you're "one flesh" with your spouse, pretty soon your redeemed behavior patterns start bleeding over into their life as well and, since you asked, you begin noticing that your wife (or hubby) hasn't looked this good in a long while.

*You decide to go all in on chasing them around more.*

You get fit from chasing your wife around and working hard at the gym, so you find it easier to go all in when playing with your kids in the backyard and, heck, since your son likes tossing the football around so much, you start wondering if maybe you should pick up coaching again. All of a sudden (except it isn't, but it'll feel that way) your whole life has that "all in" feel to it; you're achieving greatness in multiple areas of your life, and that cascading effect started with one simple decision to go all in with the way in which you approach one aspect of the mechanics of your ongoing relationship with Jesus: reading your Bible.

*Set your heart fully, and see what happens.*

Just in case you're feeling left out, because you've just been reading that whole motivational part and been thinking; "Gee, I'm not that kind of 'type A' personality; this must not be for me..." let me remind you that the Bible is beautiful, and it has *you* in mind, and it's not really about you at all.

> *"...set your hope fully on the GRACE..."*
>
> —1 PETER 1:13B ESV

And grace means "favor" or "merit" undeserved...

> *"...that will be brought TO you..."*
>
> —1 PETER 1:13B ESV

Like breakfast in bed...

> *"...at the revelation of JESUS Christ..."*
>
> —1 PETER 1:13B ESV

Thank God for the Bible. On the one hand it's saying, "You have agency, set your hope fully, go for it, make your way, be an 'Alpha

Male' or 'Alpha Female,' go out there and dominate this league for Jesus, do everything you can, every time you can, as hard as you can, as awesomely as possible, let's GO!" But, on the other, it reminds you that you're setting all this hope – with all the energy you can muster, from a life lived full out – on something you can't do.

Which is why you'll need *grace*.

That, ultimately, is why this book isn't in the "Motivational" section next to Tony Robbins and Oprah – because it's faith not in you your*self*; it's faith in *Jesus* that makes the difference. We are setting our hope fully on grace, merit or favor undeserved, that will be brought *to* us, when Jesus returns. We don't even have to go and get it; in fact, we can't.

Grace comes *to* you, like bacon and eggs in bed on Mother's Day, except the day it'll ultimately arrive is "The Day of Days," when Jesus Christ is revealed, once and for all, as Mighty God, King, and Savior for all the world to bow the knee before. That's when your hope will be *fully* realized. This means that you need to live like a long-term investor, because Christianity is not a house flip.

*It's a long-term investment.*

Set your hope fully on the *grace* that will be brought to you, fully, at Jesus' great and final triumph. And the reason Jesus' triumph is so great is because it's totally *assured*. His victory is already won; it was finished at the Cross, when He said it was. It's like you've got the GOAT in your corner.

Imagine that Michael Jordan (the greatest basketball player of all time) decided to make a comeback, and he was still awesome, and you were going to get to be on his team. He hasn't shown up yet, but you've been told he's coming, and because it's him (the greatest of all time) your victory is assured, even though he hasn't set foot back on the court yet. Your victory is assured because nobody could ever play quite like Mike: not Kobe, not LBJ, not Magic, not Bird, not the

Doctor, not Kareem, not Bill Russell. Mike was the greatest, and he can still fly, and he's coming back and you're on his team.

*Your victory is assured.*

So, you've got two possible responses here. One, you could sit back and be, like: "Good, MJ's back, he's got this. Now show me how it's done, baby!" You could think and act like a *spectator*, and it's bound to be a pretty good show. Problem is, you've been invited to *play*, on his team. See, if I got an invite to go join Michael at a celebrity charity tournament at the end of the month, you *know* what I'd be doing tomorrow at 5 a.m., right?

*I'm hitting the gym, baby.*

Let's think on this for a minute. Am I hitting the gym because, in one month, I'm going to get good enough to *actually* make a difference when MJ takes the court? Nope. The eventual victory is going to have nothing to do with me; but, since I've got an opportunity to play with the Greatest of All Time, I'm going to make sure I show up ready to go. I'm going to give the GOAT the respect he's earned (by his past performance) and bring my absolute best to the court – because I've been *invited* to play on *his* team.

The metaphor is pretty clear, right?

*Holiness is an opportunity.*

It's an invitation.

If Michael Jordan is coming out of retirement to play in your celebrity charity basketball tournament, you're going to go all out with your training in the lead-up to that event, regardless of how long the lead-up is. You've been invited to play with the Champion, so get to work!

Therein lies the how-to of holiness. Peter is telling us to boldly bet our future on Jesus' ultimate victory and to live our today all out, walking boldly – with everything we've got – *into* that victorious future.

> *"As OBEDIENT children, do not be CONFORMED to the passions of your FORMER ignorance, but as he who called you is holy, you also be holy in all your conduct, since it is written, 'You shall be holy, for I am holy...'"*
>
> —1 PETER 1:14-16 ESV

This is big.

Three things to point out here. One: obedience. Two: nonconformity to old habits. Three: the embracing of worshipful impossibility.

First: obey Jesus.

> *"As OBEDIENT children..."*
>
> —1 PETER 1:14A ESV

What does it mean to obey Jesus? Jesus Himself, in Matthew 22:37-40 reduces all the Law and the Prophets down to two great Commandments. He says,

> *"Thou shalt love the Lord thy God with all your heart, soul, mind, and strength and thou shalt love thy neighbor as thyself. On these two hang all the law and the prophets..."*
>
> —MATT 22:37-40 ESV/NKJV

*Love God. Love people.*

That's what Jesus says it looks like to obey God, and do it full out.

Maybe you're like me and the imperative of this freaks you out a bit? Think on it this way then; obeying Jesus means continuously (day by day, moment by moment, situation by situation) *learning* to love God and *learning* to love people with everything you've got. If you're doing that work, even though you never quite *reach* the goal you're striving for, you can answer our starting question with an emphatic

*"I'm living CLEAN, baby!"*

You may not *be* clean just yet, but you're *living* clean. You're living *today* in a manner *worthy* of that big and beautiful champion you're going to become someday in Jesus.

See, holiness is a process, it's a journey, it's an opportunity, it's an invitation, it's a sport! So, as long as you're in the game, on the field, on the court, in the mix, on stage, out there in the real world learning to love real people because you're learning to love the real Jesus, you're *doing* the thing that you've been invited, and created, to do. This means that each day lived this way is a day that brings you *one step closer* to that best day of all, when Jesus steps back in for His final victory lap!

That's what it looks like to *obey* Jesus.

*"How about that whole nonconformity to old habits part?"*

> *"...do not be CONFORMED to the passions of your former ignorance, but as he who called you is holy, you also be holy in all your conduct..."*
>
> —1 PETER 1:14B-15 ESV

Do not be *conformed* to your former *ignorance*.

This part right here is why scholars think Peter was writing, primarily, to a Gentile audience. Gentile culture, at the apex of Rome's rule, was pretty sick and twisted: a nasty amalgam of Polytheism (many gods), Materialism (a fixation on wealth, power, and license), and unrestrained sexuality (orgies, prostitution, sodomy, adultery), with slavery and conquest thrown in to "liven up" the mix.

Over and against this toxic brew you have the new Christians coming out of these crazed, ritualistic, nihilistic, sexually aberrant approaches to life and religion, and in most cases, they're coming out of families and social networks that had been walking out their lives and religious practice that same way for generations. These new Christians are, literally, breaking with centuries of tradition.

Anyone who's tried to change up their annual family Christmas knows how well most families and social networks embrace change.

The people Peter was writing to were literally wired, generationally, to live a certain way; Peter is taking direct aim at that way of life and saying, "Quit it!" He's calling them to walk away from the way they *used* to live and to begin walking in *newness* of life. Why? Well, because...

> *"If anyone is in Christ he (or she) is a NEW creation; behold the old has passed, the new has come..."*
>
> —2 COR 5:17 ESV

So, you're not living in a Roman District in the first Century AD. Ritual prostitution and sodomizing underage male slaves as an act of "worship" is not *exactly* something you struggle with on the daily. How are *you* to interpret and apply Peter's words here as you look to walk out a recipe for living clean?

*You try something new.*

Literally look at the order of your coming week, and *arrest* it. Think of the way you always do things and change it. Try something *new*, to the glory of God.

And I mean it: something, *anything*, new. Like maybe try *biking* to work on Monday.

*"How is biking going to help me with my holiness?"*

Try it, and you'll see.

It's all about breaking old patterns, trying something new, and seeing how God rushes in to the room you *make* for him (that's one of my Dad's sayings there).

*Try something new.*

Then, let the impossibility of "self-derived holiness" drive you to *adoration*.

> *"...but as he who called you is holy, you also be holy in all your conduct, since it is written, 'You shall be holy, for I am holy...'"*
>
> —1 PETER 1:15-16 ESV

On the surface, this is very depressing.

If you know yourself at all, you look at this and think, "Those are two of my least favorite verses right there..."

> *"You shall be holy, for I am holy..."*
>
> —1 PETER 1:16 ESV

What's the first word that comes to mind?

*Impossible.*

You know what's really funny about this? Peter here is quoting an obscure passage from Leviticus 11:44 where God is telling His people not to eat any more insects.

*That's right. Insects.*

"Bro, you gotta chill with the Praying Mantises, cool? It's getting a little out of control, this insect-eating habit of yours, man. You need to stop that and be holy because I am Holy..."

Seems ridiculous doesn't it? Like God actually *cares* whether we eat *insects* or not?

"If He's really *that* detail-oriented, we're sunk..."

Agreed.

*But it's also beautiful.*

A United Nations study found that the average human consumes about two pounds of insects (mostly fragments, like in your coffee or cereal) per year so, right there, without any further need of scrutiny, we're all sunk when it comes to attaining holiness on our own. We're lawbreakers, all of us. And here's what's beautiful about that: see, this fact of our desperate and helpless sinfulness is not meant to drive us to despair or legalism. What God wants here has nothing to do with us all adopting the wearing of complex mouth-straining systems to filter out bugs and other uncleanness.

*What God wants is adoration.*

Confronted with your helpless sinfulness, God wants you to look *through* His perfect law *to* His Perfect Son. He wants you to see Jesus – God the Son made flesh – who perfectly fulfilled God's holy law and lived in submission and connection to His perfect will at all times and in all things and then died, in your place for your sins, to make you God's friend.

*That's beautiful.*

You were always *meant* to be God's friend. That's why you look at a verse like "Be ye holy as I am Holy..." and don't lose hope. Instead, you find hope as you look to Jesus. See, the "bad news" about the "Good News" is that you'll never be good enough on your own. No matter what you do, at some point you're going to swallow a fly. You can never be good enough, *but Jesus can*. Which is exactly what Peter is talking about.

> *"...And if you call on him as Father who judges impartially according to each one's deeds, conduct yourselves with FEAR throughout the time of your exile, knowing that you were ransomed from the futile ways inherited from your forefathers, not with perishable things such as silver or gold, but with the precious blood of Christ, like that of a lamb without blemish or spot. He was foreknown before the foundation of the world but was made manifest in the last times for the sake of you who through him are believers in God, who raised him from the dead and gave him glory, so that your faith and hope are in God..."*
>
> —1 PETER 1:17-21 ESV

Basically, what Peter is saying here is that, if we *say* we have relationship with God, we ought to *act* like it, by living in "fearful hope." This can be kind of weird in our hyper-positive society where we always seem to (or are being pressured to) say to everyone: "It's all good! Everything's peachy! I'm okay, you're okay, everyone's okay and everything is awesome, as long as you follow your heart!" Which is all fine and good, of course, except when the sin and rebellion that lives within each of us rears its ugly head and somebody decides to commit a crime against God and against one of His created beings. Secular-Humanist-Pluralism works great as a worldview until some guy hikes a bunch of automatic weapons up to his hotel room in Vegas, smashes his window, and opens fire on the crowd below.

Then, face to face with evil, we have to make an answer.

And most find their worldview sadly lacking in that moment.

See, we're sinful, God is Holy, and we ought to be afraid of Him because He's fearsome. Everybody knows this, deep in their bones, even if they won't admit it.

I don't think anybody seriously believes we're here by accident or that life started when an alien starship passed overhead billions of years ago, jettisoned its septic tanks, and ET's poop fell to Earth and started a chain reaction that ended up, all these many long years later, with you sitting there reading this book.

(Yes, I actually interviewed a top evolutionary scientist/atheist on this topic years ago and, when I pushed him on the question of origins, that was his hypothesis.)

If God is, even in the slightest way, as He is described in the pages of the Bible, then we're dealing with One Tough Customer here, and Lord help us.

Which is, actually, what He did.

*Helped us when we couldn't help ourselves.*

See, in Jesus, you're almost home. How do I know?

> *"...And if you call on him as Father who judges impartially according to each one's deeds, conduct yourselves with fear throughout the time of your EXILE..."*
>
> —1 PETER 1:17 ESV

"Exile" means *sojourn.*

He's saying you don't *belong* here anymore. So, while you conduct yourselves in this place where you don't belong, or fit in, anymore, do so in fear of God but also in hope because, in the original language used, "exile" means "beside home," which sounds, to me, like you're *a lot closer* to home than you imagined.

We tend to think of God as very far away. Peter tells us we're almost home. That's where the *hope* comes from: from knowing that you're almost home. You've been set free from the painful legacy of an ugly past (like the original recipients of this letter) and been given the promise of a beautiful future in Jesus.

*So, live like it.*

That's what holiness looks like. Like someone who's living today like their future is set! I think I could live that way. I think you could too. I think that sounds a whole lot easier (and more fun) than "Abide by this, and this, and this and DON'T do that, or that, or that..."

*No more flies for you!*

Instead of trying to live that way (and ultimately failing), we live like someone who knows their future is set.

*That's what holiness looks like.*

It looks like someone so possessed by what the blood of Jesus shed for them means, so convinced that they're part of a very old story whose Author and Finisher is God, so sure that the story of life is about God and His people, and so secure in knowing that they are one of those people, that they *believe*.

You believe because you've been convinced of the power and truth of the Good News about Jesus. You believe:

> *"...knowing that you were ransomed from the futile ways inherited from your forefathers, not with perishable things such as silver or gold, but with the precious blood of Christ, like that of a lamb without blemish or spot. He was foreknown before the foundation of the world but was made manifest in the last times for the sake of you who through him are BELIEVERS in God, who raised him from the dead and gave him glory, so that your faith and hope are in God..."*
>
> —1 PETER 1:18-21 ESV

Did you *get* that part?

Through Him, you're a *believer* in God.

This means that your belief *in* Jesus is upheld *by* Jesus! Try that truth on for size this week and see how it changes your life. Your belief in Jesus is upheld by Jesus, which is why He gets glory and you get joy. He loves you so much that He carries you, and that's why you love Him. He makes you what you could not make yourself.

*Holy.*

Which is why we adore Jesus and hedge all our bets on Him. That's why we're hanging the outcome of our entire lives on His eventual victory, because He accomplished for us what we could not achieve for ourselves.

*Holiness.*

You want a recipe for living clean?

*Jesus is the recipe.*

# THREE

# LoVe Actually

Everybody's looking for authenticity.

I never met anybody who preferred fake to the real thing: never. Authentic, meaning "Worthy of acceptance, based on fact, conforming to an original so as to reproduce essential features, not false or an imitation." (Merriam-Webster)

Authentic. For *real*. As in, "Am I *really* in love?"

Do you remember the first time you fell in "love"? How old were you? I know we all thought we were in love that first time at 14 or 15 but, looking back, when did it happen *for reals*?

(Yes, I'm quoting Eskelito from "Nacho Libre.")

"Am I in love, for *reals*? How do I know?"

(Yes, I could also quote Whitney Houston.)

How about when you started following Jesus? Do you ever find yourself asking the question, "Am I really following Jesus? Like, is this for real, this whole faith thing?"

Is my faith fake or authentic? Am I in love or is it just butterflies in my stomach? On either front, how will I *know*?

Let's tackle the love question first. See, I know a few things about love. I've been married twenty-four years at this writing; that's a long time by any measure, and in today's culture of disposable relationships and casual sex, it's a dog's age.

*"Twenty-four years, will give you such a crick in the neck!"*

(Thanks, Genie.)

My sweet wife Niki and I are still very much in love, even after all this time. We often remark on this, saying things like, "Man, I feel like we're still dating..." or "I'd hoped it would feel this way after this long, but I didn't really believe it would be possible..." It's nice to be able to work through subject matter like we have on hand in this chapter with that much water under the bridge. And I'm thankful we made it this far 'cause, let's face it, when you're 22 and just married, you don't really know *jack* about love.

In my opinion, you know you're in love when *selflessness* begins showing up as your *default setting*. You find yourself doing crazy things for your partner that you would never have done before, which you would never do for anybody else, and find you didn't even have to work yourself up to it. It just happened, because you're in love.

*Like buying flowers.*

Do you remember (if you're a dude especially) the first time you went to buy flowers for someone? I do. Totally terrifying. I must have sat outside that flower shop for twenty minutes psyching myself up to go inside. I was freaked out. I had no idea what to do, no clue about what was good and what wasn't and, especially, no idea how much flowers *cost*. You guessed it; I got fleeced. No joke, I ended up spending $50 for twelve long-stem red roses twenty-seven years ago! I'm sure, looking back, that the flower-shop clerks keep a sharp lookout for seventeen-year-old rookies with no clue; that's a cash money opportunity, baby.

There are other places, besides flower shops, that are kryptonite for dudes in love. Now, keep in mind, I'm not talking to *all* men here, just dudes. If you have to ask what a *dude* is, you're not one, so you've got your answer right there; in fact, a dude already knows what my next example is going to be.

*Lingerie stores.*

My poor teenage sons. Every time we walk past one at the mall, I can feel the potent mix of interest and unease washing over them; they're equal parts intrigued and horrified. How do I know? Because I used to feel that way and kind of still do.

Twice a year a dude has to go into one of these stores, on her birthday and Valentine's Day. In my case it's three times, because I always get her something frilly for Christmas too. It's awful. In fact (and I say this as a forty-six-year-old married man of twenty-four years), this past Valentine's Day, I walked in, stood there for a second, then walked back out. I swear I could hear the attendants snickering at me as I walked away.

Flower shops and lingerie stores even smell funny to me, like flowers and girls. I prefer the smell of locker rooms and sailboats myself. And, problem is, sometimes those flowers you buy that first time, lead to a date at a fancy restaurant.

I don't like fancy restaurants.

I think fancy restaurants are a construct designed to make a dude feel uneasy in the hope that, in an effort to compensate for his ignorance and unease, he will spend money indiscriminately. These fancy waiters, all dressed up and calling you "Sir," and a menu written in a language you can't read. (It used to be just the French places that did this, but now even the Mexi-joints in town have everything listed in Spanish. I guess they think it looks more impressive that way?) Foie *Gross*? No thanks.

49

You've got seventeen utensils in front of you and no idea which one to use. Your date looks at you with a sparkle in her eye (or is she laughing at you like the lingerie clerks?) and tells you to work from the outside in.

Keep in mind that my first try at this was before the internet. These days I'm sure you'd just google it ("How to handle a date at a fancy restaurant") and you'd be fine, but back in my day it was a pretty horrible thing. Also, how does she already *know* to go from the outside in? How many of these fancy dates has she been *on*? And the problem is, if dinner goes well, it might lead to dancing.

More dude-kryptonite.

I never met a dude who likes to dance. I know men who like to dance, but not dudes. If you're one of those men who like to dance, I respect you and your dancy-ness (you probably went on more dates than me), but it's not for me. Plus, if you're dancing, you probably had to dress up and, if you were anything like me as a young man, you mostly wore track pants. Jeans were considered dressy. So, you had to go out and *buy* something fancy. Again, with the taking your money thing! And all for a girl.

If this budding relationship continues to develop, you're in for more trouble, man. Pretty soon you'll have to start cleaning your sink. I didn't even know sinks were *meant* to be cleaned until I was in love. Then, one day she'll ask you sweetly, "You know that toilet seat? Could you maybe, umm, think about lifting it?" And, newly minted husband that you are, you'll say: "Sure, honey. No problem." And then she'll ask you to put it down again after.

Now you're confused. Does she want it up, or down?

Get used to it, Brother; you're in love, and your life is over.

Also, "Up, then down..." sounds like an equation and most dudes don't like complex math. We like adding dollars and subtracting expenses to make sure the income column outsizes the payable one (that's exciting stuff), but don't push us too far now.

You'll also be asked to reduce your carb intake, and the problem with this is that most dudes don't even know they have a "carb intake" – unless we're talking about muscle cars, in which case, you've got my attention. Then you're going to have to watch "You've Got Mail," which is no fun, especially because there's football on, and after that you're going to have to meet her crazy uncle. You know the guy I'm talking about, right?

He drinks Bud Light and likes to talk about NASCAR, a lot. Problem is you don't drink much beer (you're still kind of in your "Church Guy" phase and beer-drinking hasn't been much of a thing for you) and you don't watch racing. Talking theology over a nice cup of Earl Grey is more your speed but for *seventeen* years, "Crazy Uncle" isn't going to clue in; he's just going to keep retracing the same tired themes over and over again while you try to not roll your eyes, because you're in love with his niece, so you're trying to be nice.

Then you're going to agree to have babies, buy her a house, then learn to *maintain* said house. House maintenance sucks. Remember the first time you had to figure out how to clean out the eaves troughs? Awful, stinky, you probably cut your hand six times on the edges of the trough, and you don't even *like* heights. Also, what if there's a dead squirrel, and is that *raccoon* poop? Naturally, you could always *hire* someone to clean them out for you, but you already done *spent* all your money on flowers and lingerie and dinner and dancing and a new wardrobe!

You're also going to have to learn to talk about your feelings.

You've been there, right? She asks you to tell her how you *really* feel; you talk for four minutes straight, pouring your heart out, baring every single strand of your soul. She smiles and asks you to keep going.

Really? I've been talking for *four minutes* straight, Woman!

That about covers every feeling I've *ever* had; I've got nothing left. But she insists, so you start making stuff up, because you're in love and you want her to be happy. But the thing is she can *tell* you're making it up (I have no idea how she does this; it's some sort of womanly sixth sense), so now you're in trouble.

"Why am I in trouble? I just talked to you for *four minutes* about my feelings, which is longer than I've ever talked to *anyone* in my life about that sort of thing, *and* I'm feeling kind of dizzy because this room smells funny from the flowers, *and* your uncle's going to be here any minute so I really have to google last week's NASCAR results..."

You'll know, you miserable (but happy) wretch, that you're in love when some of the things I've outlined above start happening to *you*.

*You're welcome.*

Now for some things you can expect to see showing up in your life when you're truly experiencing the Life of God *for reals*.

> *"Having PURIFIED your souls by your OBEDIENCE to the truth for a sincere brotherly love, LOVE one another earnestly from a pure heart, since you have been born again, not of perishable seed but of imperishable, through the living and abiding word of God; for 'All flesh is like grass and all its glory like the flower of grass. The grass withers, and the flower falls, but the word of the Lord remains forever.' And this word is the good news that was preached to you. So put away all malice and all deceit and hypocrisy and envy and all slander. Like newborn infants, long for the pure spiritual milk, that by it you may grow up into salvation— if indeed you have tasted that the Lord is good..."*
>
> —1 PETER 1:22–2:3 ESV

Right away here we see *three things* that show up when you're experiencing the Life of God, for real. Purity. Obedience to Jesus. Self-giving love.

> *"Having PURIFIED your souls..."*
>
> —1 PETER 1:22A ESV

*Purity* is really beautiful here in the original language. In English, it kind of sounds like something *we've* done. You'll see in a minute what our proper response is to what's been done *for* us but, for now, focus on the fact that you don't have to get out a scrub brush and work away at your soul until it's squeaky clean, because in the original it reads:

> *"Having BEEN consecrated..."*
>
> —1 PETER 1:22A ESV

That's more like it; that sounds like something that's been done *for* you, even *to* you. You were consecrated, you have been set apart – like when you're in love. True, right? Once you've fallen in love, you are set apart for that person. You see this in people all the time. If they're *really* in love, they look at each other differently, touch each other differently, are with each other in a way that is unique in all the world. Nobody else gets to them the way you do, because you're in love with them; you've been set apart for them, *consecrated*.

We hear an echo of the genius of Christian marriage here: the genius and beauty of committed, lifelong, faithful relationship. People get married for all sorts of reasons. People *stay* married because they've been *consecrated*, set apart for each other. You used to never darken the door of a flower shop; now the florist knows you by name. Something *new* has happened in your heart.

Every time I see something new happening in a Biblical story, or in my life, or someone else's, I stop and shout about it for a minute.

*Newness can happen for you!*

So, get out there and live like it this week. Change a pattern, change a habit. Do something you haven't done before; heck, go dancing! Because you have been consecrated, set apart to belong to the God who makes all things new (Rev 21:5). Newness has been accomplished *for* you, so just go out and *walk* in it. Do something new!

> *"Having purified your souls by your OBEDIENCE to the truth..."*
>
> —1 PETER 1:22 ESV

Here's the part I mentioned earlier that I'd come back to; it's the part where you *partner* with God.

Since God has set you apart, you now work *with* Him, by your *obedience* to the truth. It's important to note that we're not talking about *propositional* truth here. There is no secret set of claims that all "real" Christians subscribe to with equal fervor. So, if you've been holding your breath, waiting for me to get to the whole legalism part, exhale, because I'm not planning on going there, ever.

> *"Having purified your souls by your OBEDIENCE to the truth..."*
>
> —1 PETER 1:22 ESV

We ought to hear the entirety of the Bible's story echo in our hearts and minds when we read and interact with a particular passage in the Bible, so we should read this – that we are to be *obedient* to the truth – and hear something very specific echoing back at us from the entirety of the Bible's testimony about the truth.

> *"I Am the way, the TRUTH and the life. No one comes to the Father, except through Me..."*
>
> —JOHN 14:6 ESV

"I AM the way..." says Jesus. "I AM the truth..." says Jesus. "I AM the life..." says Jesus. "No one comes to the Father, except through ME..." says Jesus.

Set-apartness comes *through* obeying Jesus. If you want to *be* consecrated, if you want to *walk* in your set-apartness, learn what it means for *you* to obey Jesus.

Thankfully, obeying Jesus doesn't entail a list. Jesus reduced all of it (because there used to be lists, long ones, believe me) to two Great Commandments.

> *"Thou shalt love the Lord your God with all your heart, soul, mind, and strength. And thou shalt love thy neighbor as thyself. On these two hang all the Law and the Prophets..."*
>
> —MATT 22:40 ESV

As you learn to truly love God and love people, you will find yourself sticking out like a sore thumb, and this runs to the heart of what the book of 1 Peter is all about. It's written to Christians who are sticking out like sore thumbs because they are obeying Jesus, and their sticking-out-ness is causing them to come under persecution by their peers.

*"Why?"*

Because they were acting *differently* from the people around them in their contemporary culture, and their differentness was *bothering* people.

Ever been the DD? You'll know what I'm talking about if you have. The DD, the "Designated Driver." Everybody kind of treated you like a second-class citizen that night, right? Know why?

Because you were set apart; you were different from them and, by nature, the fact that you were not participating in what the rest of your friends were doing that night turned you into something other, someone like the people to whom Peter was writing.

On the night you're the DD, people who don't know that's what you're doing keep asking you, "Hey man, s'everything alright? Don't seem to be having that much fun, man! You want something?" After the third person has asked some variant of the same question you just cut to it the next time someone starts asking: "I'm the DD!"

And they look at you like you've got a disease.

See, the thing about learning to love God and learning to love people is that you can't fake it. Peter knows this.

> *"Having purified your souls by your obedience to the truth for a SINCERE brotherly love, love one another earnestly from a pure heart..."*
>
> —1 PETER 1:22 ESV

This is that authenticity piece we were talking about earlier. *Sincerity,* meaning you can't fake this stuff. Authentic Christianity is *un-fake-able,* which is why *fake* pseudo-Christianity is *so* annoying. Ever been in a "Christian context" that was clearly fake? Maybe you've known a so-called Christian who's fake. Thing is, everybody knows it but the person. Normal, non-churchy people can smell fake "churchy-ness" a mile away. Saccharine, superficial, fake. Obsessed with form and pomp. Fixated on appearance, saying the right thing and not the wrong. Focused on systems, processes, and rules.

*People see through it.*

But the authentic love of God expressed through faith, hope, and love coupled to the authentic love of neighbor? Irresistible. Only when it's real, mind you.

"So, how do we *know* when it's real?"

You know it's *real* when you have to *work* at it.

> *"...EARNESTLY from a pure heart..."*
>
> —1 PETER 1:22B ESV

Know what "earnestly" means? It means "outstretched-ly."

*True love reaches.*

Take that one all the way to the bank and build your life on it. True love *reaches*. You know it's real when you have to *work* at it, when you have to *reach*. Sometimes, to love well, you're going to have to stretch!

We all know that to be able to do this, we're going to need some miraculous help. I mean, you might be a *bit* nicer than me, but even so (and I'm not *entirely* convinced, since you asked), you're going to need a little help. You're going to need *Jesus'* story to change *your* story. You're going to need *three very special things* to show up in your life.

> *"...since you have been BORN AGAIN, not of perishable seed but of imperishable, through the living and abiding word of God; for 'All flesh is like grass and all its glory like the flower of grass. The grass withers, and the flower falls, but the word of the Lord remains forever.' And this word is the good news that was preached to you..."*
>
> —1 PETER 1:23-25 ESV

You'll know you're really tasting and seeing that the Lord is good when your life starts *transforming*. Transformation shows up through something awesome and everlasting, which is also known as "The Gospel": the Good News of Jesus.

> *"...since you have been BORN AGAIN..."*
>
> —1 PETER 1:23A ESV

You've been given *new birth*, new life, the second chance of all second chances in Jesus. He, being God Himself, became a man, entering into space-time history, and went to the cross to suffer and die in your place for your sins so that, in what C.S. Lewis describes as "The Great Exchange," Jesus' *goodness* might come to you and your *badness* might go to Him. And because He was fully God and fully man, He's big enough (as God) and man enough (as man) to take all the weight of all the sins of all the world throughout all time and let them stick to Him, so that He can pay. And then He dies, once for all, for the sins of the world, including yours and mine.

*But He doesn't stay dead.*

Instead, on the third day, He rises again in glory, defeating – in His body – the power of Satan, sin, death, and hell forever; which means that all the powers of Satan and of darkness are crushed in your life when you come to Jesus and walk with Him, and you get a second chance. You get a shot at a new life. You get a do-over or new birth because of Jesus. And this transformation – if it's the real thing – is built on something awesome and *everlasting,* and that would be the second thing we're looking for, right there. *Everlastingness.*

Peter speaks directly to it:

> *"...not of perishable seed but of IMPERISHABLE, through the living and abiding word of God; for 'All flesh is like grass and all its glory like the flower of grass. The grass withers, and the flower falls, but the word of the Lord remains forever.'"*
>
> —1 PETER 1:23B-25 ESV

Everything we have and do is subject to the law of diminishing returns. We are withering; it's just a question of *pace.* I look at my 70-year-old father and see my future. I look at my sons and see my past. I don't look as good, or as healthy, today as I did at twenty-four. I'm fatter now than I've ever been (and I work at it). I need reading glasses, and there are other realities I'm starting to have to deal with that I don't want to get into right now because this is a "Christian Living" book and it's meant to be *positive*!

Why is all this happening to me?

Because I'm like the grass of the field and the flower of the grass that Peter is talking about: I'm withering.

*News flash. So are you.*

So, go out there tomorrow and live like it. Live all the tomorrows that remain to you as if you're fading away, because everything you do, and everything you are is subject to the law of diminishing returns.

*"Hey, I thought you said this book was meant to be positive?"*

> *"...but the word of the Lord remains FOREVER."*
>
> —1 PETER 1:23B-25 ESV

I wouldn't leave you hanging, baby. There's some good news right there. You know why it's good news? Because it doesn't mean that your *Bible* is going to live forever. Christians have misused this verse for years (with authoritative, self-righteous undertones... "The *word* of the Lord abideth *forever!*")

And the clear implication those Bible-thumping preachers were trying to make was that, if you didn't listen to them and do exactly what they said, you were going to find yourself on the wrong side of the eternal scorecard.

May I remind you here that the book we call the Bible wasn't even in existence, as we know it, for most of the history of Modern Christianity or when Peter wrote his book. So, if that's true (which it is), then there's no way Peter could have been referring to the collection of documents we now call "The Bible" *before* that collection *existed*. Which means, if you ever meet a Christian who uses *"...but the word of the Lord remains FOREVER"* as a weapon to try and win an argument, you should quickly inform them that they're barking up the wrong tree.

Peter is not saying that the *document* we know as our modern Bible is going to abide forever. He's saying:

> *"...but the WORD of the Lord remains forever."*
>
> —1 PETER 1:23B-25 ESV

And, who did the Apostle John (a contemporary of Peter's) teach us that "The Word" is?

> *"In the beginning was the WORD, and the Word was with God, and the Word was God. He was in the beginning with God..."*
>
> —JOHN 1:1 ESV

The WORD is the *Logos*, the spoken WORD of God, the One who, in His Incarnation, came to us as Jesus Christ of Nazareth, our Savior: the *WORD* who abides forever!

Why is this very good news for you? Well, because the Eternal Word of God took on flesh (again we're borrowing John's words there) to become the man Jesus so that He could go to a cross to be crucified in your place for your sins. Then, because that Jesus *was* the Eternal Word of God in a body, He rose again from death the third day, defeating its power for you, then ascended back to His rightful place at the Father's right hand, where He sat down in triumph to become your cheering section (interceding for you). And He'll come again someday from that same place, stepping back into space-time with a sword proceeding from His mouth with which to slay His enemies. He is the Almighty WORD of the Father who abides forever, and:

> *"It is the WILL of Him who sent Me (says Jesus) that I should not lose ANY of all those He has GIVEN Me, but that I should raise them all to life on the last day..."*
>
> —JOHN 6:39 ESV

Don't miss this.

Who sent Jesus?

*God the Father.*

Okay, so it's the *will* of God the Father that Jesus will not lose *any* of those that the Father has *given* Him. This is your best day right here. Any time the Bible speaks in imperatives like this you should start cheering!

*You have been given, as a GIFT, to Jesus, by the Father.*

(That may be the most important thing I've ever written, right there.)

Think your salvation depends on you?

*It doesn't.*

You have been given, as part of His inheritance, to Jesus, by the Father, and Jesus has a specific *purpose* in mind for you.

> *"...but that I should RAISE them all to life on the last day..."*
>
> —JOHN 6:39 ESV

I mean, somebody SHOUT!

You belong to Jesus, and He never loses anything. We've been given, as a GIFT, to the Son, by the Father!

> *"Praise, praise the Father, praise the Son! And praise the Spirit, Three in One!"*
>
> —"ALL CREATURES OF OUR GOD AND KING" – ST. BENEDICT

And He never loses *anything*. That's the Good News that was preached to you, baby! And, now, the third thing.

*Confidence.*

Do you think knowing that you've been given *to* Jesus *by* the Father will make you more, or less, confident as you move forward through life?

*Right. More.*

That's the kind of life-changing confidence you can expect to see showing up in your life once you've tasted and seen that the Lord is good, for reals. And, that *confidence* is what's going to help you make some things *stop* showing up in your life so that one great, good, and essential thing *will*.

> *"So put away all MALICE and all DECEIT and HYPOCRISY and ENVY and all SLANDER. Like newborn infants, long for the pure spiritual milk, that by it you may grow up into salvation— if indeed you have tasted that the Lord is good..."*
>
> —1 PETER 1:22 – 2:3 ESV

Five things disappear when you're tasting and seeing that the Lord is good, for real: malice, deceit, hypocrisy, envy, and slander.

Five.

Malice disappears so, note to self, stop being evil. Where evil shows up most consistently for me is when I'm driving. Somebody cuts me off for no good reason? I go from zero to angry enough to cause an incident in less time than it takes my car to accelerate to sixty. I had a guy turn left in front of me on a blatant red light just the other day, forcing me and the driver next to me to come to a screeching halt mid-intersection; then, this yahoo has the audacity to give *us* the finger for daring to start driving into the intersection *after* our light had turned *green*. Still makes me angry, just writing this. I was ready to go to war. That urge to fight, just because somebody has disrespected me? That's evil at work in my heart, baby, and I need to stop it. You might need to as well.

Instead, I suggest we all start working on cultivating what I like to call *"relative non-evil-ness"* in our lives. I'm not talking here about ceasing to be evil altogether (because, let's be honest, fools are still going to cut me off and I'm still going to get mad enough to want to fight), but about cultivating *"relative non-evil-ness"* in our lives, like it's a delicate flower.

*"What does 'relative non-evil-ness' look like compared to going all out?"*

Well, when the dude cuts you off and then gives you the finger, you're in touch with Jesus enough, and circumcised of heart enough, to be able to resist the urge to return the favor, and/or to follow him into the parking lot where you will give him a piece of your mind or, perhaps, the "right hand of fellowship" (as my friend Mark used to say). Instead, you drive on, take a deep breath, and thank the Lord (in all sincerity) for giving you an opportunity to learn more self-control. Then, after a couple of blocks, you forget it even happened.

That's the power of God right there!

Deceit will also disappear when you're tasting and seeing that the Lord is good, in an authentic way.

*"What is deceit?"*

Guile.

So, let's start learning how to be, and *work at* being, "guileless." Stop trying to *play* people in order to get your way. Kiss manipulation goodbye. Practice guilelessness, knowing that it'll start showing up, more and more, as you taste and *see* that the Lord is good.

Hypocrisy also goes; so, become a person whose default setting is "keeping it real." I was trying to model that off the top of this chapter with how *real* I kept it, describing to you the many ways in which my "Alpha-male Neanderthal-ness" has shown up in my love life. Honest, and true. Okay, maybe also a little silly and depressing. Oh well, that's me; I can't change the essential truth of it, and neither can you, *about you*. Keep it real – tell the truth about yourself and stop pretending you've got it all together when, really, you're just trying to survive one day at a time.

Too many Christians are too uptight and upset all the time, wanting everybody to be perfect or, at the very least, *act* perfect all the time. I'm convinced that many so-called Christians are really legalists attracted to the Christian r*eligion* because they see it as an effective system of control for making people do more good things and fewer bad ones.

*Not so, those who are genuinely tasting and seeing that the Lord is good.*

Those people keep it real.

And they kill *envy* whenever it shows up in their lives.

Killing envy is super hard in our day and age. Two words illustrate this.

*Social. Media.*

Social Media is that especially awful third circle of hell where you're constantly comparing your *screwed-up life* to your friends' *awesome* one, right? You know it's true; you've spent more than a little time there developing a good dose of self-loathing as you've relentlessly compared your nondescript life to the bright lights of others. Stop it.

Let me let you in on a little secret.

*Social media is a construct.*

It ain't real. See, the problem with social media is that you're constantly being bombarded with people's *highlight reels* while living your *behind the scenes*.

Brother, Sister, you need to trade your enviousness for empathy. The Bible is explicit about this.

> *"Rejoice WITH those who rejoice, weep WITH those who weep..."*
>
> —ROM 12:15 ESV

Practice *empathy*, not envy.

And then watch – and celebrate – as slander disappears proportionately as your envy shrivels up and dies.

*"What is slander?"*

Vilification; "down-talking."

Next time you catch yourself starting to talk someone down to your own level, immediately stop yourself. Grow up already. Kids down-talk; adults should know, and *do,* better. That's a pretty big idea in play here: *growing up*. Do whatever it takes, as you walk with God, to see malice, deceit, hypocrisy, envy, and slander *excised* from your life and replaced with an undeniable *maturity* that is irresistibly showing up in your life for all to see and enjoy.

> *"Like newborn infants, long for the pure spiritual milk, that by it you may GROW up into salvation..."*
>
> —1 PETER 2:3A ESV

Charles Spurgeon, probably the greatest preacher who ever lived (not named "Jesus" or "John the Baptist"), famously jumped off this verse to remind us that all of us *always* have lots of room to grow. Say it to yourself.

"I have *lots* of room to grow..."

*Lots*.

See, the second you start thinking you've got this whole "Christianity thing" *cased*, you become annoying to everyone around you, especially to non-Christians, and I think we'd all agree that "less annoying" equals "more better." Why? Well, the less annoying we are, the fewer speed bumps and barriers we put in normal people's way to keep them from tasting and seeing that the Lord is good. Make sure you're not a speed bump, or worse still, a roadblock on someone's journey home.

We all have lots of room to *grow* in this area.

> *"...if INDEED you have tasted that the Lord is good..."*
>
> —1 PETER 2:3B ESV

We want to grow up, so we can live a pure and set apart kind of life, a life that obeys Jesus. We want a life where we sincerely give ourselves away in a love that reaches, being transformed by the awesome and everlasting *good news* about Jesus. As a result, we want to find ourselves living a life that is no longer subject to the law of diminishing returns, but one that is going from glory to glory. A life that, though for the present it is passing away, will one day put on incrruption as you stand face to face with your beautiful Jesus!

With that in mind, you start living *today* with that ultimate goal always in sight. You live like Eden's curse is no longer the *final word* for you because of what Jesus accomplished for you. Jesus became man for you, was crucified for you, rose again for you, ascended to His Father's right hand to intercede for you, and is coming back to inaugurate His Kingdom, which has a place in it for you!

*Your life should be crazy confident as a result.*

Then you need to use that confidence to *kill* malice, deceit, hypocrisy, envy, and slander every time they show up in your life.

*"Why?"*

Because you're a *grownup* now, who knows a florist by name, dresses up nice and goes to fancy restaurants where sometimes you dance afterwards, looking good and freshly shaved from a sink you cleaned after you used it, that sits next to a toilet seat that you raised and then lowered, keeping it spotlessly clean! And, at that restaurant, you will eat steak and broccoli *without* the fries, before going home with her to watch "You've Got Mail" for the fortieth time, in a living room you just cleaned because her Crazy Uncle's coming over tomorrow to see your four babies and watch the race in your lovely, well-maintained, house that kissed its diaper pail goodbye ten *years* ago, where you will spend a lovely evening talking about your feelings, because you finally *know* what it means to be in love, because you have tasted and seen that the Lord is good, *for reals*.

# FOUR

# Under ConstruCtion

There's a very good chance that – like my house was a couple of years back – your life is "under construction."

We were preparing our house to receive my mother-in-law. She'd been living with us, in our actual house, for some months while the build on her "granny flat" got going. She was, in fact, sharing a bathroom with my two teenaged daughters which – typically – led to some pretty hilarious spats over drawer space, shower etiquette, and exactly *how* the toilet paper rolls should be changed, when, and by whom.

*It was a growth opportunity.*

The build, as many builds tend to do, stretched from a planned seven months into nine months, and then ten. Mother-in-law moved into her space *just* in time to avoid any outright acts of family-on-family violence, thanks be to God. The whole "living with each other in a house that resembles a war zone" thing *did* become a bit of a trial after a while. Like I said: a growth opportunity.

If you've ever lived through renovation, you know what I'm talking about. It's not the *most* fun thing a person could ever choose to do. Granted, we hired a professional company to do the build, which was a nice change from all the times over our twenty-plus years of marriage where I'd haphazardly done my best to renovate the worst house on the best street as my sweet wife and I did our best to climb the real estate ladder on a pastor's income. I almost killed myself installing the kitchen at the second house we bought (all 800 glorious square feet of it). Lord have mercy; even now the memories are giving me chest pain. Funny thing though: I noticed – during my mother-in-law's build – that the *dust*, whether created by a rank amateur such as myself, or by the high-priced pros we hired, is still dust. More than a year later, as I write this, there is *still* drywall dust from the build in our house. Dust everywhere. Even in my ears during the height of the build.

*In my ears.*

Our garden was destroyed, they wrecked my driveway (I guess dump trucks just can't back up straight, or the drivers just don't *care* about my grass enough to *bother* to back up straight) – it was basically super fun. One day, they left the driveway so dirty that, unable to stand it any longer, I attacked with a broom and a leaf blower. The two-hour dust storm that ensued was so intense that it left the siding of my house covered and my neighbors less than impressed. But, on the upside, it gave me yet *another* job to do, which I was super-excited about.

(Come to think of it, I still haven't cleaned the siding on the second story.)

Deep breaths, Todd, deep breaths.

What's really depressing is that, two hours of sweeping and leaf-blowing later, the driveway (though slightly cleaner) *still* looked bad, because it was under construction.

We did a lot of apologizing to guests during the build.

"So sorry about our mess; someday it's going to look good though..."

*Maybe your life feels the same way.*

What's really difficult about being "under construction" is that we *feel* like it's never going to end; that's really hard for most of us because we tend to be fairly "finish-line obsessed."

I spend most late winters/early springs training to do a summer triathlon. I spend the entirety of this training time living in a state close to constant fear.

*"Why?"*

Well, because I've done seven triathlons so far, and I know, from experience, that by the time I get to within half a mile of the finish line I will basically be on the doorstep of Heaven – and not in a good way. I'll finish as a "dead man walking." Triathlons are that hard. They're near-death experiences, basically. But, over the years of continuing to do these races (I do them to impress my wife), I have slowly begun training myself to *accelerate* as I near the finish line, despite my feelings of impending expiration. My goal is to finish those last five hundred yards looking like this race has been no big deal. Yes, it's in the last five hundred yards (and at the transitions) that my wife is actually going to *see* me, which is why (you guessed it) I focus on looking good at those points in the race.

*I want to finish strong.*

Triathlons are clearly from the devil, though, because by the time you get to the finish, there's almost no joy, at least if you're me. I've seen lots of races on TV or online where the athletes look super-happy about finishing, and I can imagine being happy that you finished; but so far, for me, I'm just so spent that I can't bring myself to smile. In fact, most of the time, I end up weeping.

Getting to the finish line is hard, which makes life hard, because we're *finish-line obsessed*, and we hate being "under construction." But, if the Bible is true, maybe *under construction* is how we were meant to live all along.

> *"As you come to him, a living stone rejected by men but in the sight of God chosen and precious, you yourselves like living stones are being built up as a spiritual house, to be a holy priesthood, to offer spiritual sacrifices acceptable to God through Jesus Christ. For it stands in Scripture: 'Behold, I am laying in Zion a stone, a cornerstone chosen and precious, and whoever believes in him will not be put to shame.' So the honor is for you who believe, but for those who do not believe, 'The stone that the builders rejected has become the cornerstone,' and 'A stone of stumbling, and a rock of offense.' They stumble because they disobey the word, as they were destined to do. But you are a chosen race, a royal priesthood, a holy nation, a people for his own possession, that you may proclaim the excellencies of him who called you out of darkness into his marvelous light. Once you were not a people, but now you are God's people; once you had not received mercy, but now you have received mercy..."*

—1 PETER 2:4-10 ESV

Six verses right there full of a picture of how your beautiful, screwed-up life is meant to be. The picture painted here would have been of great encouragement to Peter's original audience.

Peter was writing to a group of people whose allegiance to Jesus was beginning to drive them away from familiarity with "life as usual" in the world around them. Maybe you can relate? The longer you walk with Jesus, the closer you follow Him, the more disconnected you will find yourself feeling from the way everyone else is "doing life." Peter's original audience had been polytheistic (many gods), materialistic (the material world is what really matters and what is really real) Gentiles (non-Jews) for generations, and their newfound allegiance to Jesus, the "Jewish Messiah," was causing them to stand out sorely from their friends, neighbors, and peers. So, Peter is writing to them during this vulnerable stage in their personal development to encourage them to hold fast to their allegiance to Jesus, even though that allegiance was making them feel like they no longer *fit in*. They might have been asking themselves, "Is this *really* how my life is meant to *be*? I mean, no one *else* I know is living this way..."

Into that tension, Peter writes the words we're going to explore here in chapter four in an attempt to paint for his audience a picture of life as it's *meant* to be.

First, life is meant to be a "Jesus-ward journey."

Your life is meant to be taking you *towards* Jesus.

> *"AS you come to him..."*
>
> —1 PETER 2:4A ESV

Sometimes, in the original language of the New Testament, the words can be different than they appear in our modern translations, but that's not the case this time; this time "As" means *as*. AS you come to Him: a *continuous* process.

*Following Jesus is a process.*

It's a *journey*, not a destination. We need to remember this with great focus and constancy. Since coming to Jesus is a journey, we need to make sure we always live like a *tourist*. And, if you've ever taken a long trip, you know that living that way isn't easy. I mean, yes, vacation is fun; it's fun to stay at a nice hotel on a nice beach in a cool city with interesting things to do and great food to eat. It's a near miracle to come back to your suite each day and find that it has "magically" cleaned itself.

Bliss.

But, you know it and I know it: after a while you just want to go home.

*"Why's that?"*

Because you don't *belong* on vacation; you *go* on vacation and then you come *home*. You know you belong at home because you *love* coming home. Your bed is the best bed in the Universe, your sheets smell better, your coffee is better, and it's a beautiful thing to have a closet with your clothes in it rather than a suitcase, and – let's be honest – it's kind of nice to not have to dress up for dinner.

So, following Peter's hint here that we are to live like tourists on a journey, like we don't really belong here (more on that in the next chapter), is going to be hard. Following Jesus means that, as far as "normal life" goes, you're always going to be just passing through. You're going to need to live like a tourist.

I watched a documentary film last year that illustrated just how difficult living that way can be. The film followed two German Millennials who were determined to try to find happiness by buying a school bus, retrofitting it into a tiny house on wheels (which sounds a lot like a crappy RV to me), and driving it across North America. What I found most interesting about the film was the ending. In the end, these two navel-gazing young adults found their happiness when they sold the bus and went *home*.

This leads me to ask myself a very important question.

"Keeping Jesus in mind, where is *my* home?"

Where do I belong? Where do you?

*With Him.*

> *"As you come to HIM..."*
>
> —1 PETER 2:4A ESV

*I could get excited about that one.*

Jesus is your home. Jesus is your destination. Jesus is the *somewhere* you're headed to. This means that we should always be doing whatever it takes to keep Jesus as the constant *trajectory* of our lives. Trajectory is important. A trajectory can't be changed once its set; once you select a target and launch that rocket, it's going to that destination or bust.

What I like about this idea of *trajectory* is that it means that, even when we stumble or pause – maybe we even wobble a little to the left or right (we're not rockets, after all) – so long as we have *Jesus* as our target, we always have a North Star to guide us back on track. Yes, something bad might happen to you; life might give you a beating and you might find yourself in one of those moments where it's all you can do to just sit still and wait for the storm to pass. But once it does, and you find yourself able to take the next step again, you'll know – without a doubt – which way to go.

Because you're headed to Jesus: He's your *trajectory*.

Make the decision to hold Him in that place, to *place* Him at the center of your life, to make Him your North Star; *decide* to keep believing in the impossible, even when nobody else does.

> *"As you come to him, a living STONE rejected by men but in the sight of God chosen and precious..."*
>
> —1 PETER 2:4 ESV

Beautiful. Jesus is *a living stone*.

Now, what do we all know about living stones?

*They don't exist.*

I picked up a stone while we were doing the construction on my mother-in-law's extension – it was a near perfect ovoid, like a small moon – from when the builders were digging the foundation. It was a "foundation stone." I noticed it sitting there in a pile of stones dug up from where the future basement would be. A white stone, perfect and round, begging closer inspection, sure, but dead as – well – a stone.

*Stones don't live.*

A "living stone" is an impossibility, but Jesus *is* "the Impossible." He is the "Living Stone," the great anachronism at the heart of the Universe. The claims the Bible makes about Jesus (and the claims He made about *Himself,* as recorded in the Bible) are plain impossible and ridiculous (a "man" *equal* with God?), unless the story about Jesus is true. If the story is true, then Jesus becomes not impossible but impossibly *remarkable*!

This is pretty encouraging stuff for you, if you've built your life on following Jesus. See, it's either/or for you. You're either completely nuts and have wasted your life on a fairytale, *or* you're totally right and have been chosen to be on the greatest and most dynastic winning team of all time. You might as well enjoy the beauty of living in that tension, baby, because there's no way you're making it go away.

I'll admit that I sometimes wish there was a middle way in between those two extremes but, if you take the big story of God and His people – as outlined in the Bible –seriously, then you have to be honest and admit that that half-hoped-for middle way just doesn't seem to exist, no matter how hard we might wish it did. Walking with Jesus is either/or, plain and simple. And the stakes are high because the story is just so crazy.

That God exists is bad enough. That He made everything that *is*, by the spoken Word of His mouth (an act of will): also crazy. He placed our first parents Adam and Eve in a garden – we lost half the readers right there. (This is just a grand metaphor, right? Nope.)

*"Dude, to be honest, I didn't even really get past the whole 'God exists' bit..."*

I get it. It's a very crazy story.

In that garden where God placed our parents were two great trees, one the Tree of Life, the other the Tree of the Knowledge of Good and Evil. Adam and Eve are told to enjoy the garden and eat of any tree in it, except for the Tree of the Knowledge of Good and Evil. That one they have to leave alone, or else they (creatures made in God's image, to live *forever* as His friends) will die.

*But they eat of it anyway.*

As a result of this disobedience on their part, they fall into sin, death, and curse. God has to kill two animals to cover up their nakedness (which is now suddenly a source of shame for them), and He banishes them from the garden and from His presence.

By the way, it was a talking snake that tempted Eve to eat of the forbidden fruit in the first place. That's right: a *talking* snake.

Crazy.

Then, in the sin and twistedness that follow that first act of rebellion, we turn from disobedient fruit-eaters into full-blown, fratricidal murderers within the first generation removed from Eden. Cain and Abel: maybe you've heard the story? And from there, just east of Eden, things get worse and worse and worse and worse until, eventually, with the story of Noah's flood, God wipes out the entire world population because it has become so sick and twisted in its sin and rebellion that He can't stand it anymore. By this point the Human Story has become so dark that God annihilates every living being except for one family and some animals He helped them herd into a homemade boat.

One dude and his family, that's it.

After Noah and his family repopulate the Earth over the centuries following the flood, guess what? Life continues to get more and more ugly to the point that God decides to call one people group to Himself as His Own Special People, through whom He will reveal Himself to the world.

You guessed it – even His "Own Special People" end up acting the fool most of the time. A favorite illustration of this, for me, is when their great leader ascends Mount Sinai to receive the Law that God has written, Himself, on tablets of stone: the Law that will govern His people's right relationship to Him. As Moses ascends the mountain, it's wreathed in smoke and fire and thunder and lightning; it's pretty obvious that *God* is on the mountain (there were no pyrotechnics or hazers or robotic lights at worship services in those days) and that nobody is faking any of this.

But Moses stays up too long.

The people begin to get nervous. Despite the supernatural storm that's still going on atop the mountain in their backyard, they begin thinking that God has abandoned them. After thinking on this awhile, they decide the really smart thing to do would be to have Aaron, their High Priest, melt down all their wives' jewelry and make a statue they can bow down to and worship right quick.

*Ridiculous.*

The thing is, that ridiculous story leads to story after story in the Bible of ridiculous people like you and me doing ridiculous things (everything we can, in fact) to ruin the world God has given us and destroy our place in its order as we, again and again, try to ascend God's throne so that we can rule and reign in His place.

Because *we've* got better ideas.

But – oh, how wonderful – God doesn't leave us alone.

In the fullness of time, as outlined beautifully in the pages of the Bible, God the Father sends God the Son into space-time history. God the Son becomes a man, known to the world as Jesus of Nazareth, worshipped by many as Jesus Christ: the Messiah, the

Savior. Because, you see, this Jesus was not just a man, not just a *good* man, not just a rabbi, or a philosopher, or a radical, or a miracle worker. He was God-in-a-body, the Word of God made-flesh; *the God-Man.*

*God in skin, walking around on the Earth.*

And He reaches out to the outcast, the downtrodden, and the oppressed; He welcomes them into fellowship with Himself, heals the sick, and tells everyone who has ears to hear that the Kingdom of God has come near, in Him. He even goes so far as to say that those who have *seen* Him, have *seen* the Father. He makes Himself *equal* with the God of the Bible, and that's what gets Him killed; because, in Judaism, to claim what Jesus claimed about Himself was not just crazy, it was blasphemy and worthy of death.

So, the Jewish religious elite peer-pressure the Roman authorities into hanging Jesus on a cross, between two thieves, to die. But as He's hanging there, the strangest thing happens. Turns out He's not just being crucified because He ticked off the religious elite of His day. Turns out He's hanging there on that tree so that the *sins* of the world – every evil and ugly thing that's ever been done, or will be done – and the death penalty that those sins so richly deserve could be laid on Him, God-the-Son-made-flesh, by God the Father. And, as described in "The Great Exchange" (C.S. Lewis), your badness goes to Jesus, and His goodness comes to you.

*Then, the Word dies.*

But He doesn't stay dead.

That very next Sunday morning, the very first Easter Sunday morning, Jesus rises again from death, defeating – in His body – the power of Satan, sin, death, and hell forever! He then proceeds to appear to His closest friends and followers (eating, and disappearing, and teaching, and reappearing, and showing off His scars, then disappearing again) before finally ascending – right in front of their eyes – back to Heaven to sit down at His Father's right hand where (His followers find out later) He begins interceding for them, and for you and me.

As Jesus' first followers stand there dumbstruck, staring up into Heaven, an angel shows up, telling them that Jesus will come again in the same way they saw Him go; at that time, He will inaugurate His Kingdom which will have no end and in which you (yes, you!) have a place!

Crazy. Ridiculous. *Mythic* even.

*Unless it's not.*

A friend of mine (a great preacher named Mark) used to put it this way when we were coming up together: "Look, we basically tell a *ridiculous* story that works, because it's *true*…"

*This ridiculous, supernatural story works.*

The second way your life is meant to be, in light of this, is *supernaturally powered*, because the story of Jesus is not *just* a story, it's true; it's not mythology, it's *reality*. And every Christian who ever *truly* followed Jesus is *evidence*.

You *are* "the impossible made possible" because of Jesus' power at work in you.

But you're thinking; "Uh, well, I haven't leaped any tall buildings in a single bound lately…"

But have you been *kind*?

Where is the room for kindness in a world without God? Where does kindness *fit* in Darwin's theory of Evolution and Natural Selection?

It doesn't.

So, kindness is *unnatural*, perhaps even supernaturally so.

What about *love*?

Have you ever shown *unconditional* love to anyone, or has anyone ever shown it to you? Or *joy*. What about joy? Have you ever felt joy (it's different from "happiness"') in the midst of an impossible situation? Ever smiled again, or even laughed, after suffering cataclysmic loss?

That's a miracle.

Just last week, in fact, I was having a really bad day, one of those days that make you hate your life and question the reason for your existence. All of a sudden, while I'm driving, the Holy Spirit shows up in my car – unannounced – and fills my heart with joy for no apparent reason. I'm weeping, smiling, feeling one hundred percent well, and nothing about the circumstances of my life had changed. I didn't ask God to show up, but like sweet spring rain, He did. Whooosh, the Holy Spirit and me, going for a drive, and all was well.

I rushed home after and told my wife.

"I just had a moment of perfect happiness..." I said.

For no apparent reason.

What about *peace*?

(You see what I'm doing here, right?)

Have you ever found yourself able to access peace in the midst of turmoil, or patience, even though you're mad as hell? Ever felt that inexplicable calmness?

("Mad as hell" is a good phrase because hell loses in the end, which is why it's mad.)

Ever been *kind* even though you wanted to be mean, or *good* even when you wanted to be bad?

For those of you who've been married for more than six minutes, have you ever been able to be *faithful*?

It's a miracle.

Just in case you haven't checked in a hot minute, *faithfulness* isn't exactly the fashion of the day. So how is it, despite the odds and the unfashionable-ness, that some people still find a way to be faithful to their spouses?

*Gentleness.*

Ever been gentle, for no reason? Even the toughest, most aggressive people are usually gentle at home with their wife and kids, or with a newborn puppy. There is gentleness in people that you never see.

One of my closest friends almost died of acute pancreatitis (I know, rare) a couple of years ago. I went to see him *every* day that he was in hospital. Every day – and it was not an insubstantial drive. I'd sit with him and sometimes talk, sometimes listen, sometimes pray, and often I'd read to him from "The Lord of the Rings" because he loves that book. I didn't do this because I'm a good or gentle person when left to my own devices. The gentleness of God *showed up* in my life (I could feel it, man) and enabled me to act in partnership with Him, sitting beside my friend, in God's (physical) place.

*Self-control.*

I did not eat the entire banana cake last night, honestly. Just *most* of it, and if you'd tasted my wife's banana cake, you'd *know* my restraint was supernatural!

These things are *impossible* without God's help in a fallen world. But with Jesus, love, joy, peace, patience, kindness, goodness, faithfulness, gentleness, self-control (Gal 5:22) are possible. You are meant to live that kind of supernaturally charged life, and that life is meant to be a work in progress.

That's your third thing right there.

> *"...you yourselves like living stones are BEING built up as a spiritual house, to be a holy priesthood, to offer spiritual sacrifices acceptable to God through Jesus Christ..."*
>
> —1 PETER 2:5 ESV

I love this.

You're *being* built up as a "spiritual house." Being built up is what your life should look like. You're *literally* meant to *be* a work in progress.

(You're welcome.)

This kind of life-changing point is super-convicting for people like (ahem) my wife, who always wants everything to be finished, and perfect, NOW! It's also convicting for people like me, who (ahem) never want to do any *work*.

The Bible says you are (present continuous) *being* built up; you are a constant work in progress.

*"But, built up into what?"*

*A spiritual house.*

You're quite literally under renovation. We should all get tattoos that read *"RENOVATION"* put on us somewhere or, at the very least, buy the t-shirt. I need that sign in my life.

"Please forgive our mess as we *renovate*, to serve you better..."

Gosh, that could be a prayer.

Have you ever dealt with a frustrating person who was never kind enough? Join the club. Thing is, they probably feel the same way about you. Maybe moving forward, having read this, you can cut 'em a little more slack, because we're all under renovation. You're literally being built up into a spiritual house to *be* something amazing. And what is that *something* you're being built into?

A Holy Priesthood.

It was the best day of my life when the reality of this started dawning in my heart about twenty years ago. Once I began realizing what "priestly" *meant*, my life began to change. The literal definition of "priestly" is *"Sacred Effect."* That's what it *means* to be a priest. It means to *be* a "Sacred Effect." In Jesus, you literally *"holy-ize"* the world around you. Yes, our holiness is rooted and grounded in *Jesus'* holiness, but since we are "in" Him, and He is "in" us (2 Cor 5:17/ John 17:21), *if* He is holy, and we are His partners on His Mission, and *if* when one of Jesus' Apostles (Peter) calls Jesus' people (us) a "Sacred Effect," he's not lying, then *we* – in partnership with Jesus – *holy-ize the world.*

So, moving forward, you need to begin seeing *everything* you do as being part of that "Sacred Effect." That means if you're going to work tomorrow to roof a house, you roof that house to the glory of God, like you're a priest! "Dr. Matt" (head and neck surgeon in our town and board member at my church) gets a text at five in the morning Sunday to come in to the ER to save someone's life; he's slated to play bass on the worship team that morning and he's been up half the night with one of his young daughters. What does he do? Because he knows he's a "Sacred Effect," he jumps up, drives to the OR, saves a girl's life, drives to church, plays bass like the "Minstrel Prophet" he is, then goes home after, snuggles up on the couch with his wife and babies and has a nap to the glory of God, because he knows he's not just a Doctor, not just a Dad, not just a Worship Team Member; he's a *Priest*!

Think you'd be a better roofer, or a more competent surgeon, if you saw yourself as a "Sacred Effect" and acted that way?

You bet.

What about if you were a corporate coach? Would it work then? If you saw yourself as being a "Sacred Effect" in the lives of the people you were training, if your input in their lives had an actual *holy-izing* effect on those future corporate leaders, do you think that might bring God much glory, you much joy, and – through their transformed lives – might do much good to the wider world?

You bet.

That's *who* you are.

A "Sacred Effect." A holy-izer. A *priest*.

Redeem your work; do it like the priest that you are from this day forward, as an act of worship!

> *"...to offer SPIRITUAL sacrifices..."*
>
> —1 PETER 2:5 ESV

Literally, you exist to worship Jesus, and you can do all this – be built up into a spiritual house, as a priest, to worship Jesus – because you've been made:

> *"...ACCEPTABLE to God through Jesus Christ..."*
>
> —1 PETER 2:5 ESV

That's amazing.

*"Why?"*

Because it means that none of this *hinges* on your "acceptability" in and of yourself, but it hinges on the fact that you've been *made* acceptable *through* Jesus Christ. So, celebrate the fact that you're "Under Renovation" by having a "Sacred Effect" – by being a "Sacred Effect" – in, and on, the world around you *while* living a life of worship which, in the original language, means to come close and *kiss* Jesus. Be close enough to Jesus that you could kiss Him, knowing that *all* of the things I've just outlined are built on *Jesus* as your firm Foundation.

*"But how do we know?"*

> *"For it stands in Scripture: 'Behold, I am laying in Zion a stone, a cornerstone chosen and precious, and whoever believes in him will NOT be put to shame...'"*
>
> —1 PETER 2:6 ESV

That's good stuff right there.

You can *count* on Jesus. Whoever believes in Him will *not* be put to shame. This affirmation leads us to the *fourth* thing that your life is meant to be, and that's *built* on Jesus as the Chief Cornerstone.

Do you know what a *cornerstone* is? It is the foundation stone at the point where two walls meet. There is an actual cornerstone in Zion and I've seen it with my own eyes and kissed it with my own lips.

I was exploring an archeological dig at the edges of the foundation walls beneath the Temple Mount in Jerusalem a few years ago and my guide had the inside track, literally. We'd become friends over several weeks of working together and he knew that I was (what he would consider) a "God-fearer" and that the significance of the ancient city of Jerusalem held deep meaning for me, as it did for him. So, as we were walking through the dig, he did a double take at a checkpoint (he was looking to see if the archaeologists could see us or not) and quickly ushered us past a "Do Not Enter!" sign into a "Restricted Area!" (yes, there were two signs). Once past those signs, we were off the reservation on an unlit thin metal catwalk inching our way forward with our iPhones for flashlights.

"This is it..." he said.

"This is what?" I asked.

"The Cornerstone..." he said. "Go ahead, jump down and take a look."

So, I did.

I turned to my left and jumped down into a live dig in the city of Jerusalem, at the base of the walls of the Second Temple from Jesus' time, took two steps forward, and knelt in the dirt face to face with the *cornerstone* of the Temple Walls. Utterly speechless, *I leaned forward and kissed the Son.*

I kissed the Cornerstone laid in Zion and, lemme tell you, I wasn't thinking about a piece of rock sitting atop the bedrock of Mt. Moriah where Abraham was led to almost sacrifice his son Isaac, as awesome as that was in itself.

No, I was thinking about *Jesus.*

Jesus, Who loved to teach no more than a hundred yards from where I was kneeling, above ground, on the Southern Steps of the Temple, at the base of the Triple Hulda Gates, the Southern Entrances to the Temple.

In Jesus' time the cornerstone would have been visible above ground level adjacent to the market area of the Temple Courts directly beneath Robinsons Arch (as it is called today), which was the primary bridge that led from the Pilgrim Road, which ascended from the Pool of Siloam – at the Southern Gates of the City – up to the Temple Courts. It's guaranteed that Jesus Himself would have taught within feet of the location I was standing, if not directly on the spot itself, at the literal meeting of the two Southern Walls of the Temple compound where the market met the steps. I had no doubt in that moment that the stone I was kneeling before was the one Peter would have had in mind, reflecting back on Jesus and His ministry, when he wrote those powerful words:

> *"Behold, I am laying in Zion a stone, a CORNERSTONE chosen and precious..."*
>
> —1 PETER 2:6 ESV

Our precious Jesus.

And you can count on Him; on that Stone that the builders rejected, because at the root of *every* triumph lies the Cornerstone. At the root of every defeat, every moment of suffering, lies the Cornerstone, and all the weight and all the pressure of the edifice that is your life, lies on the Cornerstone, just like it does in the real world with real walls.

*So, stop trying to carry the weight yourself.*

If all the weight of every good moment and all the pressure of every bad one rests squarely on the Cornerstone, that means it does not rest on *your* shoulders. The only question you really need to ask yourself is this: is Jesus truly the Cornerstone of *your* life?

If you honestly answered "No," then my follow-up is going to be simple.

"What's *stopping* you?"

*"Well, I guess I just have a hard time believing..."*

If that's your reply, let's take a moment here, as we turn the corner for home with this chapter, and explore the nature of *unbelief*.

> *"So the honor is for you who believe, but for those who do NOT believe, 'The stone that the builders rejected has become the cornerstone,' and 'A stone of stumbling, and a rock of offense.' They stumble because they disobey the word, as they were destined to do..."*
>
> —1 PETER 2:7-8 ESV

"For those who do *not* believe..."

In the original language, "unbelief" means "being stubborn." This might help us. Unbelief *is* stubbornness. Stubbornness lies at the root of unbelief; it *is* unbelief, for all intents and purposes. But *how* it manifests is equally, if not more, important than what it is.

Here's how it shows up.

*"I kind of like the sound of this Jesus that you keep talking about, but I don't want to change."* Or, *"Can I come to Jesus and keep doing everything I've been doing?"* The answer to that is, no.

*"Why not?"*

Because, if you've come to Jesus, you need to start – and it will be a lifelong process – *growing up* into Christ. You come to Jesus just as you are, to be sure, but you don't *stay* that way. The Christian life is one of ongoing transformation from glory to glory as you become more and more like Jesus and less and less like the son or daughter of hell you were before you met the King. As you are "in" Christ, righteousness now becomes something for you to taste and see more and more of as you follow Jesus, joining on His mission in culture to seek and save the lost and to work towards the renewal of all things. Holiness is now something you can *taste* as you abide in Christ, staying close to Him at all times.

As you do this, the fruit of the Spirit is going to start showing up in your life, drastically changing your relational sphere, and you're going to begin experiencing the outskirts of freedom: a freedom that will become more and more profound until that day when you awaken in Jesus' likeness and presence, one hundred percent free.

This is why Christianity repels so many.

*"I like the idea of being free, but can I keep smoking up every day?"*

Nope.

*"Why?"*

Because addiction isn't freedom and you can't name a drug, if used regularly, that isn't habit-*forming.*

*"I like the idea of being fit, but I like the idea of a cheeseburger with fries and a pop for lunch every day also."*

Can't do it.

How many people do you know who've come right to the edge of surrendering to Jesus and then have stopped at the last minute, once they've really counted the cost? If you prefer stubbornness to submission then, to you, Jesus will be a stone of stumbling and a rock of offense.

*You can't get around Him.*

I've seen this pattern at least a hundred times in twenty-five years as a pastor. Someone's starting to come to church regularly, starting to learn to worship Jesus, maybe they're checking out a smaller group meeting midweek in someone's home, and they're starting to feel compelled to make some small changes in their way of life; they are even following through on those urges a bit. Then it happens. Oops! Trip! Fall!

And what tripped them up? The Stone of Offense: Jesus. Their stubbornness ran up against God's goodness and realizing that, in light of who Jesus is and what He does, they can't "win" – can't hang onto whatever pattern of behavior has gotten them hung up – they opt out. Why?

> *They stumble because they DISOBEY the word, as they were destined to do..."*
>
> —1 PETER 2:7-8 ESV

I'm not going to get into a deep discussion of predestination and adoption here (check back with me in half a decade for a book on Romans), but let me say a couple of quick things here about why I think so many people stumble on Jesus.

First, people stumble on Jesus because they don't want to obey "the Word." Now, you probably remember that in the last chapter we established that "the Word" does not simply mean the collection of documents that is the Bible we read today. If Peter did have a collection of documents in mind as he wrote this, as an observant Jew, he would have been thinking of the Hebrew Scriptures, the Torah, the Prophets and the Chronicles, or "Writings." But I wouldn't be surprised at all to discover someday that when Peter speaks of "the Word" and the fact that stubborn unbelievers disobey it, he was actually saying that, when we stubbornly *resist* God's kindness, we are disobeying the *totality* of what God says about Himself and the *fullness* of what that means for our lives.

And, let's be honest, it's much harder to submit yourself to the totality of what God says about Himself than it is to submit to the teachings, or requirements, of a mere document. Given enough study and dedication, you can eventually wrap your arms, mind, and life around *any* document, no matter how complex. But the God of the Universe?

Somewhat taller order.

What does God *essentially* say about Himself? What kind of "Divine Totality" does this document we call "the Bible" actually testify to? Basically, from God's perspective (if I may be so bold), it says: "I'm God. You're not. Deal with it." Or –

*Submit.*

*"Yay! Such a happy, positive thought! I'm so glad I picked up this book, so that I could be told that submission is the key to happiness..."*

Look, I'm sorry, but I've spent my whole life studying the Bible and my highly non-sophisticated distillation of its one clear message is exactly as I've outlined it above, in all its inelegance.

*"I'm God. You're not. Submit."*

Yes, there's a postscript. In the Old Testament, the postscript is: "Remember Me..."

"I'm God. You're not. Submit, and *remember* Me..." That's the heart of the Old Testament right there.

In the New Testament, the core teaching is the same, but the postscript is a little more user friendly. "I'm God. You're not. Submit to *Jesus*, who *is* the Answer..." And to be fair, we should probably say that the New Testament has one of those annoying PPSs, like your high-maintenance grade-nine girlfriend used to affix to the end of her love letters.

"I'm God. You're not. Submit to *Jesus*, who *is* the Answer *and* (PPS) make sure to *love* Him and *others* while you're at it."

But we don't want to hear this, do we?

*Because none of us like to submit, to anyone, ever.*

Let me hit you with the truth about our species before we go much further. Either you're going to submit *to* God, or you're going to spend the rest of your life trying to *be* God while working endlessly (and joy-killingly) to make everyone else submit to *you*.

Have you seen that pattern in the world around you? I know you have. Maybe you see the early signs of this pattern setting up in your life.

Why does somebody cut you off in traffic? Because they want to make you submit to them. They see themselves as better than you – they deserve to turn left before you drive through – and they're going to force their will on you, if they can. Why does this make you angry? Well, if they're turning left and the advanced green has expired and it's your turn to go, you're mad because it's unjust; but what really makes you burn is the fact that their contempt for you – as they cruise through the red – screams loud and clear that they think you are "less" than them, and you don't like feeling "less" than *anyone*. So, you hate them a little (or sometimes a lot) as they blow through that intersection in front of you.

Why does everybody always try to win in a negotiation? Because they want to force you to submit your wants and desires to theirs; in however limited a way, they're playing God. Why do some use violence as leverage while others turn to manipulation? All in a quest for ultimate godlike power. They want you to submit to them, at whatever cost. Why?

Because they see themselves as God, and since – seeing as they're God – they sit in the place of highest authority, it makes *complete* sense that everyone else (including you) should submit to them.

Allow me to remind you of the key problem with playing God.

*The real God of the Universe hates it.*

He absolutely hates idolatry in all its forms. There are events recorded in the Bible where He wipes out cities and overthrows nations because of idolatry and its effects. The teaching of the story of God and His people in this area is crystal clear; God will not have his creatures "playing God."

I'm quite sure you *know* why God is like this.

*Because none of you let your toddlers run your household.*

Imagine that your two-year-old, the moment they finally learned to speak, opened their mouth and proceeded to spill out a bunch of instructions that they expected *you* to begin following as *they* took over the running of your household and life. Are you going to listen to that idiot kid, or are you going to swiftly put a whuppin' on them?

You're gonna whup that kid. You're going to whup him so good he has a "come to Jesus moment" right there on that kitchen floor.

Even as I write this, I'm mindful of how far we've fallen, in this area, here in the craven West. I was at our local Farmers Market recently; my wife and I go there every Saturday morning before the kids are up. And, yes, the fact that we have a pretty busy Farmers Market in our town means we probably live in a pretty progressive, left-leaning town. And, yes, that probably means that many of the (especially) young parents in our town don't really *believe* in disciplining their children (they've been taught to reason with them, or something stupid like that) so, yes, that means that I ran into at least six young moms who were scurrying around the market in a near panic, trying to "actively listen" to their demon-possessed offspring as they terrorized the rest of us trying to buy our eggs and bread.

Instead of just grabbing them by the arm and removing them from the situation, then taking them home, to receive their well-deserved whuppin', these poor young moms were allowing the terrorist-fruit of their loins to actively ruin their morning, and everyone else's.

Do you know what the Old Testament punishment for disrespecting your parents is?

*Death.*

I often suggest (only somewhat tongue-in-cheek) that any young parents in my congregation who are struggling with "terrorist-children" send them to Pastor Todd's house for a very special summer camp where I will go just a little bit Old Testament on them, in Jesus' name, before sending them home, good as new. I jest, but there's some truth to it. We often host the small children of the young parents in our congregation on summer afternoons so the kids can swim and their folks can get a moment to just be away from their evil brood, and the parents are always amazed when they ask us after (with a somewhat horrified look on their face in anticipation of our response) how their kids behaved.

"Just fine." We say. "No problems at all."

And they can't believe it.

Know why?

(Meaning, know why their kids behaved so well?)

*You guessed it.*

The first time they tried to throw their weight around to get me to do what they wanted me to do, they ran into the brick wall also known as a 21st Century version of an Old Testament Patriarch and realized, right then and there, that they'd met their match and then some.

Ain't no two-year-old fool-of-a-child going to boss me around.

*I'm the parent. You're the child. Submit.*

And we, my fine-feathered-pseudo-two-year-old-terrorist-friends, are *exactly* that ridiculous when we try to boss God around, continually attempting to ascend His throne so that we might rule and reign in His place and receive the glory and honor and power and praise of everyone else we encounter in the world as they bow their knee to *us* as kings and queens – as gods.

If you're not walking daily in growing repentance and humility before the *real* God of the Universe, you're acting like a two-year-old terrorist; the degree to which we fail to walk with Jesus is the degree to which we commit these crimes of pride and prejudice against the real King.

Do yourself a big favor, don't be a two-year-old-terrorist-fool.

The second reason some people "stumble" on Jesus is because they were *destined* to. That's some hard stuff right there.

*"Wait, are you saying that some people are predestined for Hell and others for Heaven?"*

I read all of the parts of the Book of Romans that deal with predestination in preparation for this moment, including chapters eight through twelve. "Predestination" and "adoption" are two of the thorniest doctrines in all of Christianity. Here's how I deal with them.

There are passages in the Scriptures where we read about God creating some "vessels" for wrath, and in that sequence, the thought is: "Well, that's not really fair. How could a good God choose some vessels to be destroyed?" What's really interesting is that the writer of Romans responds by going right *at* the questioner, asking them who they think *they* are that they should be telling the "Potter" what to do with *His* clay. Like you, I find that pretty hard stuff to deal with, especially when working to introduce new people to the beauties of Jesus.

So, let's take that ugly reality and contrast it with an idea we'll explore later in this book, an idea that comes from Peter, one of Jesus' closest followers and an Apostle of the Early Church. The idea that it is God's will that *none* should perish. Sometimes, when the New Testament talks about what Jesus did in dying on the cross, it says that He died "once for all..." for "the sins of the whole world..." (1 John 2:2), which seems to pretty clearly imply that Jesus' atoning death was for *everyone*. But then there are spots where we're told we have to confess with our mouth and believe in our heart that Jesus Christ is Lord, and that God the Father raised Him from the dead, and that only then will we be saved (Rom 10:9). And, maybe you're thinking what I'm thinking: "Doesn't it have to be one or the other?"

I feel you. If the Atonement was "once for all..." what does *my* confession have to do with anything? And the thing is, we're not Biblical scholars, we're not rabbis devoted to studying the Talmud (the oral interpretation and application of the Law of Moses), and we're not trying to be forensic about this to get every jot and tittle of the law exactly right in our life and practice, to say nothing of the fact that we're just normal people with a cranky two-year-old to raise.

So, what do we do?

I think a good starting place is to try to understand everything the Bible says through a lens that *is* the Person and Work of Jesus Christ. Who was Jesus? What did He do? What does that mean for us? Let's keep it simple. Let's keep it about Jesus. In answer to these difficult questions about who gets in and who doesn't, we say this:

Jesus Christ, God the Son, became man, suffered and died on the Cross in our place for our sin, rose again for our salvation, ascended to His Father's right hand where He sat down in victory to intercede for us – a place He will come from again in glory to judge the living and the dead and to inaugurate His Kingdom which will have no end, a Kingdom in which you have a place.

That's our response.

To all the questions about predestination and adoption we say this; "God knows those who are His..." (2 Tim 2:19).

When it comes to predestination, we know a few things for sure. We know that we are not God, so it stands to reason that we don't know those who are His. And please don't go bringing up the whole "By their fruit you shall know them..." (Matt 7:16) because, like a peach tree, I never saw a Christian who was always in bloom, always fully exhibiting all the fruit of the Spirit all the time.

So, if we agree that we are not God, then it seems pretty clear to me that we should therefore agree that our only job is to preach and live the Gospel of Jesus in such a way that everyone we meet has an opportunity to see it and to hear it.

We don't know who's "in" and who's "out" so, like the Bible tells us to, we preach the Gospel to every creature (Mark 16:15). We proclaim the good news about Jesus to everyone we can, because we don't know who's "elect" and who's not, and because we know that Jesus (and no other name) is the *hinge*.

> *"At the NAME of Jesus every knee shall bow and every tongue confess* (which means to joyfully acclaim, by the way) *that Jesus Christ is Lord, to the glory of God the Father..."*
>
> —PHIL 2:10-11 ESV

So that's what we do, and He's the One we both acclaim and proclaim. We don't worry about the details of how predestination and adoption will ultimately work themselves out, because we're not God. We leave the Godlike work up to Him and, in the meantime, we proclaim the good news about Jesus, because Jesus *is* "the Hinge."

This idea about Jesus as "the Hinge" is illustrated beautifully in "The Last Battle" by C.S. Lewis. Near the end of the story, all the creatures from Narnia are escaping their dying world and find themselves facing an open door from their country into the Higher One, and Aslan, the Great Lion and Christ figure of Lewis' Chronicles, is standing at the door so that each creature must face Him, and make a choice.

> *"...they all suddenly realized what was happening. The spreading blackness was not a cloud at all: it was simply emptiness. The black part of the sky was the part in which there were no stars left. All the stars were falling: Aslan had called them home.*
>
> *The last few seconds before the rain of stars had quite ended were very exciting. Stars began falling all round them. But stars in that world are not the great flaming globes they are in ours. They are people (Edmund and Lucy had once met one). So now they found showers of glittering people, all with long hair like burning silver and spears like white-hot metal, rushing down to them out of the black air, swifter than falling stones. They made a hissing noise as they landed and burnt the grass. And all these stars glided past them and stood somewhere behind, a little to the right.*

*This was a great advantage, because otherwise, now that there were no stars in the sky, everything would have been completely dark and you could have seen nothing. As it was, the crowd of stars behind them cast a fierce, white light over their shoulders. They could see mile upon mile of Narnian woods spread out before them, looking as if they were floodlit. Every bush and almost every blade of grass had its black shadow behind it. The edge of every leaf stood out so sharp that you'd think you could cut your finger on it.*

*On the grass before them lay their own shadows. But the great thing was Aslan's shadow. It streamed away to their left, enormous and very terrible. And all this was under a sky that would now be starless forever.*

*The light from behind them (and a little to their right) was so strong that it lit up even the slopes of the Northern Moors. Something was moving there. Enormous animals were crawling and sliding down into Narnia: great dragons and giant lizards and featherless birds with wings like bats' wings. They disappeared into the woods and for a few moments there was a silence.*

*Then there came – at first from very far off – sounds of wailing and then, from every direction, a rustling and a pattering and a sound of wings. It came nearer and nearer. Soon one could distinguish the scamper of little feet from the padding of big paws, and the clack-clack of little light hoofs from the thunder of great ones. And then one could see thousands of pairs of eyes gleaming. And at last, out of the shadow of the trees, racing up the hill for dear life, by thousands and by millions, came all kinds of creatures – Talking Beasts, Dwarfs, Satyrs, Fauns, Giants, Calormenes, men from Archenland, Monopods, and strange unearthly things from the remote islands of the unknown Western lands. And all these ran up to the doorway where Aslan stood.*

*This part of the adventure was the only one which seemed rather like a dream at the time and rather hard to remember properly afterwards. Especially, one couldn't say how long it had taken. Sometimes it seemed to have lasted only a few minutes, but at others it felt as if it might have gone on for years. Obviously, unless either the Door had grown very much larger or the creatures had suddenly grown as small as gnats, a crowd like that couldn't ever have tried to get through it. But no one thought about that sort of thing at the time.*

*The creatures came rushing on, their eyes brighter and brighter as they drew nearer and nearer to the standing Stars. But as they came right up to Aslan one or another of two things happened to each of them. They all looked straight in his face; I don't think they had any choice about that. And when some looked, the expression of their faces changed terribly – it was fear and hatred: except that, on the faces of the Talking Beasts, the fear and hatred lasted only for a fraction of a second. You could see that they suddenly ceased to be Talking Beasts. They were just ordinary animals. And all the creatures who looked at Aslan in that way swerved to their right, his left, and disappeared into his huge black shadow, which (as you have heard) streamed away to the left of the doorway. The children never saw them again. I don't know what became of them. But the others looked in the face of Aslan and loved him, though some of them were very frightened at the time. And all these came in at the Door, in on Aslan's right. There were some queer specimens among them. Eustace even recognized one of those very Dwarfs who had helped to shoot the Horses. But he had not time to wonder about that sort of thing (and anyway it was no business of his) for a great joy put everything else out of his head. Among the happy creatures who now came crowding round Tirian and his friends were all those whom they had thought dead. There was Roonwit the Centaur and Jewel the Unicorn, and the good Boar and the good Bear, and Farsight the Eagle, and the dear Dogs and the Horses, and Poggin the Dwarf.*

*'Further in and higher up!' cried Roonwit and thundered away in a gallop to the West. And though they did not understand him, the words somehow set them tingling all over. The Boar grunted at them cheerfully. The Bear was just about to mutter that he still didn't understand, when he caught sight of the fruit trees behind them. He waddled to those trees as fast as he could and there, no doubt, found something he understood very well. But the Dogs remained, wagging their tails, and Poggin remained, shaking hands with everyone and grinning all over his honest face. And Jewel leaned his snowy white head over the King's shoulder and the King whispered in Jewel's ear. Then everyone turned his attention again to what could be seen through the Doorway..."*

—"THE LAST BATTLE" CHAPTER 14, BY C.S. LEWIS

I'd put the whole ending in if I had the time. You really must read it yourself someday; it will bring you to tears and give you deepest hope. Because you see, like Aslan, Jesus is the Hinge. He is the Great Lion standing at the Door. Ultimately you have to face Jesus, and if you've ever been even *slightly* worried that you've been predestined for wrath, it's a very good sign that you *haven't* been.

Ever heard somebody spit at the name of Jesus? I mean literally, like; "Pfffftt!! Jesus! Pah! Don't bother me about Jesus! Rubbish. All a bunch of superstitious nonsense!"

That's what the damned sound like.

*"No soul that seriously and constantly desires joy will ever miss it. Those who seek, find. To those who knock it is opened..."*

—C.S. LEWIS; "THE GREAT DIVORCE"

Have you heard, or met, the other kind? The kind who at the name of Jesus exclaim: "Jesus! That sounds lovely! Who *is* this Jesus? I'm not quite sure why, but I am sure I'd love to learn more about Him. Please tell me more..."

If at the name of Jesus even the slightest sign of love or joy shows up in your heart, then the following is true of you.

> *"But you are a CHOSEN race, a ROYAL priesthood, a HOLY nation, a people for his own POSSESSION, that you may PROCLAIM the excellencies of him who called you out of darkness into his marvelous light. Once you were not a people, but now you are God's people; once you had not received mercy, but now you have received mercy..."*
>
> —1 PETER 2:9-10 ESV

The fifth thing your life is meant to be is chosen, royal, holy, owned by God so that you can be His messengers (and I realize that kind of looks more like five, six, seven, eight, and nine; but you get the idea, I think).

*You are a chosen race.*

That means God chose you, which is why you never need to allow yourself to feel rejected ever again. Let His choosing be enough for you. You are meant to be a Royal Priest. You are a "Sacred Effect" rooted in God's King-ness! Never forget that God is King, and that the Sacred Effect that you are, and have, in and on the world around you is not rooted in *your* goodness, but in *His* King-ness, and His King-ness is pretty "Kingly"; it's more than enough to deal with all of your shortcomings and mine. So, go out into your life and boldly *be* the Sacred Effect that He has made you to be because it's rooted in who *He* is, not who you are.

Also remember that you're a "Holy Nation"! That means you're a gathered, unified, purposeful people, because of Jesus. Not because we always get along, or because we agree on every jot and tittle. We are a Holy Nation because Jesus has unified us, He's gathered us, and He has sent us out on a purposeful mission.

You belong to Him; you're His own possession. You might come from a dysfunctional family, you may have been rejected time and time again in your life, but you *belong* to God Himself and nothing can separate you from His love.

He never loses anything.

A life characterized by the epic truths I've just outlined – chosen-ness, priestly-ness, holy-nation-ness, knowing that you belong to God – that kind of life leads to an existence that proclaims the excellencies – literally the "valors" – of Him who brought you from darkness to light, who moved you from not belonging to belonging, who took you from being subject to God's wrath – because of your unrelenting sinfulness –to having been shown mercy, which means to have been given favor that you don't deserve. As this kind of work happens in you, you're going to find yourself living life as it was *meant* to be: a life where you, my friend, are *under construction*, moving from being a rolling stone, to becoming a *living stone*.

# FIVE

# Live Different

Following Jesus makes life difficult.

Why?

Because following Jesus makes you *different* from the world around you.

As you follow Jesus more and more closely, you will find that proximity to Jesus changes you, little by little, into more and more of a "Little Christ" (which is what "'Christian" originally meant) and the reality is, the more you look (and act) like Jesus, the less you're going to look like everyone else around you in the real world. Following Jesus makes you different, and being different is difficult. A couple of questions naturally arise out of this.

*"Why would I do it then?"*

If it's going to make you *different* and it's going to make you stick out from the world around you, why would you do it? Also:

*"What does it look like, anyway?"*

What does life *actually* look like when you're following Jesus? What does it look like to "live differently"? Let's answer those two questions in this chapter. We'll deal with the last one first, and spend most of the rest of our time thinking about the first question.

Okay, second question, first.

What does it *look like*, to live differently?

*"BELOVED, I urge you as sojourners and exiles to abstain from the passions of the flesh, which wage war against your soul. Keep your conduct among the Gentiles honorable, so that when they speak against you as evildoers, they may see your good deeds and glorify God on the day of visitation. Be subject for the Lord's sake to every human institution, whether it be to the emperor as supreme, or to governors as sent by him to punish those who do evil and to praise those who do good. For this is the will of God, that by doing good you should put to silence the ignorance of foolish people. Live as people who are free, not using your freedom as a cover-up for evil, but living as servants of God. Honor everyone. Love the brotherhood. Fear God. Honor the emperor.*

*Servants, be subject to your masters with all respect, not only to the good and gentle but also to the unjust. For this is a gracious thing, when, mindful of God, one endures sorrows while suffering unjustly. For what credit is it if, when you sin and are beaten for it, you endure? But if when you do good and suffer for it you endure, this is a gracious thing in the sight of God. For to this you have been called, because Christ also suffered for you, leaving you an example, so that you might follow in his steps. He committed no sin, neither was deceit found in his mouth. When he was reviled, he did not revile in return; when he suffered, he did not threaten, but continued entrusting himself to him who judges justly. He himself bore our sins in his body on the tree, that we might die to sin and live to righteousness. By his wounds you have*

> been healed. For you were straying like sheep, but have now
> returned to the Shepherd and Overseer of your souls..."
>
> —1 PETER 2:11-25 ESV

That's what it looks like to "live differently."

Be. Loved.

We could end the chapter right there and you'd be good to go.
That's just about perfect right there.

Be. Loved. *Beloved*. Period.

At the end of the day, beneath all the veneer, custom, tradition,
and rules, this is what it looks like to *be* one of Jesus' people. It
means to be beloved: to be loved (this is so good it will come up
again in a later chapter). You want to live differently? Live like you
are being loved, and then *extend* it.

It's hard to love when you don't *feel* loved, right? When you come
to the powerful realization that, in Jesus, you have *been* loved,
and are *being* loved by the God of the Universe – in a way that is
greater than anyone else can love – then, and only then, do you
become *free* to live securely and, from that place of security, to
love others with abandon.

So, if you find yourself suffering from a day-to-day love deficiency,
reflect upon the beautiful story of God's love shown towards you
in the person and work of Jesus. See, there's a direct connection
between your awareness of – or awake-ness to – the power and
truth of the story of Jesus, and the security that you feel in your
life as a result; the freedom you will experience once you make
that connection is what will *enable* you to love other people wildly.

What does it look like to "live differently"?

*Be Loved.*

And then live life like it *matters*.

> *"Beloved, I URGE you..."*
>
> —1 PETER 2:11A ESV

Live life like it matters; live it with some *urgency*.

Have you ever met someone who called themselves a "Jesus-Person" but whose life seemed kind of *"meh"*? If you know someone like that (maybe it's you?), take this as an opportunity to *urge* them to give their head a shake. If you see that "meh" attitude showing up in your life, slap yourself upside the head real quick, and start living life like it matters.

Maybe start with your ear hairs.

See, I'm a preacher. That means I stand up in front of hundreds (sometimes thousands) of people and speak to them about the story of Jesus and how it might apply (in a life-changing way) to their lives. I want them to take what I have to say seriously, which means I need to preach with non-hairy ears.

Why?

Well, say someone comes up to speak with me after a sermon. Maybe they have a question, maybe they want me to pray with them. I finish with the person in front of them in line, they step up, and before they can even shake my extended hand, they notice my hairy ears. What's the first thing they're going to think?

*"Gee, this guy is sloppy. He doesn't pluck his ear hairs..."*

(Don't pretend you haven't had that exact same thought.)

Maybe it wasn't ear hairs. Maybe it was their sloppy clothes, or their breath, or their body odor, or their dirty teeth, or their unkempt hair, or the way they wouldn't look you in the eye, but kept looking over your shoulder to see who the next person approaching might be, or the way they talked over you and didn't really listen. I don't know what it was exactly, but something about that preacher made you feel uneasy, and that momentary unease might cause just a fragment of doubt to enter into your mind about what he was saying to you (and hundreds of your friends a minute ago) about Jesus.

If I'm sloppy with my ears, maybe I'm sloppy with my exegesis.

See? Everything matters. Everything preaches, even ear hair, or the lack thereof.

Let's be straight here. I don't pluck my ears and make sure I don't smell or look offensive when I preach because I'm vain or want to impress people. Heck, I wear the same outfit every single time I preach (jeans and a dress shirt) because I don't want my appearance to distract in any way, either through sloppiness or flashiness. I don't care if I *look* good, but I do care that you taste and see that the *Lord* is good, without being distracted (in *any* way) by me. I often come across as a fairly serious person; that's because I want you to take what I have to say seriously. I'm someone who talks a lot about Jesus and what He's done to save you from hell and from living a life that *feels like hell* even before you go there; that – to my mind at least – is pretty serious stuff.

I'm trying to live with *urgency* because the mission of Jesus is urgent, and the state of your soul, and of your life, is an urgent matter. I'm trying to live like Peter says:

> *"Beloved, I URGE you..."*
>
> —1 PETER 2:11A ESV

Living differently means living like everything *matters*.

It also means not getting too caught up with being comfortable in the here and now.

*"Why?"*

Because living differently means living like you don't belong.

> *"Beloved, I urge you as SOJOURNERS and exiles..."*
>
> —1 PETER 2:11A ESV

Live like an expat, like a pilgrim, like a refugee.

This is hard, especially if you happen to be reading this book from your favorite chair in your comfy house, in your nice city, in the settled, developed West.

Obvious, right?

It's hard for us to act like we're from somewhere else and we're going home, because someone like me (and maybe you) who is of North American descent, is a descendant of strangers and sojourners, of pilgrims, of refugees who fled Continental Europe to seek a new life in North America. My great-grandparents (sometimes one or more generations further removed from that) struggled to build a life here, cast into the primitive expanses of the undeveloped North America of the 1700s or 1800s. They fought and scratched and clawed an existence from the hard, unsettled soil of the Americas and made this place "home." As a result, a deep aversion to discomfort, or dislocation, has, literally, been bred into people like me for generations. We are taught to dig in, to stick and stay. We are taught that "Home is where the heart is..." and that every North American has a right to life, liberty, and the pursuit of happiness, ideally in a clapboard house, with a picket fence and a Ford Model T in the driveway.

Go to school, get a good job, get married, work hard, save your money, buy a house, raise your family, and never, ever leave where you're from, or what you do. This was the modus operandi of our grandparents and great-grandparents, and they bred it into us. This is the natural rhythm of our days.

Or maybe you're the descendant of African slaves. For you, the pressure of this feeling is generationally closer. You may be the first generation facing an equal opportunity to rise above your birth or circumstances without the stone wall of racial discrimination that your parents and grandparents dealt with, making it completely impossible; the thought of leveraging your life on anything but the best version of here and now you can attain feels like a betrayal of everything your family has done to give you your opportunity. You want your best life now, not in the next life.

Wherever you fit, demographically, into the story of the North American Experiment, the last thing any of us naturally want is to be dislocated. Our French/Irish (in my case) or Scottish or Italian or Russian or Spanish or African ancestors suffered the ultimate dislocation when they fled, or were stolen away from, their respective continents and landed on America's shores. As a result, you can bet that they swore in their hearts to never suffer such dislocation again, nor see their children, or their children's children suffer it. And that urge has descended in a direct line, right into your heart. That's why you're hating this part of the chapter.

*"Act like I don't belong? Like I'm not from here? What kind of life is that? No thank you!"*

Might as well face it, you are not predisposed to living like this world is not your home. You will find yourself resisting this teaching at every turn and with every fiber of your being.

*"Heaven is your home..."*

You won't receive it.

*"You're just passing through..."*

You won't believe it.

Instead, you will find yourself preferring comfort and sameness at almost every turn. Exactly like the people to whom Peter was originally writing.

The people Peter was originally writing to had lived in their respective Roman provinces for *generations*. The area they lived in had originally been settled by retiring Roman soldiers, and their families grew up there and stayed. This was an established pattern with the Roman Empire. The Legions of Rome would conquer a territory and the Roman leadership would allow the soldiers who had done the conquering to settle in that territory, killing two birds with one stone. On the one hand, they rewarded their soldiers with land in payment for the service they had rendered. On the other, they ensured the ongoing "Romanization" of that geographical area as their newly "landed immigrant" soldiers intermarried and built families with the women of the region, families who would be raised Roman. Over time, in the case of our original audience, what is today Northeastern Europe was made to feel a little bit like home: a little bit like Rome.

So, you can imagine how what Peter was telling these people – who used to be strangers and sojourners and who had turned their adopted land into someplace that felt like home, through conquest and the hard work of culture-building – might have come across as fairly off-putting. And the same is very true for us. With this in mind, it might be time to be asking ourselves how we can introduce some *pilgrim-ness* into our otherwise stable North American lives.

Tall order? I know *exactly* how you feel.

The more established and entrenched your life is, the more difficult this is going to be for you.

Please hear me; I'm not saying that the answer is to "up sticks" and move to New Zealand (although that does sound fun). I am saying that the answer is to live on your street, in your neighborhood, in your city or town like *Zion* is your home! Organize your life in suburban Atlanta like you're ultimately *Judean*. And, if you're feeling like that sounds a little difficult, let me remind you that living differently *is* difficult, like going to *war*.

> *"...abstain from the PASSIONS of the flesh, which wage WAR against your soul."*
>
> —1 PETER 2:11B ESV

You want to "live differently"? Live like *lust* is your enemy.

*"What is 'lust'?"*

*Epithumea.*

A longing, especially for that which is *forbidden* (Merriam-Webster). When you dig a little deeper into the meaning of "Epithumea" it means an "inordinate longing" (Merriam-Webster). This is not garden-variety *interest* we're talking about here.

Say we're using "lust" in a *sexual* sense. Sexual lust is *not* normal sexual interest. We're *not* talking here about that spike in heart rate, and desire to look, that comes upon you when a beautiful woman, or handsome man, walks past. That's a normal, built-in, response God has woven into you to make you interested in procreating on an ongoing basis, because He wants lots and lots of friends to fill His world, which is why He commanded our first parents to be fruitful and multiply, to *fill* the Earth and subdue it. If you weren't interested in sex on an ongoing basis you wouldn't be able to obey God's first command to us humans. So, the gorgeous girl jogging through the park that just set your heart racing? The handsome guy that's got you feeling all fluttery? The goal our Omniscient God (who both made her, and him, and the park they're jogging through *and* Who also knew you'd be there to see them this day) has in mind here is to set *you* racing home to your spouse to see if you can run them right into the bedroom, for God's glory, and your joy, and for the filling of the world with more beautiful creatures made in God's image and likeness.

*Lust is something different.*

Lust is an inordinate longing, a longing that becomes the center of your life, the focal point of your consciousness. A force that – given reign long enough – comes to define you as a person.

The girl in the park would become an object of lust if you lay in bed at night, not satisfied from time spent with the wife of your youth, but obsessing about the girl in the park. She would become an object of stumbling if you began planning your days around timing your arrival at the park to coincide with her nightly jogs. You would be on your way to condemnation if you were planning how to approach her, working out the right words and fantasizing about how she might reply. Now you're lusting, and it's a hop, skip, and a jump from there to adultery; God hates adultery.

Do you see the difference between *desire* and *lust*?

Sadly, lust is absolutely central to the human condition post-Eden. If you look at the story of Eden, it's the lust for knowledge, the lust for equality with God which drives Adam and Eve to disobey God's clear instruction to them to not touch the Tree of the Knowledge of Good and Evil. In fact, the serpent *accesses* their disobedience, encourages it, through the pathway of lust. He plants the idea in their minds, and that's all it takes.

"Did God *really* say?"

"You'll not *surely* die..."

And, right then and there, lust shows up in the human story, and it's been burrowing its way deeper and deeper into our inherited consciousness ever since.

In our age of the world, lust for *autonomy* is huge, and God's people may have missed this, and even contributed to it a bit. For decades the North American Church has been tightly focused on eliminating what I call garden-variety lust. Sexual lust and addiction are the top two favorites, but we've rarely focused on trying to deal with our lust for autonomy as a fundamental disconnect between us and God. The lust we all have lodged deep in our hearts that concerns me most is the lust to put ourselves on the throne and to provide for *ourselves:* the inordinate desire to protect *ourselves*, *our* families, and *our* futures at any cost. Maybe, even as you read these words, you are awakening to spots in your life where this kind of lust is lurking. Lust is bedrock to our human fallenness, and the clear teaching of the Biblical story is that lust is your enemy. If you want to "live differently," you're going to need to go to war with lust.

*"How?"*

Well, you need to understand the good news about Jesus first and foremost. You need to understand your Bible. You need to begin tasting and seeing *for yourself* that the Lord is good, as experienced in the pages of the Bible, and in the context of a local worshipping community. You need to allow God's written words to equip you with the truth about life so that you will have some weapons with which to *fight* when lust shows up. See, the only way to dethrone lust is to *know* the truth, so that – as you are set free by it – you can take up the weapons of your warfare (which are the gifts and fruit of the Spirit) as *free* men and women, and fight the good fight. I'm talking here about the Sword of the Spirit and the Word of Truth (Eph 6:17). You must learn these, embrace them, and get to know them so you can fight lust. There is no shortcut to beating lust; you've just got to stop buying Oreos.

*Oreos are the devil.*

When I was a teenager I used to take six Oreos and eat them two at a time, mixed between giant gulps out of a carton of milk. I did this almost every day. This habit was all fine and good until I hit my mid-twenties, stopped growing, and stopped playing outside linebacker. As my stomach began to balloon, I realized I needed to stop it with the Oreos. Granted, Oreos may not be your issue and, to be fair, they weren't that serious an issue for me, but they illustrate the point about lust very well. See, even now, writing about Oreos, I want to sneak upstairs and see if we have any.

But at twenty-six years of age, I got to a point in my journey where I literally had to stop buying Oreos. At that stage in my personal development (and I feel so silly admitting this) I actually couldn't resist Oreos. If they were in the house, I'd end up acting like a fourteen-year-old again, six by two with milk.

So, I did it; I stopped buying them.

Nearly twenty years later, as of this writing, I'm happy, and grateful, to be able to say that – with God's help, and because of His mercy – I've been able to conquer my Oreo-gluttony problem, to the point that, nowadays with my four kids, I can buy them Oreos and not even feel tempted. I can put those delicious cookies in their lunches (passing my addictions on to the next generation, baby!) and not even break a sweat. I'm free when it comes to Oreos. But it took a while, and I had to "fast" from Oreos for *years* to get to the point where I was free.

The point for you is simple; it might not be cookies you're struggling with, but you may find yourself in a season at some point in your life where you're going to need to apply the "stop buying Oreos" principle to whatever kind of lust you're fighting against.

*Like, internet porn for example.*

Together with my wife and two friends, I planted and then pastored a church in downtown Toronto, Canada back in the early 2000s when the internet was just starting to really pick up steam in terms of everyone having access to it, in their homes. It's hard to imagine that being a "thing," I know. Our new church was full of young people (I think the median age was 26) and I'm sure you can imagine how a church full of young people, many of them young men, fared as pornography moved from late-night cable, magazines, and video stores (I sound so *old*) onto laptops in bachelor pads.

*Sex addiction swept through my church like a fire.*

Literally every ministry time, every meeting with a young man or a young couple, this was the crucial issue.

"Dude, I just can't stop looking at porn..."

*Of course, you can't.*

You used to have to go the corner store, pretend to buy some apples and milk and, "Oh, by the way, while I'm here, I just thought I might as well pick up this copy of Playboy; for the *articles*, you know..." Or you'd sneak downstairs after everyone was asleep to try and catch a glimpse of a wayward nipple or vagina on the scrambled channel while listening for your father's dreaded tread on the stairs.

(If it sounds like I know what I'm talking about, I do, 'cause that was me, at 16.)

Fast-forward from the mid-'90s to 2001 and full-blown high-definition pornography was available on your laptop, 24/7, in the comfort of your own bedroom, and nobody had to know about it. Move the clock forward to the present day where every teen (and most children) you know own a smartphone, and it's little wonder that sex addiction has become so endemic that most North American teens consider not recycling a bigger moral failure than looking at pornography. Just this past football season at the local high school where I coach, I overheard some of my players chatting between drills about the interactions they'd had the night before on their smartphones with a woman they were paying to strip for them, whom they'd discovered on a popular porn site. Think about that for a minute. A porn star in California films a scene. The scene is uploaded to a site on the internet hosted offshore. My teenage football players see the scene on their phones. They like the girl. They google her. Turns out she has a "live-cam" site. They jump on it. It accepts Visa Debit. Boom. They're interacting with her, then talking about it at practice.

Young men (and many young women) one generation removed from my youth, where you really had to *work* for your illicit nakedness, have been absolutely inundated with full-blown adult sexuality (and "produced" sexuality, at that) from the age of 12 in most cases and, as a result, are finding themselves sexually crippled, unable to relate to young women in normal, healthy physical ways, because all they know of women and sex they've learned through what they can consume on their phones, which are with them at all times. We have allowed an entire generation to arise who are addicted to porn like I used to be addicted to Oreos.

So, what's the solution for you, if you are one of those I'm describing?

*Stop buying Oreos.*

Cut your cable. Cancel your internet, if necessary. Absolutely refuse to allow screens of any kind to leave the main floor (ideally the kitchen) of your home. Install "accountability programming" on your devices (yes, these apps actually exist) so everything you "see" is seen by a select group of your peers, and/or your spouse. Take a vacation, if you can, to somewhere where there's no internet and leave all your devices at home – seriously. You may need to cold-turkey starve yourself at first to get over your addiction. A great resource I love to recommend on this is "The Power of Habit" by Charles Duhig. Not a Christian book, but a business one, "The Power of Habit" powerfully illustrates how habits are formed and how they can be overwritten with new, less destructive, behaviors. I've given more copies of that book away than I can count. If you want some practical tools for breaking free, go buy his book.

I promise you, if you stop buying into slavery, you will get to the point (over time, and with lots of hard work) where you will find your freedom.

If you "fast from sin" long enough, it shrivels up and then dies and, because of what Jesus did for you at the Cross, in defeating the power of Satan, sin, death, and hell once and for all, if you *want* to walk into freedom, He has made a way. Step one is to stop buying Oreos.

The list gets a little tougher after that.

> *"Keep your conduct among the Gentiles honorable, so that when they SPEAK AGAINST YOU as evildoers, they may see your good deeds and glorify God on the day of visitation. Be subject for the Lord's sake to every human institution, whether it be to the emperor as supreme, or to governors as sent by him to punish those who do evil and to praise those who do good. For this is the will of God, that by doing good you should put to silence the ignorance of foolish people. Live as people who are free, not using your freedom as a cover-up for evil, but living as servants of God. Honor everyone. Love the brotherhood. Fear God. Honor the emperor..."*
>
> —1 PETER 2:12-17 ESV

Want to live differently? You need to live so honorably that even those who hate you will one day give God glory.

*Does anybody hate you?*

As someone who has a lot of haters (that's the price of pastoring a growing church, baby) I found it strange, while writing this, to find myself thinking: "Gee, you know, this analogy might not work, because there are bound to be people reading this who've never experienced real hatred before..." Which would mean – if that was true for you – that you wouldn't really get this whole section. If you are that person, I envy you. Being hated is no fun.

It's one thing not to be hated because you're kind; it's another altogether not to be hated because you're soft. There are occasions when followers of Jesus do not suffer hatred because they do not follow Jesus very *obviously*; they don't stand out.

See, the problem with faith is that – as it did with our spiritual fore-father Noah – a "living faith" condemns the world (Hebrew 11:7). This is not because it *tells* the world that it's bad (please don't misunderstand me here), but because it *testifies*, out loud and very obviously, that there is a better way. A living faith condemns the world because, over and against a secular-materialist-idolatrous self-worshipping culture that says, "Life is all about *you*!" a living faith in Jesus declares by its actions that the *exact opposite* is, in fact, true.

Your deeds, done in Jesus, say to the world around you that life is *anything* but all about them. Faithful Christianity, when it's lived out, in public, declares: "There *is* a God, He is the *King*, and *you* are His dearly-loved *subject*."

*And that's offensive.*

The life of every true Christian testifies to the world around it: "You are *not* the center of the Universe!" And, last time I checked, people don't really want to hear that one; in fact, most people will hate you for saying it, or for living in a way that shows that it's obviously true. Which is why Peter is telling his original audience –and, by extension, you – to live an *exemplary* life: a life so outstanding that, one day, even your haters will come to their senses and give God glory for how kind He's been to you.

Now, the promise we have here from Peter is difficult. Even the Biblical interpreters aren't quite sure exactly what's going on here with the whole "...in the Day of Visitation..." thing. They're not sure if it's referring to the day when your haters repent – when they finally come to faith in Jesus, realize they were wrong the whole time, and decide to give God glory as a result, because of the impact your exemplary life has had on them – or if it's referring to the End of Days.

If you take it the first way (your haters are "coming to their senses"), it certainly works. Maybe you've experienced it yourself? I certainly have, when people who hated me and expressed their hatred towards me (even acting on it in some cases) in no uncertain terms came back to me *years* later and said, "I'm sorry. I was in a bad place. I was wrong. I treated you sinfully. Please forgive me." With me, every time this has happened, it's been *ten years later*.

Those kinds of apologies are tough to deal with because the damage they did to your life and the ripple effect of their active hatred towards you has rippled *for a decade*. Their apology takes a moment, but the damage they did took *years* to bear its ugly fruit in your life, in lost opportunities, damaged relationships, and ongoing heartache. Nothing can undo what they did, regardless of their late-to-the-party apology.

Let me encourage you to do it.

*Forgive them.*

One, Jesus commands us to and, two, holding unforgiveness in your heart is like letting someone live in your mind, *rent-free*. Don't let them. Evict them with forgiveness! So, if that is what "...and they will give God glory in the Day of Visitation..." means, great; it works.

It also works if "...Day of Visitation..." is referring to the "Eschaton," the "End of the Age," the "Day of the Lord" when Jesus returns to judge the living and the dead, to set all things right, and to inaugurate His never-ending Kingdom in which you have a place. If that's what we're talking about here, we're good, because we know that on that "Day," every knee will bow and every tongue confess that Jesus Christ is Lord, to the glory of God the Father (Phil 2:10-11). And you can bet, based on the promises we have here in this section of Peter's letter, that *in* that Day, those who hated you because of your clear testimony about Jesus, will tuck their tails between their legs and give God glory.

Let me make one more point here.

We need to be very careful to not give people *cause* to hate us unnecessarily. It is true that many people hate Christians for good reason; because sometimes we act like idiots. They see us picketing, rallying behind causes they think are idiotic, or championing political candidates they find hateful. They hear us droning on about our favorite "pet sins" – the ones we are absolutely *sure* are going to be the end of Western civilization as we know it if *we* don't put a stop to them – and on and on and on.

An exemplary life does not mean you should think of yourself as, or be seen as, one of these "Team Jesus" t-shirt-wearing fools. We don't want people to notice us as Jesus' people for the things we're calling people *not to do*. I think it would be better if they noticed us for the exemplary things *we do*.

*Like plowing our neighbors' driveways in the winter.*

(Again with the not-universally-applicable analogy; if you live in SoCal, I wish I was you, but work with me here.)

My whole adult life I've been careful to plow my adjoining neighbors' driveways (the ones directly to the left and right of my house) in the winter. I never had a snowblower until my most recent house (and thank God I do because our driveway is ridiculously long), so I always just did it with a shovel. I'd go out there, shovel mine, then shovel theirs; it'd take me triple the time.

Why did I do this?

Well, see, I knew (kind of intuitively) that, sooner or later, they'd realize that I was one of Jesus' people and, worse yet, one of His pastors. And I knew that, in that moment of truth, when the hatred of all things Jesus rose up in their as yet unsaved hearts, because of all the times they'd experienced hateful so-called Christians doing hateful things (and because of the inbred sinfulness they'd inherited – just like me – from their first parents), they'd have to stop for at least one brief moment to entertain this one, simple thought:

*"Yeah, but he always shovels my driveway without me even asking; he can't be all bad..."*

And, that one exemplary (albeit small) thing – me shoveling their driveway – will set a splinter in their mind that might widen into a crack that the Light can begin seeping into, to the ultimate saving of their souls one day, leading to them giving glory to God in the Day of Visitation.

*Just because I was kind.*

So, my neighbor Bill – he's an "old" seventy – in the first crazy snowstorm that hit this past winter *sees* me out there in the middle of the night, plowing my driveway. Then I go and plow his driveway then I go and plow the other neighbor's driveway. And, let's be clear about this, I'm not doing this because I'm a good person. I'm not even naturally that nice. Even as I'm pushing the snowblower down my driveway towards Bill's lot, my selfish nature is trying to talk me out of it. But I get to the bottom of the driveway and I say to myself: "Yes, Lord! Thank You for this opportunity to celebrate Your goodness. Thank You for a body strong enough to push this snowblower that You've provided for me to use..." and I bow my knee (in my mind, not right there in the snow) to King Jesus and get to work, doing the right thing for the sake of Jesus' eventual fame.

*The Gospel compels me.*

Just make sure you don't go getting all stupid about it and place a gospel tract in Bill's mailbox, telling him that his nicely plowed driveway has been brought to Him by Jesus, and the blood He shed and that, if he would but pray this prayer, his soul can be as clean as his driveway...

God help us; that kind of "strategy" was actually taught in our churches in my lifetime.

No. Just do the right thing, don't say anything about it, and keep trying to live an *exemplary* life, one snowstorm at a time.

You resist the darkness of the world around you not by fighting it, but by doing good *to* it. You see, to "live differently" is to live a life of resistance, but not the resistance of a rebel. This is what the next section we need to explore means when it talks about subjection and, I have to admit, I kind of *hate* these verses.

> *"Be SUBJECT for the Lord's sake to every human institution, whether it be to the emperor as supreme, or to governors as sent by him to punish those who do evil and to praise those who do good. For this is the will of God, that by doing good you should put to silence the ignorance of foolish people..."*
>
> —1 PETER 2:13-15 ESV

Subjection to authority: everyone's *favorite* subject! But there's no escaping it. To "live differently" is to live under authority. This one really sticks in my craw. People often say to me, "Todd, you have a real problem with authority!" to which I reply, "I have no problem with authority, as long as I'm *in* it..."

And usually, we have a good laugh about it.

Miserable wretch that I am, it's true though. This part of the teaching is really hard for me; I'm writing this next part probably more for me than for you.

You need to submit to authority because *all* authority – even ungodly authority – is ultimately rooted (if 1 Peter 2:13-15 is to be taken at face value) in *God's* authority; that's super heavy-duty and hard to take.

All authority is ultimately rooted in God's authority and all authority will ultimately *answer* to Him. And that right there is how you find freedom. Not in rebellion, but in submission out of reverence for God, knowing that God doesn't miss a thing and will ultimately right all wrongs. We submit to authority because ultimately God is the *only* authority and we know that any authority that "is" will one day bow the knee to Him, and His authority, and have to make *answer* for what they did with the authority that had been given to them for a time.

Knowing that hard truth is what will help (and allow) you to submit to even ungodly rule without it crushing your soul, because, in your heart, you know that your submission is really to God, the *Author* of all authority.

This kind of thinking makes Christian activism very difficult and renders Christian militarism null and void. Coming from a family with a long warrior tradition, this is hard for me to embrace, but it's true.

Now, let me be clear; I do not think that this means that Christians' care for the poor should be curtailed in any way as a result of this teaching. Any "activism" that expresses itself in *doing good* should not be held back because we are learning submission as a new way of life. We know from the Book of James that "Pure religion, and undefiled, is this, to care for orphans and widows in their distress and to keep oneself unspotted from the world..." (James 1:27) We must continue to act justly, to love mercy, and to walk humbly with our God (Micah 6:8), but we must resist the urge to embrace activism as a *tool* to reshape our culture into a form we think is more fitting, or godly.

Difficult, right? But none of this is *meant* to be easy.

> *"Live as people who are FREE, not using your freedom as a COVER-UP for evil, but living as SERVANTS of God. Honor everyone. Love the brotherhood. Fear God. Honor the emperor..."*
>
> —1 PETER 2:16-17 ESV

We're called to live "free" but not "loose." That's a tough one to work out, but you can do it by focusing on being God's *servant*. You take on the identity of a servant; you see yourself as God's slave. You learn to respect your co-image-bearers (other humans, made in God's reflection) even if they sometimes act like clowns.

*"Why should we respect people?"*

Because people are made in the image of God, literally in His reflection. We respect everybody, even those who hold different opinions than us and who act differently than us (even if they act the fool) because they were made in His image; they are literally small reflections (broken and bent by sin and curse) of God Himself and are therefore worthy of respect. And that same beautiful but bent reflection is all the more lovely when it is authentically lived out, with humility, by our sisters and brothers in Christ – which is why we love *them*!

> *"...LOVE the brotherhood."*
>
> —1 PETER 2:17A ESV

Can you grow a bit in this area? Even as you sit there reading this on your train ride into work or on your back deck with your sweet-heart, is God bringing someone to mind you could love more fully? Get out there and do it!

> *"...FEAR God."*
>
> —1 PETER 2:17B ESV

Think on that this week. Ask yourself, "Am I truly afraid of God and do I *live* like it?"

> *"...HONOR the emperor."*
>
> —1 PETER 2:17C ESV

And, granted, depending on where you live and when and who happens to be "in office," that may be a bit of a tall order, but Peter's not done with you yet; he's got one more sucker punch to deliver as we wind our way towards the end of this chapter.

> *"Servants, be subject to your masters with all respect, not only to the good and gentle but also to the unjust. For this is a gracious thing, when, mindful of God, one ENDURES sorrows while suffering UNJUSTLY. For what credit is it if, when you sin and are beaten for it, you endure? But if when you do good and suffer for it you endure, this is a gracious thing in the sight of God. For to this you have been called, because Christ also suffered for you, leaving you an example, so that you might follow in his steps. He committed no sin, neither was deceit found in his mouth. When he was reviled, he did not revile in return; when he suffered, he did not threaten, but continued entrusting himself to him who judges justly. He himself bore our sins in his body on the tree, that we might die to sin and live to righteousness. By his wounds you have been healed. For you were straying like sheep, but have now returned to the Shepherd and Overseer of your souls..."*
>
> —1 PETER 2:18-25 ESV

You want to live differently? Endure injustice because God did, and remember that God will reward you when you "suffer well."

*"Why do we have to 'suffer well,' again?"*

Because, as one of Jesus' people, you're called to *copy* Him, and Jesus suffered well, fully trusting God His Father, the Righteous Judge. He suffered well because He knew that, one day, God His Father would judge rightly. In fact, in a beautifully ironic twist at the End of Days (if the picture we see in the Book of Revelation is accurate), the Father will *entrust* judgment to the Son.

So, with all that in mind, live differently, like you're beloved. Live like you don't belong, like lust is your enemy. Live so honorably that even those who hate you will one day give God glory. Live like you're under authority, like you're free, but not loose. Live like a servant, respecting your co-image-bearers – people who look like God, just like you – loving your Brothers and Sisters in God's Family, fearing God, honoring the Government (even when they act like fools), enduring injustice because God did, knowing that – one day – He will reward you for your faithfulness. Copy Jesus, who trusted His Father, the Righteous Judge.

*"Why should I live that way?"*

#becausethegospel

> *"...He himself bore our sins in his body on the tree, that we might die to sin and live to righteousness. By his wounds you have been healed..."*
>
> —1 PETER 2:24 ESV

Because He died that you might live, you should die to self and live for Him. Which is going to mean...

*Living differently.*

# SIX

# Some Counter-Cultural Advice for Husbands and Wives

Life with Jesus changes *everything*.

If the story about Jesus is true, then our lives need to change *wholesale*. If it's true that God exists, that He made everything that is, including you; if it's true that His design and desire for you is to be His friend forever; if our first parents, Adam and Eve, really fell into sin, condemnation, and curse as a result of their disobedience in the Garden of Eden; and if, as a result of their original sin, every human being since has been born with a "sin problem" – the tendency to rebel against God our Maker – then there is a problem that lies at the root of the human experience.

Our good God, who is holy and cannot tolerate sin in any form, but must punish it, has created a race of human beings to be His friends forever who've now fallen into sin; therefore, they must be separated from Him because His Holiness cannot tolerate their sinfulness. And for His justice – a key attribute of His nature as God – to be truly "just," He must not only separate Himself from them but, ultimately, they must pay the penalty for their sin, and God is pretty clear about what that penalty is: death (Rom 6:23).

This is the problem at the root of our existence, and it's our fault because we sinned and we disobeyed God: not just once (as Adam and Eve in the Garden), but again and again in our own lives. You'll know all too well from your life the ongoing tendency you have to disobey God, to do what you want, and to continually attempt to ascend God's throne so that you might rule and reign in His place and receive the worship of people like He does.

This is a very big problem. *You're a rebel.*

But God, in His goodness, did not allow that problem to run amok forever. In the fullness of time, according to the Scriptures, God the Father sent God the Son to become the *God-Man*, Jesus, so that He might live a perfect and sinless life, completely and perfectly fulfilling the will of God His Father. Ultimately, He would offer Himself up once and for all on the cross, suffering and dying in our place for our sin and rising again from death the third day – the very first Easter Sunday morning – conquering the power of Satan, sin, death and hell forever, in His Body. He then appeared to His friends, hung out, ate meals, and then ascended, right in front of their eyes, back to Heaven where He sat down at His Father's right hand and where, even now, He sits cheering for you as you make your long journey home to Him. And, one day, He's going to get up from His throne to come again to Earth in glory to judge the living and the dead and to inaugurate His Kingdom which will have no end, a Kingdom in which *you* have a place.

If that Gospel, that good news, is true, it changes *everything.*

The question for us is this: how *comprehensively* are you allowing that good news to change your life?

You'll wrestle with the tension and difficulty of that for the rest of your life.

I mean, would you let the good news about Jesus change your career choice? You think you want to do one thing with your life (be a rich and famous film director), but as the Gospel of Christ presses itself upon you over time (it takes some of us longer than others) you feel God saying: "No, I'd like you to just be a preacher..."

Maybe. Maybe I'd let the Gospel change my career.

How about your house? As in, your actual house, the one you live in. Would you think it was crazy to ask God what kind of house you should buy and in what city or neighborhood? How about the way you manage your money? Would you allow the good news about Jesus, and the imperatives that are so clearly built into it, to influence (or even dictate) the way in which you made and then spent your money?

Real "rubber-meets-the-road" stuff.

What about your approach to kids? Would you have kids, or have more kids, because of the Gospel? How would you raise those kids in view of what the story of Jesus teaches us about life and our place in it?

*Your marriage.*

Would you let the Gospel change your marriage?

*"Sure, I'd love for the story of Jesus to change my marriage; I'll take all the help I can get in that area..."*

Good. Let's get to it, then.

What if – in changing your marriage –the Gospel of Jesus asked you to do the one thing you were *least* wired to want to do?

*"Dang it, man, you set me up!"*

Yes, I did. Let me show you why.

*"Likewise, wives, be subject to your own husbands, so that even if some do not obey the word, they may be won without a word by the conduct of their wives, when they see your respectful and pure conduct. Do not let your adorning be external—the braiding of hair and the putting on of gold jewelry, or the clothing you wear— but let your adorning be the hidden person of the heart with the imperishable beauty of a gentle and quiet spirit, which in God's sight is very precious. For this is how the holy women who hoped in God used to adorn themselves, by submitting to their own husbands, as Sarah obeyed Abraham, calling him lord. And you are her children, if you do good and do not fear anything that is frightening..."*

—1 PETER 3:1-6 ESV

Six verses there for the wives and then...

*"Likewise, husbands, live with your wives in an understanding way, showing honor to the woman as the weaker vessel, since they are heirs with you of the grace of life, so that your prayers may not be hindered..."*

—1 PETER 3:7 ESV

There's nothing I can do to take the sting out of this one. I even talked it over with my wife, because I was feeling a little nervous about putting this out to the kind of wide audience that is often reached by a book like this. She smiled and said, "Just be super clear about the fact that *you* didn't write it..." And we had a good laugh about that even though I knew that, ultimately, it wasn't going to help because, though I didn't write it, I *believe* it and I have practiced it for twenty-four years of very happy marriage with Ms. Niki. So, I'm just going to strap on my "big-boy pants" and jump right into it, for God's glory and (hopefully) your joy.

*"Likewise..."*

—1 PETER 3:1A ESV

The "likewise" here is referring to the end of the second chapter of 1 Peter where the Gospel of Christ is laid out.

*"He committed no sin, neither was deceit found in his mouth. When he was reviled, he did not revile in return; when he suffered, he did not threaten, but continued entrusting himself to him who judges justly. He himself bore our sins in his body on the tree, that we might die to sin and live to righteousness. By his wounds you have been healed. For you were straying like sheep, but have now returned to the Shepherd and Overseer of your souls..."*

—1 PETER 2:22-25 ESV

Likewise, or, in the *same way* that Jesus laid down His life for you.

Peter is playing "the Gospel card" here because he knows that what he is about to teach is difficult, and because the Holy Spirit *knew* that what Peter was about to write would ultimately get added to the collection of documents that has become our Bible and would, as a result, be passed down through the generations to *my* heart and mind and, through this book, right here and now in this moment, *to you.*

He pulls "the Gospel card" because he knows things are about to get a little rough.

"In light of what Jesus has done for you. In the *same way* that Jesus laid down His life for you..."

*He's setting you up.*

He wants you to wrestle with this. He wants you wondering if you really believe this stuff, as in, do you believe it enough to *do* what it says? Because, if you do – and you're a wife – your ego is going to have to die.

Let me say something here that I'll repeat a little later in the chapter: 94% of North Americans will get married, at some point in their lifetime (Gallup/Barna). So, if you're reading this and you are not a wife yet, nor think you'll ever be, the statistics say otherwise. You are likely to be in the 94% to find yourself married at some point and, as a Jesus-loving wife, your ego is going to have to die.

> *"Likewise, wives, be SUBJECT to your own husbands..."*
>
> —1 PETER 3:1A ESV

*"Now hang on just a minute!"*

I know, it's an ugly word.

*Subject.*

No one wants to be "subjugated."

*"You got that right! Let's check 'The Message', I'm pretty sure they use a different word!"*

So, a couple of quick things on "subjugation."

We are all *subject* to somebody already. Right? You're subject to God, you're subject to the laws of nature – meaning, you can't just jump off a cliff and fly – you are subject to the government of your town, state, and nation. You are a subject.

Complete freedom is a sinful myth. The drive towards that myth is what moved Adam and Eve to sin against God in the first place. So, if you're having a reaction as you read that you are to be subject to your own husband, you need to realize that your upset-ness is a factor of your native sinfulness. We're all subject to something already, so do away with the myth of complete freedom in your heart and mind.

Ultimately, we're all subject to the Gospel. Jesus trumps *everything*. You can neither rise above the Gospel nor sink below it. The Gospel rules; you are subject to it, whether you like it or not.

> *"Every knee shall bow and every tongue CONFESS that Jesus Christ is Lord, to the glory of God the Father..."*
>
> —PHIL 2:10 ESV

And since "confess" means to "joyfully acclaim," Philippians 2:10 means that one day everyone will joyfully acclaim that Jesus Christ is Lord, to the glory of God the Father. We will recognize Christ's supremacy and be *happy* about it. So, in subjecting yourself to Jesus' rule now, you're just getting a head start on what is a joyous inevitability for the human race.

*"So, exactly what are we talking about here with this whole subjugation thing? How bad is this going to get?"*

> *"Likewise, wives, be SUBJECT to your own husbands..."*
>
> —1 PETER 3:1A ESV

*"Hupotassomenai."*

"A voluntary attitude of giving in, cooperating, assuming responsibility and carrying a burden." (Merriam-Webster)

Let's try to celebrate both the beauty *and* the difficulty of Biblical words.

I think most of us would agree that we're okay with the back half of that definition. "Cooperating" sounds nice and "assuming responsibility" doesn't sound too onerous; I think we could all get with that. There seems to be some agency implied there, like I get to *choose* to cooperate and to share responsibility.

It's just the first part that gives us hives.

*Giving in.*

Not super-fans of that part.

*"Alright, we'll do it your way, I'll help you and I'll share the respon- sibility and the burden of this choice with you..."*

That's how Peter is exhorting Christian wives to relate to their hus- bands. Very challenging. How often have you heard a Christian wife say some version of, "That was *his* decision!" or "Pffft! I wouldn't have done it that way; if only he'd *listened* to me!" A Jesus-loving wife doesn't say those things and, as she finds her way into full flower as a mature disciple of Christ, she will find herself not even *thinking* that way.

Even if it wasn't her decision, she cooperates with the decision and assumes responsibility for the decision; accepting the agency given to her by God, she carries the burden of the decision *with* her husband. Pretty heavy. Let's note a few things here. When Peter is telling wives to be subject to their own husbands, it does not mean that *all* women are subject to *all* men. That means that this point Peter is making is *not* reason for us to embrace patriarchy, nor the wholesale subjugation of all women by all men.

We're talking here about *one* wife being subject to her *one* hus- band. This also does not mean that *all* wives should be subject to *all* husbands: just one to one.

*"So, if we don't fit into that category, if we're not 'husband and wife,' how should we relate to one another?"*

1 Timothy 5:2 helps with this one.

If you're dealing with an older man, you treat him as a father; an older woman you treat as a mother. If it's a younger man in front of you, treat him as your brother – which means maybe you need a good wrestling match to settle him down. Remember giving your brother a good whuppin', or getting one? It's good for you; if it's your brother, feel free to give him a good beatdown once in a while to keep him honest. Younger women you treat as sisters: a beautiful guideline there for how older Christian men can relate to younger Christian women without sinning sexually. I mean, you love your sister, you treat her well, you even enjoy the time you spend with her once in a while when she comes to town. But there's absolutely not even a hint of sexual undertone in your relationship with her because, well, she's your *sister*. That's a beautiful – and comprehensive – ethic from Paul, in 1 Timothy, for how Jesus' people can relate to one another.

But if we're talking about your own husband? Because of the Gospel, Peter is telling you that you need to treat your husband like he's in charge.

*"But what if he's an idiot?"*

> *"...even if some do NOT obey the word, they may be won without a word by the conduct of their wives, when they see your respectful and pure conduct..."*
>
> —1 PETER 3:1B-2 ESV

"Even if some are *stubborn* in unbelief..." is what's literally being said here. Peter is urging you (if you're a wife) to practice "lifestyle evangelism" by respecting your husband practically while living a life that is pure. Not easy. But nobody ever said following Jesus was easy; in fact, following Jesus gets more and more counter-cultural the deeper you get into it. The difficult countercultural-ness, almost counterintuitive-ness, of the Christian ethic is almost what makes me believe it, if I'm being completely honest. I figure, if somebody was trying to develop a fake religion to try and enslave the masses and control them, they'd have made up something a whole lot easier than Christianity. Since we're truth-talking here, I think they'd probably invent something like the rampant self-oriented, secular-humanist , consumer-driven, sexually licentious culture that now reigns in the developed world.

If you know *anything* about "real" Christianity, you know it's impossibly tough and only works because it's true and the Holy Spirit (sent by Jesus after His ascension to be your "Helper") is real. Otherwise, what we're talking about here is the opposite of what your peers would think is the proper way to relate to an idiot husband.

I'm deeply grieved every time I hear, or see, casual contempt creep into advertising. You know the ads I'm talking about, right? The woman is rolling her eyes at her idiot husband because, like always, he's doing idiotic things – like stuffing his face with pizza, on the couch with his buddies, downing beers while forgetting about his wife's very important something or other. It's a cliché because it's just that common in our culture. Think about it: how many exasperated wives have you met? How many of them have ranted about their "man-child" husbands who just can't seem to get it together and act in a way that their wives deem appropriate?

It's an epidemic.

In the real world, when a husband acts like an idiot, we write him off as one. In a world shaped by the story of Jesus, when a husband acts like an idiot – when he will not submit to the Gospel, persisting stubbornly in unbelief – what does a faithful, Jesus-loving wife do? She wins her idiot husband over by her exemplary life. And, before you start thinking how impossible that sounds, remember we're dealing here with a promise straight out of the Bible. You *will* win him – by respecting him and living a life that is pure.

*"But he hasn't earned my respect..."*

So, let's filter that objection through the Gospel. Are any of us worthy of respect? No.

> *"For ALL have sinned and fall short of the glory of God..."*
>
> —ROM 3:23 ESV

In and of ourselves, we are all hopelessly lost, bereft, far from God, in every way alone. None of us are *worthy* of respect; only Jesus is. So, even if your husband is a prize idiot, you can respect him because God *told* you to, and *God* is worthy of your respect. This is the same deal as in the last chapter where we were all commanded to be subject to the government because all of us are subject to God, who will one day judge everyone, including corrupt politicians or fool husbands.

Building on that idea, Peter is saying to wives that, even if their husband is being difficult, they should respect him because God has commanded it, and God is supremely worthy of our respect.

*"So, how do I do that, practically?"*

Maybe one small step at a time.

Nobody's all bad. I've met, interacted with, and even had to work with some pretty despicable people, but nobody is all bad. I'll never forget watching a World War II documentary that featured some candid film footage of Hitler dancing with his niece and nephew on a terrace overlooking a mountain valley. He was smiling, laughing, clearly happy, and even kissed his niece gently at one point: the most evil man in modern history, enjoying the day, being happy and sharing it. That's the most extreme example I can think of and leads us to be able to make the – perhaps slightly exaggerated – point that your husband is probably going to be a little easier to love than Hitler.

*Nobody is all bad.*

Surely you can find one thing with which to begin rediscovering the admiration you once had for your husband. You married him; there must have been something you liked about him that made you take that drastic step. My wife and I learned this from a friend of ours. She's been on a journey for years, trying to learn to respect, and love, her husband again after discovering more than a decade of serial infidelity on his part.

*"Why doesn't she just leave him?"*

Well, because they have four kids together – kids whom they both love very much – and they've built a life together and have a strong friendship that underlies their marriage; it's just that he's been a fool when it comes to sexual fidelity. So, she decided to try and stay with him and work things out, and she knew intuitively that her marriage had no hope of resurrection if she went on despising him over the long term, for his admittedly despicable actions.

Don't miss this. He's *worthy* of being despised because what he's done is truly despicable, but nobody can love someone they despise and nobody wants to live with somebody they don't love. So, unless she wants to leave him (which she doesn't) she has to find a way to learn to love him again.

*So, she went and got herself a glass jar and some pieces of paper.*

Every day, she makes a point to notice one good thing about him. She writes it down, and puts it in the jar.

*"He has nice arms..."* was the first one.

One good thing. Put it in the jar.

*"He has a nice smile..."* was another.

Put it in the jar.

*"He's gentle with the kids..."*

And so on.

Little by little she began accumulating signs that he wasn't a *complete* idiot. Little by little she gave herself a whole jarful of reasons not to *completely* despise him.

That's a godly woman, living a pure life right there. That's the Gospel at work. That's the power of redemption doing what only the power of redemption can do.

Most people aren't all bad. Start with one good thing, no matter how seemingly insignificant, and build from there.

And, as you commit to doing the relational heavy lifting required to see the Gospel work this impossible change in your heart, keep at it, and stop trying to impress people.

> *"Do not let your adorning be EXTERNAL—the braiding of hair and the putting on of gold jewelry, or the clothing you wear— but let your adorning be the hidden person of the heart with the imperishable beauty of a gentle and quiet spirit, which in God's sight is very precious. For this is how the holy women who hoped in God used to adorn themselves, by submitting to their own husbands, as Sarah obeyed Abraham, calling him lord. And you are her children, if you do good and do not fear anything that is frightening..."*
>
> —1 PETER 3:3-6 ESV

You can see how some pretty severe and weird expressions of Christianity came out of proof-texting and misapplying these verses. But you can be sure that those who apply these verses legalistically do not do so *uniformly*, because, given that we're instructed here not to wear jewelry *or clothes*, that would make for some pretty fun nudie PTA meetings, and we all know that fundamentalists – their name notwithstanding – don't like fun.

And if you don't think being naked is fun, you've just proved that you're a fundamentalist.

Let's be clear about this passage. It's not meant to be a tool in your hand to help you keep your women "modest" or "plain." What it *is* saying is that we need to avoid high-class affectations: the overt – and show-off-y – symbols of the wealthy. The braiding of hair in question here was the kind of thing that would take a team of slaves most of a day to do before the wealthy woman headed out into public to parade around, flaunting her status and position.

*"Look how rich and powerful and fabulous I am! This hair took all day; isn't it gorgeous?"*

Basically, Peter is telling us to avoid "red carpet" living.

Avoid "Awards Show Christianity" like the plague. You know what I'm talking about here, right? The Golden Globes, the Oscars, the GRAMMYs, social media, fashion and lifestyle magazines that idolize wealth and comfort. Flee them. Don't "braid your hair." Any time you're tempted to do something outwardly (and for show) that will exalt you and demean others, don't do it.

*It's better to be naked than to wear fancy clothes.*

If you're a woman reading this and you've been told your whole life to dress more modestly, or plainly, told to slouch so your breasts don't cause some man to stumble, told to be careful about how tight your jeans are at church (believe it or not, there are some who say women should only wear skirts to church; I call these fanatics "Skirt-Wearing Homeschoolers"), told to be careful about your makeup or that wearing anything beyond a modest string of pearls is sinful; and if, as a result, you've developed a complex that feminine beauty is in some way "sinful" or "bad," let me be the first to tell you that your beauty is God-given and that all of us redeemed men consider it a gift to the world. We see in your loveliness a picture of our first Mother Eve and an echo of the beauty of God Himself in Whose Image our first Mother – and you – were made. Eve was so naked and gorgeous when God made her in the Garden that Adam burst into *song* the moment he saw her!

> *"Surely now this is bone of my bone and flesh of my flesh! She shall be called Woman for she was taken out of Man!"*
>
> —GEN 2:23 ESV

*Your beauty makes us sing.*

God forbid we should have a world without women in full flower. I'd rather go see Jesus right *now* than live in a world without Daughters of Eve. Take me to where the ladies are, man; I want to see the glory of God writ large in His girls.

But exhibitionism, showing off, flaunting your looks to gain so-called "status"? Let's not do that.

Literally here, when Peter uses the word "clothing," it is rendered "clothing system" in the original language. All these many years later, Peter's choice of words reminds us not to buy into the materialistic *system* that everyone around us seems to have bought into, wholesale. You don't have to keep up with the Joneses. You are great and awesome just as God has made you; you don't have to impress anyone, ever! You don't have to do *anything* to enhance your worth, your value, or your awesomeness. You also don't need to artificially hide it, or pretend God didn't give you what He gave you. You are amazing just as God has made you; you are a gift to the world. You are the glory of God at work in our everyday.

*Because your worth is rooted in Him.*

> *"...but let your adorning be the hidden person of the heart with the imperishable beauty of a gentle and quiet spirit, which in GOD'S sight is very precious..."*
>
> —1 PETER 3:4 ESV

Again here, it comes down to God. If the story about Him is true, if He made you – literally *forming* you in your mother's womb – then, as the One who knows *everything* about you, it's pretty clear that His opinion of you is the *only one* that matters. You see, God *is* the Gospel, and only His story matters. He drives what's right and wrong, and His expectations should be the ones that move your life.

> *"For this is how the holy women who hoped in God used to adorn themselves, by submitting to their own husbands, as Sarah obeyed Abraham, calling him LORD. And you are her children, if you do good and do not fear anything that is frightening..."*
>
> —1 PETER 3:5-6 ESV

What I find really astonishing here is not that Sarah called Abraham "lord" – that would have been very common in the culture in which Abraham and Sarah had been raised – and it's not common today, as it would have been even when Peter originally wrote these words, so I'm pretty sure his point wasn't to ensure that twenty-first-century wives used an Ancient Near Eastern honorific for their husbands.

What I find amazing here is that the *faith* of the Matriarchs allowed them to endure fear without it driving them to dismay. Sometimes our English translations of the Bible fall a little short of the resonance that the original language would have had in a particular instance, and this is one of those moments.

> *"...as Sarah obeyed Abraham, calling him lord. And you are her children, if you do good and do not fear anything that is frightening..."*
>
> —1 PETER 3:6 ESV

You read that and you think: "Do not fear anything that is *frightening*? That doesn't make much sense. If it wasn't frightening, I wouldn't be *afraid* of it in the first place!"

So, what does this really mean?

> *"...and do not fear anything with DISMAY..."*
>
> —1 PETER 3:6B ESV

144

*There* you go; now we're onto something. Do not fear anything with *dismay*. We're all afraid of things; some of us are afraid of *many* things, and sometimes that fear can drive us to dismay. And so great is our aversion to dismay that we'll do anything, including trying to control *everything*, in order to avoid it.

How many women do you know who are highly controlling?

*A few?*

Seems to me, from my limited experience, and also from the clear teaching of scripture here that, more often than not, a "high controller" is really just afraid.

*Afraid of dismay.*

They're so afraid of it that they spend their lives trying to control everything. The problem with seeking to control everything is that, ultimately, it's idolatrous. When you're a "high controller," you're trying to put yourself in the supreme position of power, a position that only (and rightly) belongs to God. At the root of the problem is this simple fact: a "high controller" thinks they can do a better job at being God than God.

If that's you, you need to stop it.

And you can be *empowered* to stop it by recalling the example of the Biblical Matriarchs who, yes, suffered fear, but – because of their deep faith – did not allow themselves to be driven to dismay.

If the Good News about Jesus is true, you never need to fear to the level of dismay again. If the story about Jesus is fact, you don't need to let fear control you ever again; you can trust Jesus *entirely* and that "entire trusting" will be what enables you to voluntarily give in to your husband, cooperating with him, even assuming responsibility with him, and carrying the burden of your life together. Because you will no longer be dominated by dismay-inducing fear that your husband is going to screw it up. You can have freedom from fear and from your urge to control everything, because of Jesus.

*"And what about the husbands?"*

> *"...Likewise, HUSBANDS, live with your wives in an under-standing way, showing honor to the woman as the weaker vessel, since they are heirs with you of the grace of life, so that your prayers may not be hindered.*
>
> —1 PETER 3:7 ESV

I may be a little more direct with the dudes here than I have been so far with the ladies.

How many men have you ever heard say, "I see no clear evidence of God's hand at work in my life..." or maybe "God's ignoring me..." or "I keep praying but God never answers. He must not be listening..." Or my favorite, "If God was real, you'd think He'd show up once in a while..."

I've heard lots of men say these things.

So many men are hard-hearted. You know why? Because life is hard. I get it. If you're a man reading this, especially if you're a husband, have you ever felt abandoned by God?

*It might be because of how you treat your wife.*

> *"...Likewise, husbands, live with your wives in an UNDER-STANDING way..."*
>
> —1 PETER 3:7A ESV

I love how *impossible* the Bible is. It is impossible to *understand* my wife. I know this without equivocation; I've been married for twenty-four years. She still does things, every week, that leave me at a loss. She'll be sitting at the dinner table studying (she's doing her master's degree in Psychotherapy) and suddenly burst into tears. "Why are you crying?" I'll ask.

146

"Because I'm so sad..." she'll say.

"Why are you sad?" I'll ask.

"I don't know..." she'll say, before succumbing to more tears.

*I don't understand.*

But what's beautiful about the Bible here is that it's going right for my jugular because it's not telling me to tolerate her; it's not telling me to put up with her or to ignore her. The Bible is commanding me to *understand* her. The very thing I find most difficult to do is *the* thing it's telling me to do.

*I'm going to need some grace.*

I believe the extreme difficulty of this particular instruction to the men – to understand their wives – echoes how difficult it is for a wife to submit to her husband: the *one* thing *she* does not want to do. This goes right back to the curse, recorded in Genesis chapter three. When God curses Eve, He tells her that her desire will be for her husband to *rule* over him, but that *he* will rule over her. So, every Daughter of Eve ever born has this inbred desire to *conquer* and *subdue* her husband. This is why it's no mistake that Peter – an Apostle of Jesus, the Great Teacher of "Death to Self" and "Self-Giving Love" – goes right for our jugular.

*"That's the one thing I don't want to do!"*

Exactly.

And the husbands are getting a straight shot to the neck too, because he's not telling them to put up with their wives, not to tolerate them, but to *understand* them – which is impossible.

But, because of Jesus, you owe it to her. Because of Jesus, you owe it to her to do the heavy lifting required – however long it takes to master it – to come to the point where you *understand* her. That means working to come to the point where you *relate* to her in a way that is as easy and as natural as the way in which you relate to *yourself*.

See?

You understand what you do *intuitively;* you don't even have to think about what you do most of the time. With Jesus' help, you need to become *such* a husband that you treat your wife in a way that is *so* good – but you don't even have to think about it; it just comes naturally because you *understand* her.

> *"...showing HONOR to the woman as the weaker vessel..."*
>
> —1 PETER 3:7B ESV

*Honor* her, which means value her.

What have you said or done lately that makes her feel valued? And, men, let me remind you that you *value* what you *spend time on*. Take a look at your weekly schedule and you will discover your value system. Go back and examine the last month of your life – if you're really brave, go back six months – and shudder as you realize how little of your time has been spent with the wife of your youth. It's little wonder she's feeling insecure, which is making her fearful, which is triggering her "Eve Default" to become domineering. You haven't spent any *significant* time with her in *months* and she knows intuitively that that means you don't really *value* her. *You better repent quick, Buddy.*

Value her. Honor her, as the "weaker vessel."

That whole "weaker vessel" thing is a phrase *so* abused by my grandparents' generation that it still kind of lives in infamy in most of our hearts and minds the moment we hear it.

*"Well, you do know, son, that the Bible says the woman is the WEAKER VESSEL..."* as if somehow implying feminine inferiority as some kind of twisted, God-ordained thing.

148

*Pshaw*!

All this means is that, as a man, you are *physically stronger* than her, which anyone with half a brain knows without being told; so, you need to be *careful* with how you *handle* her, physically. What we have here is a command to husbands *not* to use their physical strength as a tool to gain leverage over their wives. To the members of Peter's original audience, raised in the context of Roman culture where the husband/father was the "Paterfamilias" and enjoyed absolute, life-or-death power over all the members of his household, what Peter is commanding here would have seemed totally ridiculous. *"Value her. Honor her, and never, ever, use your strength to gain leverage over her..."* says St. Peter the Just. And, in an afterthought that I think has particular resonance in our day and age:

*"Enjoy her..."*

> *"...since they are joint ENJOYERS of the allotment with you of the grace of life..."*
>
> —1 PETER 3:7C ESV

Isn't that awesome? The original language keeps surprising again and again. We would totally miss this if we just stayed in the English. "Heirs" means "Enjoyers of the Allotment." All the good things in life that you don't deserve – and none of us really *deserve* anything good, if you think about it – are *gifts* of God to you. That lovely breakfast you enjoyed today? Gift. That body of yours that works well enough for you to walk your kid to school? Also, a gift.

And Peter's point here is clear; every good thing you've been given that you don't deserve, you are meant to enjoy *with her*. Your whole existence is meant to be *with* her as your partner. We know this from the story of our first Father Adam upon whom the Lord God looked, after He had made all things and called them "good," and realized it was *not* good that man should be alone. Adam needed a helper suited to him, or – from the Hebrew – a partner who could stand face to face (or go toe to toe) with him. Adam needed a best friend *with whom* he could be fruitful and multiply, fill the Earth and subdue it.

*He needed a wife.*

Husbands, you are meant (designed, even) to *enjoy* your wives. This is so true of our human partnerships that nothing crushes a wife's soul more than realizing that her husband doesn't *enjoy* her anymore. So, all you men, out of reverence for Christ and His Gospel, determine right here, right now, to enjoy your wives like you never have before! Enjoy them, celebrate them, pursue them, glory in them, make them your second-highest priority, after your fixation on the Lord God.

Enjoy your wife.

There should be absolutely *nothing* in life you enjoy *more* than your wife. If, being honest about it, you know that you like your hobbies more than you enjoy your wife, quit them. Or, never get married; stay a boy forever. Mark my words, the happiness of your marriage (and ultimate fulfillment of your life) will be inversely proportionate to your golf game. Crappy golfer: good husband, happy wife. Dynamite golfer? Probably a crappy husband with a miserable wife.

Yeah, I said it.

Ladies, if you are really committed to preferring the illusion of autonomy that the prevalent culture of our day is so intent on selling you at any cost, never get married; stay a girl forever.

Autonomy is a myth, an illusion, and if you bring that illusion into marriage, you're going to be miserable, and – as you continuously work to gain autonomy over your husband – he will grow to hate you.

Strong words for the women and for the men, and I believe every one of them.

Husbands, *enjoy* your wives.

Wives, kiss your desire for autonomy *goodbye*.

Because 94% of you reading this will, at some point in your life, get married, which means, for 94% of you, the issues we've explored here are going to be real struggles and actual opportunities in your day-to-day life – which is why you'd better *get* the Gospel, quick. Because, life with Jesus? Well, it changes *everything*; especially marriages.

# SEVEN

# The Good Life

Have you ever found yourself in a situation where you realize there's no way you're going to win, so you decide to stop competing and just try to have a good time instead?

It happens to me a lot as a football coach. I often find myself coaching a game where I realize we can't win, and it's very difficult as a coach to concede defeat, so you work really hard to turn your attention to helping your players to just have a good time, grow as people, learn something as players and, hopefully – despite the defeat – enjoy the moment.

This was especially true when I was coaching my son's team of eight- and nine-year-olds. Coaching little boys that age is like herding cats. I think it's probably true that most eight-year-olds should not be playing tackle football. Between tantrums, crying, getting hurt feelings when someone looks at them meanly, and just generally staring off into space when they should be sealing the edge, it's going to take a while before you can run "Fake twenty-five, quick inside hit, eight Sally..." And, if I'm honest about it, I find it very difficult to manage the waiting period between when coaching is no more than babysitting terrorists in pads, and when the mangled mess we are putting on the field each Saturday morning, from week one through week four, actually turns into something that somewhat resembles the game that I love.

It was usually eight weeks before I was completely happy.

And between weeks one and seven, as I realized that the experience I *thought* I was going to have (imagining what it would be like to coach football) just wasn't going to happen, I had to shift my mindset, saying to myself something like:

*"Look dude, no matter what you do, you're not going to win this game – you're probably not even going to get a first down today – so you might as well accept it, and focus instead on just trying to have a good time."*

Same thing with the "baby stage."

The moment you have kids you are officially defeated. You're not going to win the diaper battle. The day you open the first truly nuclear deposit your newborn makes, you think to yourself: *"My life is over."* And you're right. Once kids show up in your life, it's over. Your house is never going to be clean again, your furniture is going to be destroyed no matter what you do, so take it from me – don't buy anything nice until they move out! In fact, if you have little kids, I have three words for you that will change your life.

Slip. Covered. Furniture.

You're welcome. They barf on it? No worries; just wash it.

(And I'm speaking *from experience* here, people.)

But slipcovers are more than just a way to barf-proof your living room; they are a white flag symbolizing your acceptance of defeat.

There's no way we're going to win, so we're going to shift our focus to just trying to have a good time. The problem, mind you, if you're a young couple, when you decide to shift your focus towards trying to have a good time, is that the more "good times" you have, the *more* kids keep showing up, which does nothing to alleviate your excessive-kid-population problems.

*Same with triathlons.*

My first triathlon, I almost died. I actually blogged about it the day after and my opening line was awesome, and humiliating.

*"When I got passed by the seventy-four-year-old woman and the one-legged man, I knew it was going to be a very long day."*

See, for no reason I can think of other than that triathlon organizers are sick and twisted people, they write every competitor's age on the back of their calf. Maybe this is so that, when the seventy-four-year-old woman blows past you on the bike like you're standing still, the deep self-loathing that washes over you will drive you to greater heights of athletic exploit!

*Or they do it just to make you feel small.*

So, after the near-death experience that was my first triathlon, I came much more prepared to my second one. People would ask me, once they found out I was doing another race, *"So, what's your goal? Do you have a time you're trying to hit? A place you're looking to finish?"*

Yes.

"Finish" sounds nice. I'll go with that option. I'd just like to *finish*. Not dying would be a bonus.

That, my friends, is the attitude of a broken man, and I think it's a healthy one. Sure, I had delusions of grandeur when I first started to race. I wanted to be a top finisher in my age category, get sponsored, that sort of thing. But then, once I was actually in it, the realities of the race kicked in, and I realized that just finishing was going to be a pretty tall order all by itself and maybe, just maybe, a noble endeavor in and of itself.

*Same thing when you turn forty.*

As kids we all think we're going to grow up to be JFK or Martin Luther King Jr. I was going to change the world. I was going to be Stephen Spielberg meets Billy Graham! Then, at some point between age 35 and 45 you begin to realize that JFK's probably not in the cards after all so, if your head is screwed on right, you trade your lofty goal of conquest for: *"You know, I'm just happy to be here; let's try and have a good time..."*

If what I've just described sounds like defeat to you, don't beat yourself up about it; it's just because you haven't lived (or suffered) enough yet to know better. Trust me, you will. Once you're a little older, wiser, and more beat up you'll come to see what a beautiful thing learning to just simply enjoy the journey can be.

The kind of surrender I've outlined above is what the story of Jesus is looking to teach us. Jesus' story teaches us something both difficult and beautiful. It tells us that God exists, and that He made everything that is, including us, and that we have been made to be God's friends. That's beautiful. The story goes on to tell that we messed it all up when our first Parents, Adam and Eve, sinned against God in the Garden of Eden, disobeying His one clear command not to touch the Tree of the Knowledge of Good and Evil. Our first Parents' sin was, ultimately, that they wanted to be equal with God. They figured: "Why should God have something that we don't?" So, from jealousy, from pride, from a desire to ascend God's throne for ourselves, sin and rebellion and curse and death came into the human story, and it's been with us ever since. That's why your life is always difficult, that's why our world is always miserable: because we have a sin problem that we inherited from our Parents. So, we kill each other and we oppress one another and we fight for power and influence. That's the difficult part of the story.

But, a little good news here. God did not leave us alone.

*Because you're His friend.*

You've been restored, in Jesus, to right relationship with God Himself so, as a result, you don't have to live as a slave to sin anymore; you don't have to let the "way of the world" ruin you, and you don't have to participate in "business as usual."

The Gospel teaches us that God wins and, ultimately, you're just fortunate to be His friend.

Do you *feel* that way, fortunate to *be* His friend? I sure do. God wins; we're just lucky to be His friends. The sooner you can learn and begin applying this great truth to your life, the happier you're going to be. So, let's get to it.

> "Finally, all of you, have unity of mind, sympathy, brotherly love, a tender heart, and a humble mind. Do not repay evil for evil or reviling for reviling, but on the contrary, bless, for to this you were called, that you may obtain a blessing. For 'Whoever desires to love life and see good days, let him keep his tongue from evil and his lips from speaking deceit; let him turn away from evil and do good; let him seek peace and pursue it. For the eyes of the Lord are on the righteous, and his ears are open to their prayer. But the face of the Lord is against those who do evil.' Now who is there to harm you if you are zealous for what is good? But even if you should suffer for righteousness' sake, you will be blessed. Have no fear of them, nor be troubled, but in your hearts honor Christ the Lord as holy, always being prepared to make a defense to anyone who asks you for a reason for the hope that is in you; yet do it with gentleness and respect, having a good conscience, so that, when you are slandered, those who revile your good behavior in Christ may be put to shame. For it is better to suffer for doing good, if that should be God's will, than for doing evil..."
>
> —1 PETER 3:8-17 ESV

There's a countercultural recipe right there for living the good life, having hope and doing good. Let's take a look at the whole "countercultural" thing first.

> *"Finally, all of you, have unity of mind, sympathy, brotherly love, a tender heart, and a humble mind. Do not repay evil for evil or reviling for reviling, but on the CONTRARY, bless, for to this you were called, that you may obtain a blessing..."*
>
> —1 PETER 3:8-9 ESV

Christians are supposed to be contrarian; we're supposed to live differently from everyone else. One of the central tensions that the original audience to whom Peter was writing would have been dealing with was the increasing *cultural distance* that was creeping in between them, as Jesus followers, and their neighbors, family, and peers. This distance was being created as the story of Jesus began leading them into living, more and more over time, in a way that was *noticeably different* from the way in which most of their peers were living. Most importantly, that difference between the early Christians Peter was writing to, and their peers, was beginning to cause them to experience alienation, and that was troubling because, let's face it, nobody likes to be alienated.

Peter is writing to comfort Christians who are feeling ostracized.

In addition to comfort, he is writing to encourage them to continue doing what they have been doing, as followers of "The Way" of Jesus, in spite of the fact that they were beginning to find doing that difficult.

Can you relate? It's difficult to live differently, but that's what a Christian is called to do.

> *"Finally, ALL of you, have unity of mind, sympathy, brotherly love, a tender heart, and a humble mind..."*
>
> —1 PETER 3:8 ESV

Six signs right there of what it looks like to live differently, like life isn't all about you, like the "we" is more important than the "me," like it's *all* of us that matter.

I find this difficult.

Peter is commanding *all* of us to agree to agree, to have *unity* of mind. I think you and I both know that, most of the time, the best we and our peers can do is to agree to *disagree*, and often we do that with acrimony, not harmony. We are being urged here to develop *unity* as a core value, as a "way of being," and unity is just the start.

In addition to being unified, we are to live like *compassion* is the primary way in which we relate to one another. That's what "sympathy" means here in the original language: *compassion*. Would your friends say that having compassion on your peers is one of your defining characteristics? If the answer is no, then you and I both have some work to do.

*The goal is to look like we're from Philly.*

That's the next word here: "Philadelphioi," *brotherly love*. So maybe this week you need to meditate on this *while* eating a Philly Cheese Steak to the glory of God. Seriously, go to lunch (take someone with you), eat a cheese steak and determine to *love* your sisters and brothers better from that day forward. Put a cheese steak on it.

Me? I live like I'm stuck in traffic in L.A. more than I do like I'm from the "City of Brotherly Love" ("Fly Eagles fly," baby), so I could really use a lunch break too.

We need to live like we're from Philly: like people marked by a deep, profoundly felt, and consistently walked-out brotherly love.

How many of us treat one another tenderly and courteously as a matter of course? Tenderness. Courtesy. These are the *ways of being* implied in the phrase "a humble mind..." Maybe you're good with one or the other. Maybe courtesy comes easy to you. I think courtesy can be *learned*. There are certain things we do that can help us be (or at least come across as) courteous. Hold a door open and let someone else go first. Wait your turn in line and don't rush to take the next register when the clerk says they'll take the next customer; let someone else take that spot. These are *politeness* things that can be taught.

But to *have* a tender heart? That's a whole other level. You can't fake tenderness. It's like the difference between a perfume and a stench. When someone is tender, it's like they smell like lavender or eucalyptus; they have a lovely air about them. When someone lacks tenderness, you can feel their hardness of heart radiating off them like a smell. In light of this, we must ask ourselves on a regular basis what it is that we can be *doing* to live more like we smell beautifully of tenderness.

Because that's how Jesus' people are supposed to be.

And they're *not* to:

> *"...repay evil for evil or reviling for reviling, but on the contrary, BLESS, for to this you were called, that you may obtain a blessing..."*
>
> —1 PETER 3:9 ESV

Jesus' people don't get even.

I was deeply troubled recently listening to Sports Talk Radio discuss the sale of the Carolina Panthers' NFL franchise. Maybe you heard the story?

The longtime owner of the Panthers was forced to sell the team due to some issues of personal conduct and workplace discrimination that came to light and caused quite a firestorm in the media and online. So, forced by the league to sell his team, he found a buyer: a Hedge Fund Guy. And if you're thinking, "Great, this is going to go *real* well because Hedge Fund Guys are known to be such sweethearts..." you might be a prophet. This is the NFL we're talking about here; get rid of one maniac, hire another. But I'm getting ahead of myself.

So, this new guy, earlier in his financial career, was passed over for a promotion while working his way up at Bear Stearns in New York. He was up for a partnership – a move that would have cemented his wealth for generations – and he got passed over by his direct boss. Obviously unhappy about this, he left in a huff and started his own firm. Eventually he grew it into the mid-fifty-million-dollar range – a very small firm by comparison to a giant like Bear Stearns, but *his*, something he'd built from scratch. Then the 2008-2009 housing crisis hit, and this guy realized that the U.S. Banks were likely to fail due to their exposure to the tanking real estate market. He acted on his realization and made a huge bet (short selling) against the American banking system. He was counting on one thing: that the American government would not allow their banking system to fail, so they would step in to prop it up, buy it out, or essentially bail it out.

Sure enough, that's exactly what happened, and Mr. Future Carolina Panthers sees his firm's valuation grow from fifty-odd million to several billion dollars: billions of *U.S. taxpayer dollars*, to be exact. So, in some sense (because the bailout was with taxpayer dollars) *you* own the Carolina Panthers.

But it doesn't end there.

Flush with his newfound riches, Mr. Hedge Fund makes an offer that can't be refused to the wife of his former boss at Bear Stearns to buy their family home, a home that used to be the pride and joy of his former boss. No sooner has he taken ownership than he tears their family house down and builds one twice its size in its place. Smug with his victory, he is quoted as saying, looking at his monstrosity of a house, *"Looks like there is some justice in the world after all..."*

Reading that account, I thought to myself; *"No sir, what you've just proved is that there is vengeance in the world after all."*

Jesus' people need to flee from that kind of behavior. Stories like the one you've just read should freeze your blood and make you recoil in horror.

*Jesus' people don't get even.*

Granted, your life may not be on the scale of a Billionaire Hedge Fund Guy, but that same urge to get even lurks in your heart the same as it does in mine and we know that, from God's perspective, evil is evil. Period. You will be tempted to try to get justice for yourself from time to time and Jesus' people don't do that. If you want to live counterculturally, leave *justice* (and the "getting" of it) to God. Realize that you were called to bless and that blessing is the pathway to *blessing*.

> *"...but on the contrary, BLESS, for to this you were called, that you may obtain a blessing..."*
>
> —1 PETER 3:9B ESV

Blessing is the pathway to *blessing*. And, we'd all rather be blessed than cursed, right? Or, put another way, we'd all like to live "The Good Life."

Here's how we can.

> *"Whoever desires to love life and see good days, let him keep his TONGUE from evil and his lips from speaking deceit; let him turn away from evil and DO good; let him SEEK peace and pursue it. For the eyes of the Lord are on the righteous, and his ears are open to their prayer. But the face of the Lord is against those who do evil..."*
>
> —1 PETER 3:10-12 ESV

You want "The Good Life"? Watch what you say, watch what you do, and chase peace like you chased your wife when you met her at seventeen. Let's break each of those down a little bit.

> *"...let him keep HIS tongue from evil and HIS lips from speaking deceit..."*
>
> —1 PETER 3:10A ESV

Manage what *you* say. Make sure *you* stop lying.

How many times in your life have you tried to manage what *other people* say? Lots of times! I've done it lots. I think if Christians tweaked this one aspect of their collective character the overall reputation of Christ and His people in the world would go up by a considerable margin. How often are Christians quoted shaking their figurative finger at something evil someone has said in mainstream culture? You see it all the time: outraged Christians, on TV or online, protesting, yelling, waving placards.

*Spare me.*

Have you ever stopped to think how stupid it is to somebody who's "perishing" to have someone who's been "redeemed" telling them how to act? Someone who loves Jesus sees the world completely differently from somebody who doesn't. You might as well be from Venus and they from Mars. Maybe, instead of shouting at people who don't believe the Gospel or really know anything about the story of the Bible, Jesus' people could focus on *reading* the Bible more for themselves? If we did this, we'd quickly realize that the Bible says that the Good News about Jesus is foolishness to them that are perishing, but to those who are being saved it is everlasting life (1 Cor 1:18).

So, if your approach to someone who is "perishing" is to *scold* them for their "bad behavior," you're really doing no good at all; you're just wasting everyone's time, while bringing shame, not fame, upon

Jesus' Name. It would be kind of like yelling at someone in a foreign language; they can tell you're angry but have no idea what you're talking *about*. You may be yelling pure wisdom but, since they don't share a common language with you, all they get is that you're angry.

*Stop scolding people.*

Instead, manage yourself: what *you* say and what *you* do.

> *"...let HIM turn away from evil and do good..."*
>
> —1 PETER 3:11A ESV

Let *him* turn away.

Stop trying to turn *other* people away from doing evil. *You* turn away from evil and do good. And what's really beautiful about this is that, in Jesus, you're actually free (as in, able) to do this.

Did you know that the Bible says that those who are unredeemed, those who are not yet Jesus' friends, are sold as *slaves* to sin? (Rom 6:20) This means that all the people that those annoying Christians are scolding *can't help* but sin. They're *enslaved* to sin; they have no choice. Once you're in Jesus, though, it's a whole different ball game. Once you belong to Jesus, you are His slave, and no one (or *no-thing*) else's. While it's true that, even once we've become followers of Jesus, we continue to struggle at times with sin and its aftereffects, it's key to remember that once we've found freedom in Jesus, we are free to choose not to sin; this option wasn't available to us before we met Jesus. Also, the beautiful thing about a Jesus who died for us *while* we were yet sinners (Rom 5:8) is that, as we walk with Him, He will show (and *has* shown) us everything we need for life, righteousness, peace, holiness, and joy in the Holy Ghost (Rom 14:7).

*You don't have to sin anymore if you don't want to.*

Instead, because you are now free in Jesus, you can practice doing the right thing, moment by moment, day by day, this week, this month, this year, walking in newness of life. You can *be* free. You can live a new way now; just ask yourself, one moment at a time, "What's the *right* thing to do?" Then go do it.

Let's be really clear about this; this may be *difficult*, and it may change what you do in a way that makes it harder than what you were going to do before you started thinking about being righteous. This is why so many Christians lack so much in righteousness, because doing the right thing is harder than sinning, nine times out of ten. Doing the right thing often means entering by the narrow gate (not the wide) and taking the difficult way (not the easy) that leads to life (Matt 7:13-14).

Okay, so we've covered "Manage what you *say*" and "Manage what you *do*," which brings us to *chasing peace* like she's the wife of your youth.

> *"...let him turn away from evil and do good; let him seek peace and pursue HER..."*
>
> —1 PETER 3:11 ESV

That's right, it's not a typo. Peace is a *Her* in the original language, and that changes everything. You can see it, right?

*Peace has a personality.*

That's encouraging, because peace as an abstraction, peace as a "concept," or as an "it" is not highly relatable. I can't catch it. But if peace is a "person" (her), that makes things much better. If peace was an "it," telling us to catch it would be like telling us to try to catch the wind, except worse because the wind is physical and peace, as an abstraction, is even less tangible than a summer breeze. I believe it is no mistake that, as he was writing our source letter, Peter was being inspired by the Presence and Power of the Holy Spirit to give peace a personality, on purpose.

Seek Peace and pursue Her. Chase her like she's the wife of your youth, knowing that, in Jesus, and because of what He's done, you can actually *catch* her.

> *"Peace I leave with you. My peace I GIVE to you..."*
>
> —JOHN 14:27 ESV

Jesus Himself has left you *His* peace. You can no longer consider it just an abstraction.

And, look, if all this positive reinforcement – "Recipe for the Good Life" – stuff isn't quite getting to you yet, Peter reminds us what's at stake in verse twelve.

> *"For the eyes of the Lord are on the righteous, and his ears are open to their prayer. But the face of the Lord is AGAINST those who do evil..."*
>
> —1 PETER 3:12 ESV

*That ought to sober you up right quick.*

The face of the Lord is *against* those who do evil. If that's true, then you'd better ask yourself one key thing this week: *"Am I living in such a way that I'm making God my Adversary?"* Honestly, I hadn't ever really actively thought that was even possible until I began studying this chapter. To be fair, it's not a common theme in Sunday School, nor do we see many best-selling Christian books titled: *"How to Make God Your Enemy in Seven Easy Steps."*

Now, let me say, I don't think we're talking about salvation or damnation here; this is not heaven or hell-type stuff. What I think *is* in play is the kind of life you're going to live here in the Shadowlands. I was reading about this in Leviticus chapter twenty-six this morning in fact. God sets before His people a pretty clear choice in that chapter. On the one hand, obey God, honoring Him by keeping His commandments, and your fields will be full, yielding their crops, and you will have peace in your land. Or, disobey and dishonor Him, and all your work will be for nothing (Lev 26:20). Either, or. You're going to have to choose whether you want to be God's friend, or His enemy.

The beautiful thing about living differently, about living the truly "good life," is that living that way leads to having hope and doing good. One plus two leads to three.

> "Now who is there to harm you if you are zealous for what is good? But even if you should suffer for righteousness' sake, you will be blessed. Have no fear of them, nor be troubled, but in your hearts honor Christ the Lord as holy, always being prepared to make a defense to anyone who asks you for a reason for the hope that is in you; yet do it with gentleness and respect, having a good conscience, so that, when you are slandered, those who revile your good behavior in Christ may be put to shame. For it is better to suffer for doing good, if that should be God's will, than for doing evil..."
>
> —1 PETER 3:13-17 ESV

Here we have 1) a promise, 2) another promise, 3) an exhortation, 4) some life coaching, 5) a missional reminder, then 6) a command, 7) a practical reminder, and finally 8) an assurance of victory. Let's go at them, point by point.

## A Promise

> "Now who is there to harm you if you IMITATE for what is good?"
>
> —1 PETER 3:13 ESV

That's right, "zealous" in the English translation is more properly rendered *imitate*, which is much more powerful because it means that, if you do things Jesus' way, you can't lose. If you *imitate* Jesus, you're going to win, because Jesus has won, and will be the Ultimate Victor when History's final page is written. So, stop thinking of yourself as a loser and – because you are Jesus' friend – start thinking of yourself as victorious! I'm not a "Prosperity Gospel" kind of guy, but I'm certainly going to take this opportunity (from the text) to remind you (and me) that there *is* some *prosperity* in the Gospel.

*Jesus wins and, as you are in Him, so will you.*

## Another Promise

> *"But even if you should SUFFER for righteousness' sake, you will be blessed..."*
>
> —1 PETER 3:14A ESV

Right here we see why no one should ever be full-blown "Prosperity Gospel" in their thinking because, almost every time the Bible says you're going to be blessed, it also says you're going to suffer. Life ain't all tea and crumpets. Sometimes you still suffer, even when you do the right thing, so don't let suffering discourage you when it comes your way.

It's like we're being given advanced warning.

Have you ever felt ripped off by suffering? Like, a *"I'm doing the right thing here, Lord, so why do bad things keep on happening to me?"* type thing. If you've ever felt that way, it's only because of Biblical ignorance, which you and I are both set free from because Peter has been kind enough to teach us that sometimes we will still suffer, even while doing good.

*Thanks, Peter.*

Next time you find yourself suffering despite your best attempts at doing the right thing, you don't need to fall into despair, or think that you've somehow been cursed. You haven't "brought this on yourself";

it just happens. The world is broken post-Eden; "'The Fall" is real. Don't be discouraged. Know that your victory is assured in Jesus! This is why the words of 2 Corinthians 4 have such powerful resonance.

> *"So we do not lose heart. Though our outer self is wasting away, our inner self is being renewed day by day. For this light momentary affliction is preparing for us an eternal weight of glory beyond all comparison, as we look not to the things that are seen but to the things that are unseen. For the things that are seen are transient, but the things that are unseen are eternal..."*
>
> —2 COR 4:16-18 ESV

Your suffering may be heavy, but Jesus is in the business of turning heaviness into *glory*. Glory means *weight*; it means heaviness, and Jesus turns heaviness into *glory*! And that beautiful promise leads us to:

## An Exhortation

> *"Have no FEAR of them, nor be troubled..."*
>
> —1 PETER 3:14B ESV

Have no fear, because your suffering will be turned to glory one day. That's definitely the best thing I've read in a while.

*Do not be afraid.*

Ok, time for:

## A Little Life Coaching

> *"...but in your hearts honor CHRIST the Lord as holy..."*
>
> —1 PETER 3:15A ESV

The way you survive the Shadowlands (that C.S. Lewis loved to talk about) is to make much of Jesus. You hold Jesus in your heart and let your dazzling love of Him be your testimony both to your own questions and doubts and to a lost and dying world. Which leads to:

## A Missional Reminder

> *"...always being prepared to make a defense to ANYONE who asks you for a reason for the hope that is in you..."*
>
> —1 PETER 3:15B ESV

That, right there, is what "evangelism" is meant to look like. You're living your life, building relationships with people, doing real work in the real world, and making a difference while you're at it when, suddenly, your peers start asking you questions.

*"Umm, how come life doesn't seem to make you as miserable as it does me?"*

If you're one of Jesus' people, this is your golden moment and *this* is your answer: *"Well, since you asked, I've got to tell you the truth. It's because of Jesus."*

Full stop.

*It's because of Jesus.*

That's all you need to say. You don't need to give them a tract. You don't need to use this moment of vulnerability on their part to correct a moral failing you've noticed in their life that's been bothering you, and you don't need to do an "altar call" right there on the shop floor. Just tell them any goodness they've seen in your life is because of Jesus. Full stop.

Now, sure, there's a chance your friend may find your response a little weird, or they may not even one hundred percent understand it right away, but they're your friend, they know you. They know you're not crazy because, maybe it wasn't the shop floor you were on when they asked you; maybe it was by the pool at your house while you were flipping burgers and sharing a cold one with them. If that was the case, it's even better. The more down to earth you've been in your relationship with them, the better it's going to be when you introduce Jesus into the equation, because they won't be able to suddenly decide that their friend and co-worker of more than a decade has now lost his mind. Especially if – immediately after you tell them it's all because of Jesus – you say, "Hey, could you pass me another Bud Light?"

That'll blow their mind.

*"Umm, can I ask you something? How come your marriage seems so happy?"*

It's because of Jesus.

I mean, go ask my wife, or have your friend ask her. My happy marriage is definitely not because of me and – lovely as she is – it's also not because of my wife. Left to our own devices we're both no more than human, which means prone to selfishness and broken in more ways than we're whole.

*Our marriage works because of Jesus.*

I have a friend who practices what I call "Culinary Evangelism." He constantly has people over to his house and cooks the most amazing meals for them; I'm talking meals so awesome they're fit for the Wedding Supper of the Lamb!

*"Umm, why do you go to all that trouble? They're just coming over for a meal..."*

And – I've seen him do it – he'll look you straight in the eye and tell you it's because of Jesus.

*"How come you adopted the kids you were fostering when you knew that would mean the government would cut off your foster parent payments and you'd end up losing money?"*

Because of Jesus.

You tell people that your *beautiful screwed-up life* is because of Jesus enough times and eventually they'll ask you one more question.

*"So, can I meet this Jesus you keep talking about?"*

I thought you'd never ask.

Once they do, you take them to your church, where – in worship, and the Word, and sacrament, and community – they will *taste and see* that the Lord is good for themselves and they will, eventually, meet the Good Jesus they have seen so clearly at work in you.

And all this testifying to the difference Jesus has made (and is making) in your life, you do gently, with respect and in as authentic a way as possible; but you *do* it.


## A Command, a Reminder, and an Assurance of Victory

The Command: *do* everything I've been writing about...

> *"...so that, WHEN you are slandered, those who revile your good behavior in Christ may be put to shame..."*
>
> —1 PETER 3:16B ESV

The Reminder: you *will* be slandered because you are a Jesus-Person, but you will be vindicated. So, don't bother trying to live some kind of weird undercover Jesus-life. Don't bother trying to soft-sell your allegiance to Jesus, or waste any time trying to appear "normal" to your friends, peers, and coworkers, because you're not. If you belong to Jesus you *will* be slandered, but those who revile you will be put to shame.

Because, ultimately, God wins! Ultimately, it's His will that bends the Universe.

So, while...

> *"...it is better to suffer for doing good, if that should be God's WILL, than for doing evil..."*
>
> —1 PETER 3:17 ESV

Let's just agree that, whatever God's will *is*, that's what we want. Right?

*We want what He wants.*

Because He is ultimately in control. He's ultimately going to win. So, you might as well just stop competing and, instead, just try to focus on having a good time.

# EIGHT

# Victory Lap

Do you have any memories from the back seat?

*When you were kids!*

I mean the back seat of your parents' station wagon, when you were growing up: *those* back-seat experiences. See, I was a kid before minivans were invented. I still remember the first time I saw one of those abominable inventions. It was a Plymouth Voyager, fake wood paneling and all. I remember thinking, *"Wow, that's a strange-looking car..."* then I got inside, and everything changed.

These days, if you have kids, you probably drive a minivan. They are as ubiquitous today as station wagons were when I was a boy and, let me tell you, kids these days have it *made* compared to what we had to deal with in the back seat of our parents' Buick Estate Wagons, or in my case, a Volkswagen Passat Wagon. My two siblings and I spent a lot of time crammed into the back seat of that cool, but not large, station wagon rolling our way door to door as my father enthusiastically put his fun-to-drive VW through its paces on the winding roads of the State of Israel in the mid-1980s. The switchbacks leading up the Mount of Beatitudes (where Jesus preached the Sermon on the Mount) were always a particular highlight when we drove north for a swim in the Sea of Galilee.

Once we moved back to North America, because my dad had always preferred small sporty cars, he bought the first generation of Honda's Civic Si hatchback – the one still prized by teenage boys everywhere – to drive his three, now teenaged, kids around. That's right, a family of five (with two boys over six feet and two hundred pounds) crammed into a tiny (but sexy) hatchback rolling to church and back on hot summer Sundays. I can close my eyes and still smell the new car smell of it. That car was as awesome as it was small and I loved it, even though I was always cramped in its non-North-American-sized back seat.

Even in a bigger car, the back seat always sucks when you're a kid. It's cramped, and if you happen to have a brother like mine, it's stinky, and your sister usually ends up drooling on you when she falls asleep in the middle, because she's got no window to lean on so you're the next best thing. On long trips your legs cramp up, your butt gets sweaty and, if you're like me, you end up sticking your nose out the window like a dog to fend off car sickness. The back seat is not much fun, except for one thing. *Someone was always taking you somewhere.*

And, for our purposes today, that someone is *Jesus* and that somewhere is to *victory*.

> *"For Christ also suffered once for sins, the righteous for the unrighteous, that he might bring us to God, being put to death in the flesh but made alive in the spirit, in which he went and proclaimed to the spirits in prison, because they formerly did not obey, when God's patience waited in the days of Noah, while the ark was being prepared, in which a few, that is, eight persons, were brought safely through water. Baptism, which corresponds to this, now saves you, not as a removal of dirt from the body but as an appeal to God for a good conscience, through the resurrection of Jesus Christ, who has gone into heaven and is at the right hand*

*of God, with angels, authorities, and powers having been subjected to him..."*

—1 PETER 3:18-22 ESV

We've got eight big ideas to work through here. 1) Jesus identified with you, so now *you* can identify with Him. 2) The story about Jesus is *really* true, so you can really build your life on it. 3) He's so stoked about His story that He actually took a "victory lap" through hell to preach about it. 4) By the way, while we're talking about God, let's make sure we talk about and remember His patience. And, 5) let's remember that salvation, both in its outer manifestation, and in the inner work it is based upon, relies on – and is rooted in – the resurrection. 6) Jesus rose again to go *somewhere* (back to His rightful place) and, 7) to *do* something, which was to sit down at the Father's right hand to rule and reign, or in other words, *continue* His victory lap. We'll leave point number eight for the end of this chapter.

In the meantime, let's find points one through seven in the text.

*"For CHRIST also suffered once for sins, the righteous for the unrighteous, that he might bring us to God   "*

—1 PETER 3:18A ESV

*We always start with Jesus.*

"For *Christ*..."

Anytime a writer begins with Jesus they are beginning in the right place. This is true for you as well. Begin with Jesus. Everything you do in life should be because of what Christ has done, and I mean *everything*. Think about everything you do in the course of an average week: wake up, shower, have breakfast, pack lunches, do devotions, get the kids out the door, get to work, do your work, break for lunch, fight traffic on the way home, have an afternoon workout, eat dinner, manage kids' activities, maybe have a date night, Netflix, sleep, repeat. And that's just a high-level view; I didn't get into laundry, or chores, or conflict at work, or bills, or meetings, or school, or a social life. Everything outlined above and everything I've left out should be done *because* of what Jesus has done for you.

This of course begs the question: *"Umm, what exactly has Jesus done for me?"*

Jesus has identified with your sufferings and, not just that, He has suffered and died, in your place for your sins. Often, when speaking about the death of Christ, we ask the question, *"Why did Jesus have to die?"* For the answer to that we have to dig a little deeper into the Bible for some of the reasons Jesus had to die.

> *"For all have SINNED and fall short of the glory of God..."*
>
> —ROM 3:23 ESV

God is Holy. He cannot tolerate sin in any form, but must punish it. God made us to be His friends forever, but we fell into sin and death as a result of our first Parents' sin in the Garden of Eden when they disobeyed God's clear command to them to not eat of the Tree of the Knowledge of Good and Evil. As a result of their first sin, we now have a sin problem and it's a very big problem. A Holy God made humans in His image and likeness to be His friends forever, but that entire race is now bent and broken by sin, and His holiness demands that sin be punished.

> *"For the WAGES of sin, is death..."*
>
> —ROM 6:26 ESV

*Sin comes with a price tag.*

You know the truth of this from your own life. When you sin against someone, something dies in that relationship. If anyone has ever sinned grievously against you, you know this to be true. Even when forgiveness enters the picture (and that sometimes takes a while), that relationship is never quite the same as it was before the original sin was committed, because something dies when sin enters in; it's a concrete law of God's Universe.

The wages of sin, is death.

Ultimately, sin, unrepented of, will lead to everlasting death, separation from a Holy God, forever – a prospect too horrible to contemplate. And every time you do contemplate it, you must also dwell on this:

> *"But, WHILE we were yet sinners, Jesus Christ died for us..."*
>
> —ROM 5:8 ESV

That fits our source material for this chapter pretty nicely, doesn't it?

> *"For Christ also suffered ONCE for sins..."*
>
> —1 PETER 3:18A ESV

Jesus entered into space-time history; God became a man, to ultimately go to the cross, where, as He hung there, God the Father would place on Him (God the Son) the iniquities of us all. In the beautiful horror of God's ultimate plan of redemption, Jesus Christ would suffer and die in *your* place *for* your sins. Peter is here emphasizing that Jesus died *once* for sins. The idea was that the original audience would hear this part of Peter's letter read out loud and go, *"OH! He's dealt with it once and for all!"* This is why the story of who Jesus is and what Jesus did is such Good News. Jesus has dealt with not just my sin problem, but yours also. Borrowing a phrase from C.S. Lewis, Jesus has performed "The Great Exchange":

> *"The RIGHTEOUS for the unrighteous..."*
>
> —1 PETER 3:18A ESV

In that great exchange, as described by arguably the greatest Christian writer of the modern era, Jesus' *goodness* comes to you, and your *badness* goes to Him, for all time. Jesus is the Righteous dying once for the unrighteous. Why?

> *"...that he might bring us TO God..."*
>
> —1 PETER 3:18 ESV

*Jesus' death had a destination built into it.*

Simply put, Jesus has brought you home.

God Himself entered into the human story deeply, in Christ. He has identified deeply with the pain and suffering of our shared story as humans and He has introduced a whole new way for us to be "human" – through His incarnation, in His sinless life, His death, His resurrection, and ascension. Which kind of takes us all the way back to where we started this chapter.

## 1  Jesus has identified with you, so now you can identify with him.

*"What does this mean practically?"*

Practically, this means you should go out and live your life this week as if *"I'm a Jesus-Person now!"* is tattooed on your soul. Because Jesus has deeply identified with you, you can, should, and *must* identify with Him. You're a Jesus-Person now. And I think it's important to remind you that this story that you are now identifying yourself with is not some kind of *fairy tale*.

> *"...being put to death in the flesh but made ALIVE in the spirit..."*
>
> —1 PETER 3:18B ESV

What's the point here? The point is that, this Jesus we're talking about, He *really* died and He *really* rose again.

*"But how do we know?"*

Let's remember who is writing our source material here.

*Peter.*

Who, in Luke 22:54-62, is with Jesus at His arrest and, during the sequence recorded there, sees the crowd begin to beat Jesus and spit upon Him just prior to bringing Him to His first mock trial. Peter, standing right there and seeing it all with his own eyes, infamously denies any association with Jesus when he's asked, in that heated moment.

*Peter.*

Who, in Luke 23:49, is with the crowd of all of Jesus' acquaintances, friends, followers, and family as they watch Jesus die upon the cross.

*Peter.*

Who, in Luke 24:12, runs to the empty tomb to see for himself that Jesus has risen again from death.

*Peter.*

Who, in Mark 16:14, is at dinner with the other ten remaining disciples when the resurrected Jesus shows up, rebukes their unbelief, and gives them The Great Commission.

*Peter.*

Who, in John 21, is fishing – after Jesus' resurrection – back home on the Sea of Galilee, when Jesus suddenly shows up. Peter is so excited to see the Lord that he jumps out of the boat, swims to shore as the rest of the guys bring the boat back in – loaded with an incredible catch – and ends up dragging the near-bursting nets to shore all by himself so that he can make Jesus breakfast.

*Peter.*

Who, in Acts 2, filled with the Holy Spirit, preaches the first sermon of Jesus' new Church, and three thousand people give their hearts to Jesus that day, turning the 120 disciples into a Mega-Church in one day.

*Peter.*

Who, in Acts 10, has a vision from God that leads him to realize that the Good News about Jesus is for everyone, not just the Jews, which leads him to say the following:

> *"So Peter opened his mouth and said: 'Truly I understand that God shows no partiality, but in every nation anyone who fears him and does what is right is acceptable to him. As for the word that he sent to Israel, preaching good news of peace through Jesus Christ (he is Lord of all), you yourselves know what happened throughout all Judea, beginning from Galilee after the baptism that John proclaimed: how God anointed Jesus of Nazareth with the Holy Spirit and with power. He went about doing good and healing all who were oppressed by the devil, for God was with him. And we are witnesses of all that he did both in the country of the Jews and in Jerusalem. They put him to death by hanging him on a tree, but God raised him on the third day and made him to appear, not to all the people but to us who had been chosen by God as witnesses, who ate and drank with him after he rose from the dead. And he commanded us to preach to the people and to testify that he is the one appointed by God to be judge of the living and the dead. To him all the prophets bear witness that everyone who believes in him receives forgiveness of sins through his name.' While Peter was still saying these*

*things, the Holy Spirit fell on all who heard the word. And the believers from among the circumcised who had come with Peter were amazed, because the gift of the Holy Spirit was poured out even on the Gentiles. For they were hearing them speaking in tongues and extolling God. Then Peter declared, 'Can anyone withhold water for baptizing these people, who have received the Holy Spirit just as we have?' And he commanded them to be baptized in the name of Jesus Christ. Then they asked him to remain for some days..."*

—ACTS 10:34-48 ESV

Those are Peter's own words right there.

*Peter.*

An eyewitness, telling you that:

## 2  The story of Jesus is *really* true, so you can *really* build your life on it.

So, based on all that firsthand evidence you've just read, go out into your week – this week – and find *one thing* you can do to build your life on Jesus, and His story of triumph. And we're talking *real* triumph here, triumph that's worth getting excited about – like *as excited* as Jesus was after the Holy Spirit woke Him up that very Easter Sunday morning.

*"...but (He was) MADE alive in the spirit..."*

—1 PETER 3:18B ESV

What a beautiful moment that must have been.

Did you know it was the Holy Spirit who raised Jesus from the dead? Sometimes we think that Jesus had enough power, in and of Himself, to raise Himself from the dead, but it wasn't Him, it was the Holy Ghost. Who rolled the stone away? Well, according to Matthew 28:2 the Angel of the Lord did. But before he got there, the Holy Ghost must have shown up in that tomb and seen the Logos still slumbering all wrapped up in His grave clothes. I imagine the Holy Ghost standing there, or just filling the space with its nonmaterial Presence, and saying with great authority and glee: *"Wakey, wakey Logos! We got some WORK to do!"*

"Logos" is the name for the Second Member of the Trinity: God the Son, the Word of God, the *Logos*. And that's who the Holy Ghost walked into that tomb, that Sunday morning all those years ago just, outside the walls of downtown Jerusalem, to awaken from death!

In that great moment, you can picture the Logos jumping up, freed from death and His grave clothes, and probably shouting back in reply to the Holy Spirit; *"Whooooo! Let's go!"* And the Holy Ghost in return saying; *"Okay! Where do you want to go first?"* and the Logos saying, *"I want to go to HELL!"* And the Holy Ghost would be like, *"Really? I wasn't expecting that would be Your first choice. Why there?"* And you can picture the Logos smiling that gorgeous smile of His back at the Holy Ghost and saying; *"Because I feel the urge in Me to PREACH!"* And, with that, the Logos descended unto hell, by the power of the Holy Spirit and did what?

> *"...went and (preached) to the spirits in PRISON, because they formerly did not obey, when God's patience waited in the days of Noah..."*
>
> —1 PETER 3:19B-20A ESV

Most of the Bible interpreters I read on this agree, and I tend to agree with them, that the "spirits in prison" Peter is talking about here are the Nephilim, the fallen angels of Genesis 6, who were sleeping with the Daughters of Men, giving birth to the race of giants who plagued God's people throughout their history in what would become Canaan, or the Promised Land: what is, today, Modern Israel.

God wasn't happy about this interbreeding of the angelic and the human, so the spirits in question were sent into "prison" until the Day of Judgment would come. Little did they know that *their* day of judgment would be when the Logos descended unto hell to say, *"It is finished! I have won! I have the keys to death and hell! Behold my awesomeness! Get ready for what's about to come! Y'all didn't see this coming, now did you? Happy Easter, baby!"*

(Or something like that)

Never forget the fact that Jesus is a *Preacher*. He was so excited about His resurrection that he took *a victory lap* through hell to preach about it to the fallen angels. He's not being super-efficient here. He's not serving any clearly grand purpose with this victory lap; He's just *exulting* in it. Take a page from Jesus here. Next time you find something to celebrate in your life, *celebrate it*, in Jesus' Name!

Next time something beautiful happens to you, *celebrate* like it's Easter! If God's been good to you, *shout* it out like a preacher!

And, since we're preaching here, let's preach for a moment about God's patience.

> *"...when God's PATIENCE waited in the days of Noah..."*
>
> —1 PETER 3:20A ESV

God's patience *waited.*

I love that. Patience personified. Like God's patience has a personality and it's waiting, back in the days of Noah, for the ark to be finished. God's patience is relaxing for a minute; it's waiting. Meanwhile, these fallen angels are up to no good, acting the fool with a bunch of human ladies and you'd think, to look at it, like the world had gone astray, off-kilter, like God was somehow asleep at the wheel, because why else would He be letting something that twisted happen? Let me remind you here that sometimes God is just being patient; He's in no rush. All the power, authority, dominion, rule, reign, and glory are His – and His alone – throughout all time. Nobody can touch what's His. He's got nothing to worry about; He can relax and wait.

*"But why does God wait?"*

Romans 11:25 gives us a clue. He's waiting for the *fullness* of the Gentiles to come in. That's a beautiful picture right there, especially if you're not Jewish. If you're a Gentile this is very good news, because He's waiting for you. He's waiting for your families. He's waiting for your friends. God is waiting for the fullness of the Gentiles to come into His Family, and that ingathering is taking some time. So, God waits.

He's waiting because it's His will that none should perish, but that all should come to repentance (2 Peter 3:9). Maybe today is *your* day to stop testing God's patience. Maybe today is your day to repent, to admit to God that you can't fix yourself and you need some help. And the salvation that is the root and source of that help, in both its outer manifestation and its inner work, is based on, relies upon, and is rooted in (in its entirety) the resurrection of Jesus.

The outer signs of salvation, the way in which somebody's life *visibly* changes after they begin following Jesus, and the inner work – the stuff that changes in you that no one but you and God know about – *both* of these realities rely upon the resurrection of Jesus for their power, period. This is why Peter says what he does about baptism.

> *"Baptism, which corresponds to this (referring to Noah's flood), now saves you..."*
>
> —1 PETER 3:21A ESV

Then he qualifies it, lest we should think, *"Oh! Baptism saves us. Quick, let's run a bunch of illiterate European peasants through a*

186

*river while a priest makes the sign of the Cross over them and –*
*POOF – we'll have us a 'Christian Continent'..."*

(Wait a minute...)

> *"...NOT as a removal of dirt from the body but as an appeal*
> *to God for a good CONSCIENCE, through the resurrection*
> *of Jesus Christ..."*
>
> —1 PETER 3:21B ESV

Baptism, from Peter's point of view, saves you not just by ceremonially "cleansing" you, but because baptism is an *outer sign* of an inner work whereby you are *appealing* to God – praying with your body – for a good conscience. And God, because of His goodness and His grace, rushes in to meet you in the waters of baptism, jumping onto your public declaration of faith, affirming it with His Presence, like He did when Jesus was baptized, and fans into flame the inner working of His Holy Spirit *in* you that then *drives* all of the outer manifestation of "New Life in Jesus" that shows up in your life – for the rest of your life – as you learn to love, serve, follow, obey, and enjoy Jesus forever!

*All of this hinges on the resurrection.*

Why?

Because the resurrection of Jesus is the ultimate evidence of God's power at work, and it is that power – that same power that raised Jesus Christ from the dead, in the words of Romans 8 – that dwells *in* you and gives life to *your* mortal bodies.

> *"If the Spirit of him who raised Jesus from the dead DWELLS*
> *in you, He who raised Christ Jesus from the dead will also give*
> *life to your mortal bodies through His Spirit who dwells in you..."*
>
> —ROM 8:11 ESV

*Did you catch that?*

The same Spirit that woke the Logos Easter Sunday morning is the *same* Spirit that dwells in you! The *power* of God is alive and at work *in* you, giving you *power* to live.

So many Christians live disempowered lives because they are disconnected from the Holy Spirit. Why else would the Scriptures teach us to "Be *being* filled with the Holy Spirit..."? (Eph 5:18)

*Because we leak.*

To be filled at conversion is not enough. The constant imperative, and pattern, in the Scriptures when speaking about our interaction with the Holy Spirit is to be presently, and *continuously* "Be BEING filled..." with the Holy Spirit, because you're a sieve.

As we walk *with* Jesus, He fills us up little by little, but we are not yet what we shall one day *be* when we awaken in His image and likeness, knowing Him fully even as we have always been fully known (1 Cor 13:12). So, in the meantime, we leak and we need to be *being* filled with the Holy Spirit so that we can live lives of power. Do you lack power for living? Ask God to fill you with the Holy Spirit. Do you lack joy? Ask God to fill you with the Holy Spirit. Love, joy, peace, patience, kindness, goodness, faithfulness, gentleness, self-control: what *are* these? They are the fruit of – you guessed it – the Holy Spirit!

*"Fill me Lord!"*

*"Help me Jesus!"*

These should be your daily, recurrent prayers.

Why is this so important? Because living life to the fullest is what this is all about. How do I know that's what this is all about? Because of my favorite part from this section of Peter's letter.

*Jesus did not resurrect to retire. He resurrected to go somewhere.*

> *"... who has gone into HEAVEN and is at the right hand of God..."*
>
> —1 PETER 3:22A ESV

Jesus resurrected and returned to His rightful place at His Father's right hand where, as I love to tell it as often as I get the chance, He sat down in victory to begin interceding for *you*! He did not resurrect in order to retire.

> *"What then shall we say to these things? If God is for us, who can be against us? He who did not spare his own Son but gave him up for us all, how will he not also with him graciously give us all things? Who shall bring any charge against God's elect? It is God who justifies. Who is to condemn? Christ Jesus is the one who died—more than that, who was raised—who is at the right hand of God, who indeed is interceding for us. Who shall separate us from the love of Christ? Shall tribulation, or distress, or persecution, or famine, or nakedness, or danger, or sword? As it is written, 'For your sake we are being killed all the day long; we are regarded as sheep to be slaughtered.' No, in all these things we are more than conquerors through him who loved us. For I am sure that neither death nor life, nor angels nor rulers, nor things present nor things to come, nor powers, nor height nor depth, nor anything else in all creation, will be able to SEPARATE us from the love of God in Christ Jesus our Lord..."*
>
> —ROM 8:31-39 ESV

Who can *separate* us from the love of God in Christ?

Nobody.

See, Jesus resurrected to continue His victory lap, ruling and reigning over angels, authorities, and powers (1 Peter 3:22). All authority in Heaven and on Earth has been given to Him.

> *"Go therefore and make disciples of all nations, baptizing them in the name of the Father and of the Son and of the Holy Spirit, teaching them to observe all that I have commanded you..."*
>
> —MATT 28:18B-20A ESV

Which means, because He has *identified* with you, and now *you* can identify with Him; because the story about Him is *really* true and you can therefore really *build* your life on it; because Jesus is so stoked about the *implications* of His story that He took a victory lap through hell to *preach* about it; because God is patient; because salvation – both in its outer manifestation, and in its inner work – depends *completely* on the resurrection; because Jesus rose again to go somewhere (back to His rightful place at the Father's right hand) and to *do* something (to rule and reign), continuing His victory lap, *you might as well just jump in the back seat and let Him drive you on home, to Glory.*

# NINE

# God's Future Is My Future NOw

How you *see* the world hugely impacts your experience *of* it.

Take a juicy, delicious, perfectly cooked steak, for example. Can you see it in your mind's eye? If you have a strong imagination like I do, maybe you can almost *smell* it. Are you salivating? Good. Let's talk about that steak for a minute. Is it a delicious part of a wonderful meal, or is it a charred piece of flesh sundered from one of God's living creatures?

Or how about that workout your trainer has lined up for you to do? You know the one I'm talking about, right? It's going to leave you panting, sweat-soaked, and sore in every limb; you're going to feel the aftereffects for days. Is that workout an opportunity for you to get stronger, for you to push yourself, to learn what your limits are and then redefine them, or is it willingly subjecting yourself to an activity verging on torture, designed to induce misery and despair?

What about life in the big city? You know, condo life, downtown, walking distance from shops and cafes and groceries just around the corner with your boat docked three blocks down in the marina (yes, that's the dream for our golden years; you caught me fantasizing there for a minute). People and noise and busyness everywhere; that's life in the city. Does that sound like excitement and awesomeness to you, or do you read that and think: *"Congestion, pollution, and never-ending people: no thank you!"*

So maybe you like the country better? Ten acres, farmhouse, your own gardens to grow your own food, maybe even an old barn out back you can convert into a studio to do some painting or writing in. Would that kind of thing seem idyllic and peaceful to you, or would even thinking about it for too long make you want to slap yourself from boredom?

Okay, last one.

Say I went out and bought that 2008 Porsche 911 Targa 4S I've been dreaming about since I was twelve. Would I be purchasing a piece of mechanical art, a part of automotive history, something to cherish and enjoy to God's glory because of its beauty and awesomeness and the joy it births in my heart, or would it be an act of ostentatious frivolity? I mean, maybe you drive a beige Toyota Corolla. If that's the case, let me ask you this: Is your homely, boring Corolla a pedestrian and unimaginative "old person's car," not much better than a sewing machine, or is it practical, good enough, and responsible?

Ah, but I can't resist.

Picture a woman. Her cheekbones are still high and fair and her lips full, if not quite as lustrous as in yesteryear. Her eyes, wrinkle-circled though they might be, clearly used to sparkle with mischievous anticipation whenever her husband entered the room and the kids were out. Her arms, which sag a little now on the underside, used to be firm, and she moves quite a bit more slowly and carefully these days than she did forty years ago. Is this woman I'm describing an "old woman," or is she the wife of your youth?

*What about Jesus?*

Is Jesus a curious figure from an ancient fairytale, or is He *the key* to changing your mindset so that you get the most out of life?

Let's see what our text has to say.

> *"Since therefore Christ suffered in the flesh, arm yourselves with the same way of thinking, for whoever has suffered in the flesh has ceased from sin, so as to live for the rest of the time in the flesh no longer for human passions but for the will of God. For the time that is past suffices for doing what the Gentiles want to do, living in sensuality, passions, drunkenness, orgies, drinking parties, and lawless idolatry. With respect to this they are surprised when you do not join them in the same flood of debauchery, and they malign you; but they will give account to him who is ready to judge the living and the dead. For this is why the gospel was preached even to those who are dead, that though judged in the flesh the way people are, they might live in the spirit the way God does..."*
>
> —1 PETER 4:1-6 ESV

Here's the deal with this chapter: I want to help you learn to keep Jesus' suffering, and His victory, in mind as a *tool* to help you adopt His *mindset* as the key weapon you're going to need in your quest to *really* live. See, Jesus *really* suffered, so you can *really* bank on the fruits of that suffering. In the same way, Jesus *really* was victorious in His resurrection, so you can *really* build your life on the hope that is to be found in who Jesus is and what Jesus did.

And what was victorious Jesus' mindset really like? I think you can capture Jesus' victorious mindset beautifully from His words in the Garden of Gethsemane the night that He was betrayed.

> *"Nevertheless, not My will, but YOURS be done..."*
>
> —LUKE 22:42 ESV

Jesus was suffering in the Garden. He knew that the next day He was going to the cross and that it was going to be a very ugly death. To the degree that He knew that the Father was going to lay the penalty for the sins of the world throughout all time on His shoulders during His crucifixion, you can bet that the prospect of it was stressing Him out, to say the least. So, as He's praying in that Garden, the night before, in anguish He cries out:

> *"Father! If it is possible, let this cup pass from before Me!"*
>
> —MATT 26:39 ESV

He's basically asking God the Father if there's *any* way around what's about to happen to Him. But He follows it up with those immortal words:

> *"Nevertheless, not My will, but YOURS be done..."*
>
> —LUKE 22:42 ESV

*That's Jesus' mindset, right there.*

Elsewhere in His story, as captured in the pages of the New Testament, we see Him saying He only does what He sees the Father doing (John 5:19-20). He is constantly in communication with God the Father, seeking to *know* and to *do* the Father's will. *Not My will, but Yours be done.*

God-the-Son-made-flesh *knew* that the Gospel is ultimately about God: His glory, His fame, His will, His activity, His people, His redemptive work, His future. Never forget that, in being adopted into God's family, you have been adopted into the future of God. God's future is your future now, because of Jesus.

*#godsfutureismyfuturenow*

Put that on a bumper sticker or on a t-shirt or, better yet, sear it on your heart and (most importantly) go out into your week and start *living* like it's true! How would your life, and the *stresses* of your average week, change if you *truly* believed (and were counting on the fact) that God's future is *your* future now? You see, the moment you begin to adopt a "God first" mindset, is the moment you will find yourself really on the way to living.

It's also worth noting that, if you're living with a "God first" mindset, it is impossible to live with a "Me first" one. "God first" and "Me first" are mutually exclusive; you're going to have to pick *one* as your way of living.

The reason, of course, that this is so important is that destroying selfishness is the key to killing sin.

> *"...for whoever has suffered in the flesh has CEASED from sin.."*
>
> —1 PETER 4:1B ESV

Pretty audacious stuff from Peter right there. I'm thinking; *"Really? Whoever has suffered has ceased from sin? That's all it takes? A little suffering? Because, man, I've suffered quite a bit by this point in my life, and I still sin..."* So, is the Bible *wrong* here, or is Peter lying to us? If we dig a little deeper into the original language, we might find us some help.

> *"For whoever WILLINGLY accepts suffering, has ceased from sinning..."*
>
> —1 PETER 4:1B, ADAPTED FROM THE GREEK

To *willingly* accept suffering means something more; there's a kind of miracle to it. There is a very clear difference between the way one of Jesus' people *accepts* suffering and the way someone who's not yet one of Jesus' friends *deals* with it. The "Jesus-Person" accepts suffering and clings to hope *through* it.

This happens to me frequently, especially when the traffic in my city is trying to crush my soul. Does this ever happen to you? You really need to get somewhere, maybe you're even running a little bit late and, in that moment, the slowest-driving old lady in the *world* settles down right in front of you (yes, it's a one-lane road) and proceeds to lead you through town, doing ten under the speed limit. And, to add insult to injury, because she's oblivious to the fact that the stoplights are timed, she doesn't speed up to catch the next one, and you end up hitting all the reds.

(I have decided that these kinds of moments are sent from the devil to test me.)

It's in those petty moments of inane suffering (because, let's face it, we all deal with things much worse than old ladies and red lights) that your relationship with Jesus can come in most handy. When you call Jesus to mind, even when crawling in traffic behind that demon-possessed old lady, the realization of the epic salvation that He has accomplished for you will wash over you and you will find yourself able to hold onto your joy: not because you are good, but because Jesus is.

The thing about Jesus' beauty and His fame is that, as you walk with Him, some of His greatness begins seeping into *your* habits, changing you little by little until you find yourself able to accept the suffering you run into in your day-to-day life while holding on to hope. This is where the "Christian Genius" begins to take flight.

*Life is hard, but God is good.*

As you grow in faith, eventually you find yourself able to exchange one word for another.

Life is hard *and* God is good.

It may take you half a lifetime to switch the "but" for an "and," but once you get there? Life's gonna be *alright*.

This is the Christian response to suffering: "Life is hard *and* God is good." The non-Christian response always involves some version of

*"Umm, well let me see if I can save myself first."* Faced with suffering, most people *react*, then, they begin working to try to save *themselves.* The Christian says: *"Life is hard and God is good. I'm not sure how I'm going to get through this, but I am sure I am not the answer. I think I'm going to wait and trust God instead..."* The more you suffer without losing hope, the less of a grip "self" is going to have on you, and this is a very good thing because selfishness is very nearly the *root* of sin.

We know this from the first story in the Bible.

*"Gee, you know, the fruit of that Tree of the Knowledge of Good and Evil looks mighty tasty..."*

Nevertheless, not my will but *Yours* be done.

If Adam and Eve had had the mindset of the Logos – the mind of Christ (Phil 2:5) –and if they had adopted His way of seeing life, they would have looked at that tasty fruit the snake was suggesting they try and said, *"No Sir, no thank you, I think not..."* And the serpent might have cocked a crooked eye at them and asked, *"Why not, doesn't it look good?"* And Eve might have looked a second time at the fruit and seen that it was indeed desirable to make one wise (Gen 3:6), but then she would have thought in her heart: *"Nevertheless, not my will, but Yours be done..."* And she would have said no a final time to the snake and the whole long, sad story of the humans would have looked completely different than it does.

*If she'd but had the mindset of the Word.*

The only reason I can write something so bold and direct about the sin of our first Parents (I'm going to have to meet them someday, after all) is because their sinfulness is so clearly still alive in *me.* I know that, placed in the garden with my lovely naked wife at *my* side, I would have fared no better, and I'm a fraction of a fraction of the kind of quality of man that the first man, Adam, surely was.

*The weight of their choice lives in me still.*

When you get a whole new mindset, in and because of Jesus, you'll be able to *watch* as suffering becomes the pathway to freedom in your life. You could easily call this chapter "Redeeming Suffering." But I'm probably going to have to show you how suffering leads to freedom first, before you fully jump on board.

> *"...so as to live for the rest of the time in the flesh no longer for human passions but FOR the will of God..."*
>
> —1 PETER 4:2 ESV

If you think like Jesus, and suffer your way through, joyfully, to selflessness, you *will* find yourself free from slavery to sin.

It's important to say here that you will never be free from slavery. You can be a slave to sin or you can be God's slave. This is clearly taught in Scripture.

*We are the servant race.*

You can no more deny your servant-ness than you can deny your existence or your need to breathe. Yet, most of humanity spends most of its time doing everything they can to ascend God's throne for themselves so they can rule and reign in His place, while making as many people as possible as *subject* to them as possible. This is the great, foul, and blasphemous spirit of our age of the world. This is "anti-Christ"; its spirit is alive and well in the world around us, and if we're not careful, in our own hearts as well.

You gotta serve *somebody*. Dylan said it. You can be a slave to sin or a slave to God. We're the servant race and, chances are, you've spent more than a little of your life enslaved to sin.

> *"For the time that is PAST suffices for doing what the Gentiles want to do, living in sensuality, passions, drunkenness, orgies, drinking parties, and lawless idolatry..."*
>
> —1 PETER 4:3 ESV

Here's the point: you *used* to do what everybody else does, living the same way as them. How did everyone else live in the Roman culture that Peter was writing to? Wretched, sensual excess was an everyday way of life. We're going to need some very careful definitions for the words Peter uses here because we want to get this *right*; the stakes are high.

The people Peter was writing to were used to making the *experience* of sensuality an *end* in itself. For them, the ultimate expression of human dignity and worth was to be found in the throwing off of restraint: no limits, no restrictions, total and absolute freedom to do whatever one wanted, whenever one wanted, with whomever one wanted, for whatever reason seemed fit.

*Sound familiar?*

It's really scary how familiar it sounds! It sounds exactly like *our* world.

Now, look, I don't want to make this whole chapter about sexual sin (everyone's "favorite" subject in a "Christian Living" book, I know), but I do want to point out that this is a very big issue, both in the original audience that Peter was writing to and in the audience reading this book today. The problem they were facing is the problem we are facing.

*"How's that?"*

Well, you see, look: God makes Adam and Eve *naked* in the Garden of Eden and *commands* them to procreate. Obviously, He thinks sex is a good idea, and He's efficient; He didn't waste any time (or opportunity for Adam, His friend) with giving our first Parents clothes. God also cared about Adam and Eve (and their future descendants) so much that He designed our human physiology in such a way that we would really enjoy sex – so much so, that even in our fallen world, sex still makes the world go 'round.

*Why would God have designed us this way?*

Because He's good, and He's kind, and He wants you to have joy – but mostly He wants you to fill the Earth and subdue it. Why? Because I think He wanted (and wants) many, many, friends – women and men – descendants of those first two naked humans from the Garden, made in God's image and likeness, to be in fellowship with Him, as His friends, forever. He must have a *very* large banqueting table in Glory, because He's chosen you as his partner in co-creation to help Him fill it up.

So, He made you *able* to procreate and designed you to really, really *like* it so that you'd do it, lots. And we take that noble, beautiful, life-oriented impulse and we turn it into a game, an industry, a pastime, a mechanism for power, a commodity to trade for money, an escape, an addiction.

*And it's not just sex we ruin.*

God creates wine to make glad the heart of man (Psalm 104) and "make glad" in the Hebrew is *Ye-sameach,* which means "to *make* happy," which means to intoxicate. The kind of warm fuzziness that comes after a nice glass of wine is *celebrated* in Psalm 104. Further, Jesus, at the first miracle He wrought in Cana of Galilee (John 2:1-12) makes *more* wine at a wedding after all the wine has already been drunk. If you've ever been to a Jewish, or Polish, or Italian, or Greek wedding, you know *exactly* what was happening in John 2. Big party, all the wine's gone so they turn to *Jesus* for help. Does He wag His finger at them saying *"Tut, tut..."* and urge moderation on them? No, He calls for water so he can turn it into round two and the party can keep going. But we take what I like to refer to as "Biblical Intoxication" and we turn it into habitual drunkenness.

*Silly rabbits.*

From this twisting of something good we get alcoholism, destitution, spousal abuse, poverty, slavery – the list could go on and on – because of all the ways we ruin something God made *good* in the first place. We forsake the worship of God and put things and self on the throne, and it leads to all manner of abusive evil as we seek to live life in *our* own name, for *our* glory. And here's the rub:

*None of it ultimately satisfies.*

Study addiction ("The Power of Habit" by Charles Duhig is a good place to start) and what do you find? Put *very* simply, we take the pleasure responses that God has built into our physiology to encourage us to procreate, so He can have an Earth full of people to love, and turn those pleasure responses into false gods. We stimulate and we stimulate and we stimulate and we stimulate until, eventually, the pleasure centers in our brain become (in layman's terms) *calloused* to the point that regular, God-designed inputs no longer work. So now a glass of wine needs to become a "drinking party" and sex with our spouse needs to become an orgy (do a little *careful* research of articles online relating to this and you'll be shocked to see how common this kind of thing has become in our generation). A good meal with friends is no longer satisfying so we gorge ourselves at feasts fit for Rome in her fallenness, while the poor get poorer and thousands starve worldwide every year.

My friends, in almost every way that counts, we're still living in Rome, and it's still the 1st Century AD. We *are* Babylon the Great, and our wickedness ascends to Heaven like a stench.

We take the good things God has made, turn them into "god-things" and, as such, they quickly become *bad things*. My friend Mark was the first one I ever heard say it that way, so let's give credit where credit is due. Nice work, Mark. Love you, buddy.

What happens when your senses get dulled? Well, you have to stimulate them more and more and *more*, futilely consuming *more* to get the same response until, eventually, your supremely dulled senses (a direct result of your supremely practiced addiction) give you nothing back, and you end up a full-blown addict, trapped in despair.

Do you know what the closest bedfellow of sex addiction, especially through pornography, is in North American Men?

*Depression*.

Pornography addiction is now seen, by most experts, as *equivalent* to heroin addiction in terms of how hard a habit it is to break. We've dulled ourselves, through continual sinning, to the point of literal despair.

Then Jesus walks into your life – thank God – and things begin to change.

*"Why? How?"*

Because you start (and sometimes it is just a start) to find your satisfaction in God Himself. Has that begun happening in you, even just a little bit? Sure, it has. We've *tasted and seen* that the Lord is good. And I get that sometimes redemption's creep into your life is just in small measure – and sometimes you feel like it's not enough – but God *knows* this, and that's why He says:

> *"Blessed are those who hunger and thirst for righteousness for they SHALL be filled..."*
>
> —MATT 5:6 ESV

Jesus walks with you for the entirety of your life and He will continue to be your Friend and Lord into Eternity. To say He's committed to you for the long haul is a huge understatement. So, don't despair that you don't get all the riches of Eternity now – it would probably cause you to disintegrate if you got all of what Eternity holds in the balance for you all in one fell swoop anyway. God is with you now, and will be with you forever; so, take what He gives you now, be thankful for it, knowing that much more is coming in the future, and just faithfully keep moving forward.

As you start finding your satisfaction in God Himself, you will find that your interest in "self" and in stimulation begin to pale in comparison to the beauty of God, the awesomeness of His will and the greatness of His Creation, which includes you!

*This is incredibly freeing and empowering.*

What will happen is that the Beauty of God will begin to *eclipse* your lust for lesser beauties and, eventually – as God's redemptive power works its way out in your heart – anytime you see anything beautiful, you will see the hand of God in it. This will increasingly make it more and more difficult to sin *against* God in making an idol of that thing because now, that beautiful thing is eliciting a pleasure response inside a God-designed brain that is more and more surrendered to the will and power of Christ. That's because you've looked upon the Beauty of Jesus *enough* that His Beauty is beginning to *eclipse* all other beauties for you – even that extra ice cream sundae or that girl at the beach. And you know what's funny about this? Your "normal" friends are not happy about this transformation that is happening in you. Why?

Because, like I already told you, everybody *hates* the "DD."

Have you noticed how everyone treats the designated driver at a party? Everyone's trying to get them to *drink*! (Okay, maybe not everyone, but definitely their buddies.) It's almost like a game· "Hey, let's see if we can get the DD to drink, that sucker!" This leads to a very deep question about human existence: *Why do drunk people always have a hard time with non-drunk people?* You've noticed this, right? I'll tell you why they don't like you; *your non-drunk-ness condemns them.* Your very presence is harshing their vibe.

It's not a problem if everyone is drunk, but even one sober person in the room, one person not joining in the "fun," is enough of a killjoy to cause problems. The DD's abstinence – by its very presence – condemns everyone else's licentiousness. Your nonparticipation condemns them (implicitly) as lawbreakers and rebels against God and, last time I checked, nobody likes feeling that way and nobody likes a "Party Pooper."

Peer pressure is nothing other than sinners trying to get others they *perceive* as "non-sinners" to join in the "fun."

> *"With respect to this they are surprised when you do not JOIN them in the same FLOOD of debauchery, and they malign you; but they will give account to him who is ready to judge the living and the dead..."*
>
> —1 PETER 4:4-5 ESV

Or, "They are surprised when you do not *lodge* with them in the *same un-saving puddle...*"

My big takeaway from this is pretty deep; get ready for it...

*Don't live in things that don't save.*

Even though your friends will blaspheme you for it.

That's what "malign you" means here; they're literally going to blaspheme you because you don't participate. You will become the object of blasphemy. Anyone else come to mind to Whom that has happened? That's right, your Friend Jesus Christ. Put quotes around His name and end it with an exclamation mark:

*"Jesus Christ!"*

And it's blasphemy.

And you hear it every day.

This is the kind of thing the Bible is talking about when it refers to us entering into the "fellowship of His sufferings" (Phil 3:10). As you live a life that echoes who Jesus is and what He does, more and more, you will be blasphemed just like He was. But why? Why do people blaspheme you when you refuse to lodge with them in the same un-saving puddle?

(I'm going to write about judgment now, then we'll go to hell for a minute; you've been warned)

204

Everyone hates the DD because they feel *judged* by the DD's nonparticipation. When you don't participate with someone who's acting the fool, your nonparticipation makes them *feel* judged; nothing you can do about it. A quick word on "judgment" might be helpful here.

> *"...but they will give account to Him who is ready to JUDGE the living and the dead..."*
>
> —1 PETER 4:5 ESV

Here's the thing: I don't judge you, and you shouldn't judge others, but the Judge *exists,* and His Name is God. This is a very unpopular opinion to hold in popular culture. What's interesting about this – and it may help you deal with your friends' objections to this way of thinking – is that, since we're all made in the image of God, we kind of "act" like Him as we mirror (in whatever broken and small way) his God-ness. This is evidenced by the fact that we *all* judge *every-thing*, all the time. Steak: great meal, or violence against animals? City or country? Old woman, young woman? Porsche? Corolla?

*You see what I did there, right?*

Everybody judges everything all the time; they just don't want you (or anyone else, including God) to judge them when it's *inconvenient.* Even if you don't *actively* judge them, they don't even want your actions to *remind* them that there *is* a Judge at all. Thing is, I'm a Gospel Preacher writing a book about the Gospel, so I'm definitely going to go there.

> *"Then I saw a great white throne and him who was seated on it. From his presence earth and sky fled away, and no place was found for them. And I saw the dead, great and small, standing before the throne, and books were opened. Then another book was opened, which is the book of life. And the dead were judged by what was written in the books,*

> *according to what they had done. And the sea gave up the dead who were in it, Death and Hades gave up the dead who were in them, and they were judged, each one of them, according to what they had done. Then Death and Hades were thrown into the lake of fire. This is the second death, the lake of fire. And if anyone's name was not found written in the book of life, he was thrown into the lake of fire...*"

—REV 20:11-15 ESV

In the next chapter (Revelation 21) they go to the New Jerusalem and everything is *all right* – but first, you've got to get through Revelation 20. First sermon I ever preached in my life (and I've been preaching since I was 19) was from Revelation 20. We're talking about the "Great White Throne Judgment" here; it's super-epic and serious and I want to point out two things from it.

First, books are opened, death and hell give up their dead, even the sea does the same, and *everyone* gets judged according to their deeds. Now, before we go a little deeper, and because I'm trying to be both faithful and not an idiot here, let me remind you that the Book of Revelation is a vision, a dream, that John (probably the Elder) has in his later years while imprisoned on a Greek Island called Patmos. I figure, if you *have* to be imprisoned, might as well be on a Greek Island. So, since John is dreaming here, let's at least *try* to agree to not be dogmatic about what we read. Let's at least *try* to keep in mind that we're looking to interpret and apply an Apostolic *dream* here. So, we're not going to *build* our actual "life and practice" around the details we find here ("Locusts and dragons and prophets, oh my!") but instead, we are going to let the details of this vision *inform* our life and practice. I'm talking about a good ol' dose of "Christian Moderation" here, although – depending on where you're from and the tradition you grew up in – *moderation* might not be something you're used to.

It's how I like to roll, so we'll do it that way.

So (still on the first point here), the books are opened and every-one is judged according to their *works*. This means God is keeping track of what's going on in your life and in the world; He knows and, someday, everybody's going to know. If you were looking for a "Practical Theology" of how to motivate yourself to *be* righ-teous that doesn't involve endless rules and regulations, this is it. You're welcome. If what's pictured here plays out like it's pictured, it sounds an awful lot like somebody might actually *read* those books of collected deeds, including everything *you* ever did, in front of that assembled throng.

Whoa. It makes me sick thinking about it, even now, as I write.

That's absolutely horrifying right there, no? If that's how it's actually going to go, as those books are being read, what's everyone in the crowd thinking?

*"They know it all! They haven't missed a thing. I'm sunk!"*

That's a recipe for Christian humility right there. Live like everyone is going to *know* how you lived.

Ultimately, what's happening in that crowd, (again) if the scene pictured by John in Revelation 20 is an accurate reflection of a future event that will *actually* take place, is that everyone there, from the most famous figures of history down to the most obscure nobody who ever lived, is realizing, absolutely without exception, that they have no hope. By the time they get to the C's, I'm already going to be on my face, because I've *lived* my life; I *know* what's coming. I imagine the same will be true for every soul in that crowd. I expect, by the time they get to the end of that great and awful reading, the entire throng will be on its face.

> *"And every knee shall bow and every tongue confess that Jesus Christ is Lord, to the glory of God the Father..."*
>
> —ROM 14:11

And, if I'm picturing it right, I think there will probably be a *pause* between the first sentence (And every knee shall bow...) and the second (and every tongue confess....) because to "confess" means to joyfully acclaim, and I can't picture much joy in that moment, after all the long sordid tale of fallen humanity has been read for all to hear.

*Unless there's another book.*

(Have you ever thought about how the Two Books of Revelation 20 *echo* the Two Trees of Eden? Funny right? And books are *made* from trees. I wonder...)

There is a second book, The Book of Life.

The Book of Life gets opened during that pause and (if C.S. Lewis is right in how he pictures this same scene, in the Last Battle) it's a pause that echoes into eternity: a pause so long, nobody can count it, but also seeming to last only a moment, ultimately lost in the glories of Eternity to come. But in that moment, another set of names are read and, this time, when they approach the C's I'm waiting for it, ready to jump up screaming, *"LORD HAVE MERCY! CHRIST HAVE MERCY! LORD HAVE MERCY!"* Because I *know* that I belong to Jesus and, when I hear my name read from the Lamb's Book of Life, you can bet your butt I'm going to be ready to joyfully acclaim Jesus Christ as King of Kings and Lord of Lords, the Lamb that was slain, Lion of Judah's Tribe who made a way for *my* sins to be forgiven, indeed forgotten, cast into the sea of God's forgetfulness (Micah 7:19) – a sea which will be no more, come to think of it (Rev 21:1) – such that I can be welcomed into the undying realm of a Holy God and His blood-bought people!

So, as the Angels of God come to cast those whose names are *not* written in the Lamb's Book of Life into the Lake of Fire with the devil and his angels – like Passover – they PASS ME BY *because my deeds are recorded in the First Book but my name is written in the Second!*

Friend, there is a Judge and there is a Judgment coming and, if you confess with your mouth that Jesus Christ is Lord and believe in your heart that God raised Him from the dead, you shall not perish but have everlasting life (Rom 10:9)!

> *"Jesus said to them, 'I am the bread of life; whoever comes to me shall not hunger, and whoever believes in me shall never thirst. But I said to you that you have seen me and yet do not believe. All that the Father gives me will come to me, and whoever comes to me I will never cast out. For I have come down from heaven, not to do my own will but the will of him who sent me. And this is the will of him who sent me, that I should lose nothing of all that he has given me, but raise it up on the last day. For this is the will of my Father, that everyone who looks on the Son and believes in him should have eternal life, and I will raise him up on the last day...'"*
>
> —JOHN 6:35-40 ESV

Friends, God is real, He is holy, you're a sinner, and Jesus has made a way! There is a *choice* that looms before you, and C.S. Lewis said it best:

> *"There are only two kinds of people in the end, those who say to God, 'Thy Will be done' and those to whom God says in the end, 'thy will be done.' All that are in hell choose it, without that self-choice there could be no hell. No soul that seriously and constantly desires joy will ever miss it, those who seek will find, to those who knock it will be opened..."*
>
> —"THE GREAT DIVORCE," C.S. LEWIS

Come to Jesus, my friend. Return to Jesus today. Jesus, and Jesus alone, can deal with your sin problem; you do not have the resources equal to that task. Even as you sit there reading, say it with me:

*"Jesus, I need You to save me. I need forgiveness for my many sins and my sinfulness. Please forgive me. Lord Jesus, allow Your work at the Cross to be applied to my life today. I surrender my will to Yours now. Today I give you my life! Fill me with Your Holy Spirit, and make me Yours forever. Amen."*

I know it sounds simplistic, but it's not. If you just prayed those words along with me (I was praying them as I wrote them) then your name is now writ in the Lamb's Book of Life. You belong to Jesus now. Maybe send me an email to let me know; I'd love to celebrate with you (*toddcantelon@gmail.com*).

See, we only *need* the Gospel because judgment is *real*. If we gloss over the realness of judgment, we miss the absolute beauty of the Good News about Jesus.

> *"For this is why the gospel was preached even to those who are dead, that though judged in the flesh the way people are, they might LIVE in the spirit the way God does..."*
>
> —1 PETER 4:6 ESV

The Gospel was preached to the *friends* of the people listening to Peter who had died, and he's reminding them of this to drive home the point that everybody dies because sin has consequences. All of us will one day die because sin was born into the world as a result of Adam and Eve's sin but, thanks be to God, in Jesus Christ, grace has been born into the world also.

Grace has been poured out in our hearts, which means that, though we will all die one day, we shall all be made alive by the power and presence and working of the Holy Spirit, because of what Jesus did for us. This leads me to the final point: a point I *really* don't want you to miss.

*Everybody dies, but not everybody really lives.*

To do that – really live – you'll need to get a new *mindset* in Jesus. You'll need to embrace suffering as the *pathway* to freedom. You'll need to stop living like you used to live, or like everyone else – who are busy worshiping self and experience and doing whatever the heck they want to do – because the Judgment is *real* but, thank God, so is the Gospel. My dear friend, live like you're tasting the firstfruits of Eternity even *now*. Free your mind and get the most out of life by following Jesus, the One who is *the Key*.

# TEN

# Playing for Keeps

Nothing lasts forever.

Take a first date, for example. Remember that first moment when you were sitting close to each other (not "on" each other, yet) and you spent the first twenty minutes of the movie agonizing over whether or not (and how and when) to take her hand? Tough moment. Remember how it felt when you actually *touched* her hand for the first time? Rapture! Transport! Angels singing, blood racing! You could've died then and there a happy man. Maybe that first date led to a second date, maybe even a third. Maybe a relationship began to develop; you got engaged, married, started to build a family, build a life. Nothing lasts forever though. Forty, fifty years, later one of you is going to find yourself alone.

Or, say you go out and buy something new and beautiful; it's shiny, fabulous, a status symbol even. Maybe for you this purchase is the fulfillment of a lifelong dream. You always wanted one of these (you've been talking to God about it since you were twelve) and we're not talking vanity here; this is the real deal for you, this "thing" symbolizes God's kindness and provision to you as you've spent your life working to be obedient to Him, doing what He called you to do.

No matter how nice that thing is at first (even if you buy it *used*) after a freak accident occurs, or just in the natural passing of years, that beautiful piece of mechanical art is going to become just one more piece of scrap for the heap. Birth leads to death, new becomes old, and there's nothing you can do to stop it. You can't win.

*But you can play for keeps.*

> *"The end of all things is at hand; therefore be self-controlled and sober-minded for the sake of your prayers. Above all, keep loving one another earnestly, since love covers a multitude of sins. Show hospitality to one another without grumbling. As each has received a gift, use it to serve one another, as good stewards of God's varied grace: whoever speaks, as one who speaks oracles of God; whoever serves, as one who serves by the strength that God supplies—in order that in everything God may be glorified through Jesus Christ. To him belong glory and dominion forever and ever. Amen..."*
>
> —1 PETER 4:7-11 ESV

That passage *sings* real good right there. I've got seven points from this to help you play for keeps.

### #1 Recognize how it *is*, and live accordingly

> *"The END of all things is at hand..."*
>
> —1 PETER 4:1A ESV

The End Is Near.

Turns out the Fat Guy in the end zone was right all along (especially for him, if he keeps eating all those chicken wings). It's too bad this phrase has become overused to the point of caricature because, at the heart of it, it's true; the end of all things *is* at hand.

The concept of *Imminence* was *the* driver for the growth and expansion of the Early Church. Imminence refers to the *imminent* return of Jesus Christ, as in, it's going to happen *any* minute.

*He is coming quickly!*

The End Is Near. Jesus' return is imminent; it could happen any day now. This sense of urgency was absolutely catalytic to the urgent mission of Jesus' first followers. When you study the life of the Early Church, most scholars (in fact, I didn't find even *one* who wasn't in agreement on this) say that the Early Church mothers and fathers, those who founded our movement, were convinced that Jesus was returning in *their lifetimes*. Imagine how different *your* life would look if you were similarly convinced. When you think about it like that, it helps you understand why the first followers of Jesus were so "crazy."

Look at the stories of the Apostles, or the other members of that first Church in Jerusalem: the things that they did, the lengths to which they went to see the story of Jesus proclaimed and embodied to as many people as possible. Consider the absolute conviction you see portrayed in their lives in the pages of the Book of Acts. Their actions speak louder than words; it's entirely clear that they believed that the end truly was near. The difficulty for us, two thousand years later, is to find a way to live with that same kind of urgency because: *"Umm, what happened to their original timeline?"* Right?

*Did we miss it?*

It's funny – as you study the New Testament, many of the writings deal with that same kind of skeptical insecurity. Even some members of the original Church, meaning *during* New Testament times, a Church that had spread from Jerusalem into the entirety of the Roman Empire, were concerned that they had somehow missed Christ's return.

*"I mean, it's been seven years; surely He must have come back by now?"* And then, approaching their golden years: *"Umm, it's been forty years now; do you think we missed it?"* And things started getting *really* tense when that first generation of Jesus' followers – Jesus' contemporaries – began *dying* of old age, and still the Savior whose promises they'd staked their lives on (at very great practical cost) hadn't returned to inaugurate His New Heavens and New Earth. Those would have been some *very* difficult days to live through as a Christian.

*People started getting squirrelly.*

So, for their sake, and ours, a few words on how we might *reconcile* that difficult timeline:

> *"But do not overlook this one fact, beloved, that with the Lord one day is as a THOUSAND years, and a thousand years as ONE day..."*
>
> —2 PETER 3:8 ESV

Time runs differently from God's perspective; it's a little more *elastic* for Him, it's fluid. He, the *Maker* of space-time, experiences it *differently* than we do, as creatures *of* it. A simple way to think on this is to imagine God as inhabiting "The Eternal Now," the Eternal *Present.* Think of it this way; God lives *at* the Speed of Light, and anyone who's done Grade 12 Physics knows what scientists believe *happens* at the Speed of Light. Time slows down, until it doesn't really exist anymore as we know it here within the confines of space-time. If God lives *at* the Speed of Light, everything is "'Yes and Amen" to Him.

*One day with God truly is like a thousand years.*

Jesus Himself hints at this.

> *"But concerning that day and hour no one knows, not even the angels of heaven, nor the Son, but the FATHER only..."*
>
> —MATT 24:36 ESV

216

Even Jesus said He didn't know when the End of All Things was coming. Granted, Jesus says this in His Incarnation, during the time of His Self-limiting, but Peter clearly believed that Jesus was coming back soon.

> *"The end of all things is AT hand..."*
>
> —1 PETER 4:7A ESV

For you and me today, here's the big idea connected to this; everything begins, moves towards culmination, and then ends. We who follow Jesus need to let the current "cycle of life" drive us towards urgency. Because everything begins, moves towards its culmination, and then ends, we ought to *live* like it, with some urgency: like we're on borrowed time. The simple truth of it is that you don't have all the time in the world to get right and start doing something important with your life. Time is limited. Start today.

What could you do this week to start living with more urgency?

Just because you can't win and can't escape the cycle of beginning, movement towards culmination, and end, does not mean that you shouldn't be playing for *keeps*.

You can't win, but you can play for keeps.

> *"...therefore (in light of the fact that the end is near) be self-controlled and SOBER-MINDED for the sake of your prayers..."*
>
> —1 PETER 4:7B ESV

Because the end is near we live like *sane* people. "Sober-minded" means *sanity*. Why should we live this way? The text isn't super-clear at first reading, even if you dig into the original language. If you do, *"For the sake of your prayers..."* means *"So that watch unto prayers..."* which doesn't really help. Maybe we should try stripping it right down to its *simplest* meaning:

217

*So that we can talk to God and God can talk to us.*

For the sake of your prayers.

Have you ever felt like God has shut you out, like you're praying to a glass ceiling? It might be because you need a little more sobriety – sanity – in your life.

Next way to play for keeps?

## #2 Live like the one sane person in your crazy world

What would "sanity" look like for you this week? You're going to need to ask yourself that question and then find the answer quick, because it's guaranteed that you're going to find yourself in a moment this week where you want to act crazy. It might be with your kids, your job, or how you respond to an unmet expectation or unfulfilled dream. Maybe you'll suffer the biggest betrayal of your life this week or it might just be some dude who's rude to you, for no reason, in the line at the grocery store. In the pressure of that moment (whichever moment it ends up being for you), it's going to be too much to bear and you're going to need to *choose* sanity.

The only way to survive our crazy, crazy world is to choose love.

> *"Above all, keep loving one another earnestly, since LOVE covers a multitude of sins..."*
>
> —1 PETER 4:8 ESV

Thank God for bottom lines.

Bottom line? Here's how to play for keeps.

## #3 Keep loving one another earnestly

Or, from the original (and this is *so* great):

*"Keep INTO-selves love, OUTSTRETCHED-ly..."*

—1 PETER 4:8A GREEK

*"Keep into-selves love..."* you gotta keep love *in* you.

*"Outstretched-ly..."* so you can *spread* it.

That's "Gospel Living" in one ancient Greek sentence right there: the continuous receiving and giving of love. *Continuous,* mind you. Receive it, give it away. Receive it, give it away. In and then out. In and then out.

*Like the tide.*

The "tide" analogy works real good, if you ask me. The tide never stops. Sometimes (depending on where you are) the tides are big, or noticeable; it's like this with love. Sometimes you feel *very* loving: big waves rolling in, a powerful riptide flowing back out. Other times you won't feel very loving: the tide is barely noticeable that day, just a ripple. But it's still there, coming in, and flowing back out.

*Be like the tide with your love.*

And, remember, this works because *Jesus* worked.

*"...since LOVE covers a multitude of sins..."*

—1 PETER 4:8B ESV

This is literally the best.

We think "Love *covers* a multitude of sins..." so *we* need to be *more* loving. The truth is, we don't need to be better "lovers"; we need to be better theologians.

Let's play a game. I'll write the first part and you say the second part (in your mind) before you read what I wrote next. Cool? Okay, here we go.

*God is...*

(Say it in your mind before you look.)

*Love.*

(Good, you're getting the hang of this. Next one, ready?)

*Jesus is...*

(This one's a bit tougher.)

*God.*

(Nice work; you don't even need to go to seminary if you got that one all on your own. Okay, last one; it's a "one plus one, equals two" kind of thing.)

JESUS *is...*

(That's right, you just had an "aha moment," didn't you?)

*Love.*

*God is love. Jesus is God. Jesus is LOVE.*

LOVE covers a multitude of sins.

(That's worth the price of admission right there, if you ask me.)

How about it? Doesn't that make *all* the difference in the world? You don't have to work yourself up to be more loving so that *you* can cover a multitude of sins. You just need Jesus and His story.

> *"This is the message we have heard from him and proclaim to you, that God is light, and in him is no darkness at all. If we say we have fellowship with him while we walk in darkness, we lie and do not practice the truth. But if we walk in the light, as he is in the light, we have fellowship with one another, and the blood of Jesus his Son KEEPS ON cleansing us from all sin..."*
>
> —1 JOHN 1:5-7 ESV

I added the ALL CAPS there to reflect what that phrase sounds like in the original language. We're talking absolutely life-changing stuff right there.

The blood of Jesus *KEEPS ON cleansing us* from all our sin.

*Love covers a multitude of sins!*

Because of Jesus, your sins are covered. Because He first loved you, you love Him. Because you love Him, you're *learning* to love others. Look, it's pretty simple really; the more "Gospel" you get in your heart, the less other people's sins will bother you because you'll know, deep down in the guts of you, that only Jesus is the Answer. Better behavior from the people who are bothering you is not really the answer. Better behavior from you is not the answer.

*Jesus is the answer.*

Do you see, in light of all this, how the Gospel of Jesus allows you to be like the tide, continuously receiving and giving love? This is the miracle of Christianity that not enough people talk about anywhere *near* enough.

*Continuously receptive and outstretched love drives everything.*

> *"SHOW hospitality to one another WITHOUT grumbling. As each has received a gift, use it to serve one another, as good stewards of God's varied grace: whoever speaks, as one who speaks oracles of God; whoever serves, as one who serves by the strength that God supplies—in order that in everything God may be glorified through Jesus Christ. To him belong glory and dominion forever and ever. Amen..."*
>
> —1 PETER 4:9-11 ESV

If you want to play for keeps:

## #4 Let the *inside* drive the outside

"Show hospitality without grumbling..." means *do* the right thing *and* be happy about it.

*"That's gonna be a bit of a stretch."*

I know, right?

The hardness of this command is why Christianity so often lapses into stupidity. Because we can't – or won't – do the *inner* work, we codify a series, or system, of *outer* works that *we* (and this differs from person to person, tradition to tradition, sect to sect, denomination to denomination, movement to movement) decide "represent" actual Christianity.

*"Do this work, this work, this work, this work, this work, and this work, and you're good..."*

Sometimes we even twist it a little into something even more insidious.

*"Don't do this work, or this work, or this work, or that work, or this one, and you're good..."* This annoys everybody, because it's *idiotic* instead of *Christian*.

The *actual* Gospel of God in Christ is much more complex and beautifully simple at the same time than a list of dos and don'ts.

> *"Show hospitality to one another WITHOUT grumbling..."*
>
> —1 PETER 4:9 ESV

Do the right thing *and* be happy about it.

This speaks to *alignment* between an inner work of God's grace and the "outer works" that you do in *response*. There's no room for legalism, hypocrisy, or "duty-bound-ness" in God's Church. You can't just play ball, you need to *be* the ball.

*"Dude..."*

(Shout-out to "Turtle Crush")

If it was a sport, Christianity would be about *being* the ball; doing *your* job.

(Shout-out to Bill Belichick)

> *"As EACH has received a GIFT, use it to serve one another, as good stewards of God's varied grace..."*
>
> —1 PETER 4:10 ESV

Each has received a gift. What is a gift? It's a "grace-effect."

A grace, *effect*.

You need grace *first*, then the *effect* of that grace *follows*, allowing you to do what you've been made to do, using your "grace-effect" to serve others. That's good stuff right there. Use at least *some* of the grace you've been given for the benefit of *others*. If we're honest, we'll know that, most of the time, we use most of the grace we're given for *our* benefit.

*That's not Gospel living.*

Keep in mind that grace is multi-faceted, like a diamond.

> *"...as good stewards of God's VARIED grace..."*
>
> —1 PETER 4:10B ESV

You want to play for keeps?

**#5 Recognize your gift, understand it's "of grace," and do what it requires for the benefit of others, keeping in mind that god's grace is multi-faceted, like a diamond**

#godisadiamond

I don't really need to say much more than that. Just don't forget that God's grace is multi-faceted; you'll never completely figure it out so don't become an idiot. And while you're at it (busy *not* becoming an idiot) if you want to play for keeps:

## #6 Get some urgency and some *power* in your christian walk

> *"...whoever SPEAKS, as one who speaks ORACLES of God; whoever serves, as one who serves by the strength that God supplies—in order that in everything God may be glorified through Jesus Christ. To him belong glory and dominion forever and ever. Amen..."*
>
> —1 PETER 4:11 ESV

If you're going to speak about God and His Kingdom, do it like an Oracle, like a Prophet, forth-telling the glory of God with power, passion, and conviction! God *loved* His Old Testament Prophets, powerful, weird, difficult, awesome people that they were. Most of them died young because they ticked so many people off, but they were *friends* of God.

Whoever serves? Do it like the Strong Right Arm of God Himself!

> *"With the POWER that God supplies..."*
>
> —1 PETER 4:11B GREEK

You need to know that every time the Bible uses the word *power*, it means it. *Dunamis* is the most common word for power used in the New Testament, and from it we get the word (of course) "dynamite." Live a *dynamite* life as you serve Jesus! Get some *power* in your practice, baby. You want to play for keeps?

*Achieve greatness!*

*"Sounds great! How do I do it?"*

Think about it, then do it.

I don't know exactly what tone or texture "achieving greatness" is going to take for you, because we're all uniquely made, but I *do* know that it's going to be *awesome* because the Fingerprints of an Awesome God are all over you! So, if you're going to make someone a chocolate cake, make an awesome chocolate cake to God's glory! You get to mix sound at church this Sunday? Make that mix as awesome as you can; bend your whole life and gift-mix into it. Raising kids? Raise *awesome* kids. Managing a factory? No, you're *awesomely* managing a factory.

When God's people put *greatness* into the things that they are able to do by His grace – even if it's as simple as parenting or baking a cake – God gets His glory.

*Make a decision to be great.*

*"Why, because I'm so great?"*

No, because *God* is.

> *"...that in everything GOD may be glorified through Jesus Christ. To him belong glory and dominion forever and ever. Amen..."*
>
> —1 PETER 4:11C ESV

You want to play for keeps?

Recognize how life *is* and live accordingly, with urgency and self-control, with continuously receptive and outstretched love, letting the inner work of God's grace *drive* the outer works that you do. Recognize your gift, remember it's "of grace," and *do* what it requires, for the benefit of *others*. Keep in mind that #godisadiamond, doing what you do like the prophets of old, or like you're the Strong Right Arm of God Himself! Achieve *greatness*, for God's glory.

## #7 Because eternity hangs in the balance

Which of course means that, after all, *some things do last forever*.

# ELEVEN

# God's Neighbourhood

What makes a place *good*?

Think about a "good" place that you know and love. What is it about that place that makes it someplace *good*? Maybe the weather is always awesome. Even when it rains, the sun comes back out, dries it all up, and you can go back to the beach. Yes, I'm talking about Miami. I love Miami. I should have been born there. Sadly, where I was actually born, we have this thing called "winter" and it's plain awful. Just this morning, in fact, I spent nearly two hours digging our driveway out from a snowstorm. Last winter I did this *twenty eight* times. No, I don't live in Minnesota, but I might as well, given the weather I have to deal with. Maybe it's the weather that makes a place into someplace *good*. I wouldn't know for sure though, because I don't live there.

Maybe it's the natural setting that makes a place into someplace *good*. I kept my sailboat on Georgian Bay a couple of summers back. Georgian Bay is "lake country" where I live, an inlet of Lake Huron (cousin to Lake Michigan), where crystal water works with jagged granite and windswept pines to create the perfect setting, especially in the summer. Some travel magazines refer to the area we kept our boat as "Caribbean North"; that's how awesome it is, and much of that has to do with the *setting*. Anchored in a little cove, with nothing but the sound of wind on the bow and your children splashing in the sparkling water to slowly lull you to sleep in the cockpit of your boat while your wife lays out in the sun...well, you get the picture; *definitely* someplace *good*.

Speaking of my wife, to her, someplace good always involves *people* – the more the merrier – and lots of things to do. As long as she has activities lined up and *people* to do those activities with, she's good. So, for her, you could say it's what you put *in* the setting that really matters. My wife is such a busy bee that she often ends up in conversations with people asking them how they can *stand* taking more than one week's vacation? They end up looking at her like she's some strange workaholic alien as she regales them with tales of how she's typically bored by day three on a vacation and just wants to get back home to her "people" so she can start *doing* stuff.

So, as you can see, my life *rules*. I live in "not-Minnesota-but-might-as-well-be," never taking vacation, with a wife who considers busting your butt for two hours to shovel the driveway a good time; mind you, she's already onto the *next* task so she's *forgotten* how hard shoveling the driveway was.

Pray for me.

Maybe it's the history of a place that really gets you going. Have you been to Paris? I like Paris; it's just *Parisians* I have a hard time with. You can't believe how rude the McDonald's lady was. What we were doing eating at McDonald's while in Paris is another story. I speak passable French but, no matter what I did, the Parisians looked down their noses at my linguistic attempts and very obviously wished me a very speedy return back across the Atlantic to the Colonies. It's like they could *smell* the prairies on me.

I like London, and I could live in Barcelona, but Rome is *amazing*! Italians are uniformly friendly, and the food rocks. Jerusalem (where I grew up) is my hands-down favorite, of course. Growing up there, with 120 feet of climbing rope at our disposal (thanks Dad) and endless unguarded archaeological digs for my brother and I to explore equaled one heck of an awesome childhood. But I think my wife is ultimately correct; what really and truly makes a place into *someplace good*, is its *people*.

*Its suffering people.*

> "Beloved, do not be surprised at the fiery trial when it comes upon you to test you, as though something strange were happening to you. But rejoice insofar as you share Christ's sufferings, that you may also rejoice and be glad when his glory is revealed. If you are insulted for the name of Christ, you are blessed, because the Spirit of glory and of God rests upon you. But let none of you suffer as a murderer or a thief or an evildoer or as a meddler. Yet if anyone suffers as a Christian, let him not be ashamed, but let him glorify God in that name. For it is time for judgment to begin at the household of God; and if it begins with us, what will be the outcome for those who do not obey the gospel of God? And 'If the righteous is scarcely saved, what will become of the ungodly and the sinner?' Therefore let those who suffer according to God's will entrust their souls to a faithful Creator while doing good..."
>
> —1 PETER 4:12-19 ESV

Here's the big idea that's in play this chapter: *suffering* is the secret to becoming "God's Neighborhood" and, of course, God's Neighborhood is the *ultimate* someplace *good*. A little-known fact about God's people is that they (which means, you) are in the business of making the whole world into God's Neighborhood as they learn to suffer, *well*.

Here's how.

> *"Beloved..."*
>
> —1 PETER 4:12A ESV

I know I've mentioned this before, but it's worth pointing out again, and again – each time you come to it – in the Biblical text. *Beloved* should always be broken down and understood as:

*Be. Loved.*

Beloved. Be. Loved. That's how you suffer well; know that you are dearly, and deeply loved by God Himself.

*Be. Loved.*

You are loved by God and by *many* of God's people. I can't write "all" because, let's be real, not everybody loves you. Even now (like me) you're probably thinking of all the people you know who seem to loathe you entirely. It's not fun and nobody would ever ask to be disliked, but it's simply true; some people aren't going to like you, no matter what you say or do. But God loves you (and if God really exists, that's about the best news anybody will ever need to hear) and many of His people do. Every time you run into someone nasty, or get treated really badly for no good reason, take a moment afterward to remind yourself of the love of God, and then maybe call or text someone who you know loves you. They'll remind you that you are not, in fact, scum of the Earth.

If God loves you, *live* like it.

*#liveliketheloved*

What would it look like, this week, for you to live that way?

> *"...do not be SURPRISED at the fiery trial when it comes upon you to test you, as though something strange were happening to you..."*
>
> —1 PETER 4:12 ESV

Ever feel that way? *Surprised* by suffering?

*"Why is this happening to me?"*

I've felt that way, you have too. Everybody goes through this, and that's kind of what Peter is getting at. He's reminding us not to be surprised when *serious* suffering comes our way, even a "fiery trial."

Do you ever have those "house on fire" dreams? I have them a few times a year. I'm racing through the house trying to save my wife and kids and keep forgetting one of them and having to rush back in to get the last one. Invariably, once I'm back in the house, I can't find them but I can hear their screams. I usually wake up at that point, gasping and weeping. Awful stuff. That kind of feeling is what Peter is referring to here when he uses the term "fiery trial." Don't be surprised when your life gets hit with that kind of bleakness.

Suffering is probably the most undersold aspect of the Christian life. You don't hear many sermon series on it and not too many Christian best sellers have catchy titles like: *"Fiery Trial: Seven Keys to the Good Life"* or *"House on Fire: How Suffering and Salvation Are Inextricably Linked"* (actually, I kind of *like* that title; think I'll file that one away). Yeah, not many of those are sitting on the coffee table of your average suburban Christian housewife in Atlanta. Because of this – our reluctance to talk about suffering – many Christians *are* surprised when bad things happen to them and the shock of it is often as bad as, if not worse than, the event itself. It's almost like we're *offended,* as if this sort of bad thing isn't *supposed* to happen to Bible-believing, conservative, football-coaching, picket-fence-painting, minivan-driving, small-group-leading, tithing, date-night-ing parents of four like us!

This is why Peter is warning you not to be surprised when suffering comes your way. He wants to help you avoid the *"Why me?"* reaction. The *"What did I do to deserve this?"* reaction. The *"Am I cursed?"* reaction. The *"Do I have any unconfessed sin?"* reaction, or the *"Maybe I'm not walking inside the perfect will of God..."*

reaction. Especially if you grew up in a family or tradition that was heavy on legalism and guilt, the whole, *"This is all my fault..."* reaction is going to be a very real struggle for you.

> *"...do not be surprised at the (suffering) when it comes upon YOU..."*
>
> —1 PETER 4:12 PARAPHRASED ESV

Suffering is coming, it's inevitable, it'll be hard – because it's a "fiery trial" – and it's going to be personal because it's going to come upon you. You are going to suffer, badly. Maybe it's time to shift your mindset and expectations a little bit.

*Being Jesus' friend does not equal bliss.*

*"But why do we have to suffer?"*

Because it's a *test*.

> *"...do not be surprised at the fiery trial when it comes upon you to TEST you..."*
>
> —1 PETER 4:12A ESV

Suffering is a test.

In light of this, you'd better ask yourself if your love of Jesus, and your trust in Jesus, are *conditional* on having continually good times.

How convicting is that? I need to just sit in that, like a toddler in mud, for a minute. Is *my* love of Jesus, *my* trust in Him, *conditional* on me enjoying good times? If I'm completely, dangerously, honest I would have to say yes, yes it does. Every time I sing a worship song about the love of God never failing me yet, I always find myself thinking about the time that I felt like the love of God did fail me (and my family) when my beloved brother-in-law (husband to my little sister) died in a freak building accident overseas. He was working on a "Prayer Tower" as a Missionary Bible College Professor, Farming Instructor, and part-time Construction Manager – for God's glory and the good of the people of Africa – with my sister and their three little kids (aged 6, 4, and 2 at the time). A poorly-maintained grinder exploded in his hand while he was cutting a steel beam for the roof of a prayer room (the irony is sickening) on the Bible College campus grounds, and a flying piece from the blade hit him in the chest like a piece of shrapnel; he bled out in a minute-and-a-half.

Phone service was spotty that day so the first we heard of it was by email, just after breakfast at home with my wife and the kids. I opened up my Gmail and there it was, from my sister Kate.

*"Guys, I'm SO sorry to have to do this, this way, but the phones are out. Robbie died today."*

Even now my heart is racing just writing those words and it was 2011 when it happened. Rob Hall, one of the absolute best, most Jesus-loving, kind, full-of-life, great husbands, and awesome father dudes *ever*! Truly a friend of God all his life, Robbie was cut down in the *prime* of his life for no good reason, leaving my sister a widow and my niece and nephews fatherless.

When Robbie died, I remember thinking, *"Man, if God can let that happen, then all bets are off..."* I realized in that moment – personally – that anything can, and will, happen to anyone, at any time.

*The love of God failed, for me, in 2011.*

But only for a time, and only from my perspective. Yes, I went into three years of depression after Robbie's death (which was really tough to deal with while pastoring a church) and, yes, I nearly lost my faith in the process (only the kindness of God – as I look back in hindsight – got me through) but, ultimately, even though it felt like it at the time, looking back I can testify with Martin Smith (the iconic British Worship Leader) that Jesus' *"love never fails me..."*

I look back and see (to borrow an image from a famous poem) only one set of footprints in the sand as my Good Jesus carried me and my sister, and her kids, and our broken family and shattered circle of friends who loved Robbie as their own, through our heartbreak and temporary loss of faith into something new and more powerful after we'd survived the fiery trial.

So, I'm glad to say, I can sing in worship again. Took me two years though. Imagine that, me, a formerly worship-loving preacher/pastor, standing there (we'd closed our church plant down by this point) in another man's church, hands at my side in worship like a statue unable to sing. It was dark. I used to look at so many of the men in church who stood there like statues and wonder what was wrong with them; now I know, because I've been shattered too.

One Sunday, seemingly no different from any other, the Presence of God settled on me in a way I could feel, as I stood there like a statue, and I just started crying. And it wasn't that I hadn't cried since Robbie's death; I'd cried a lot. But I had been mad at God in worship, standing there like a stone, with a stone for a heart. But the kindness of God reached out to me, all on its own, and I realized in that moment that, even though Robbie was still gone, *God was still good.*

One time, Robbie visited me in a dream. He was mad at me.

*"Here I am enjoying the Presence of God Himself, and you're still moping about it? Get over it, dude, and get back to preaching!"* And then he anointed my feet with a mixture of hummus and myrrh (no joke) and told me, one last time, to get back to work. A very weird dream, but I listened to it (and in case you think *I'm* weird, go back and look at all the times in the Bible when God communicated with His people through dreams, either directly, or through a messenger).

*Suffering is a test.*

Many of us trust Jesus to the point of suffering, but not beyond. Always hovering in the back of our minds is that insidious question; "But what if something *bad* happens?"

> *"Now there was a day when the sons of God came to present themselves before the Lord, and Satan also came among them. The Lord said to Satan, 'From where have you come?' Satan answered the Lord and said, 'From going to and fro on the earth, and from walking up and down on it.' And the Lord said to Satan, 'Have you considered my servant Job, that there is none like him on the earth, a blameless and upright man, who fears God and turns away from evil?' Then Satan answered the Lord and said, 'Does Job fear God for no reason? Have you not put a hedge around him and his house and all that he has, on every side? You have blessed the work of his hands, and his possessions have increased in the land. But stretch out your hand and touch all that he has, and he will curse you to your face.' And the Lord said to Satan, 'Behold, all that he has is in your hand. Only against him do not stretch out your hand.' So Satan went out from the presence of the Lord..."*
>
> —JOB 1:6-12 ESV

To find out what happened to Job, turn to the middle of your Bible and find out for yourself. I will say this; Satan opened up a can of whup-Balaam's-you-know-what on Job and some *very* bad things happened to him, as a *test*.

Suffering is a test.

*So, prepare for it.*

Now that you know that suffering is a test and, like midterms, it's on its way and there's nothing you can do to stop it from coming, *prepare* for it!

*"But how?"*

By remembering, and counting on, Jesus.

> *"But REJOICE insofar as you share Christ's sufferings, that you may also rejoice and be glad when his glory is revealed..."*
>
> —1 PETER 4:13 ESV

How should a Christian respond to suffering?

*With rejoicing.*

Counterintuitive, right?

*"Why would I rejoice in suffering?"*

Because we share in Christ's suffering; that's why. When you suffer, if you hold in your heart the fact that all suffering is *partnering* in Jesus' suffering, all of a sudden, you'll find *meaning* and purpose in your suffering; if the Bible is true, you'll also find joy.

> *"Indeed, I count everything as loss because of the surpassing worth of knowing Christ Jesus my Lord. For his sake I have suffered the loss of all things and count them as rubbish, in order that I may gain Christ and be found in him, not having a righteousness of my own that comes from the law, but that which comes through faith in Christ, the righteousness from God that depends on faith—* **that I may know him** *and the power of his resurrection, and may share his sufferings, becoming like him in his death, that by any means possible I may attain the resurrection from the dead..."*
>
> —PHIL 3:8-11 ESV

That's one of the great, testifying, *shouts* of the New Testament, right there.

*"That I may KNOW Him..."*

—PHIL 3:10A ESV

If the *price* of friendship with God is suffering, are you willing to pay the price?

If your answer is "Yes," then every time something bad happens to you, learn to immediately find the way that that something bad is helping you to *know* God more. This can be as innocuous as dealing with a series of red lights or as serious as out-and-out disaster that strikes you and your family when you least expect it. Begin learning how each moment of suffering is bringing you *closer* to Jesus, and know that the price is worth it.

*"But rejoice insofar AS you share Christ's sufferings, that you may also rejoice and be glad when his glory IS revealed..."*

—1 PETER 4:13 ESV

There are twin inevitabilities at play here. You *will* suffer, and God's glory *will* be revealed.

*Suffering is inevitable, but so is Glory.*

In the same way that there is no escape for us from suffering, there will be no escape (for anyone) from Jesus' victory! This is so good that I have to visit 2 Timothy for a minute.

*"Remember Jesus Christ, risen from the dead, the offspring of David, as preached in my gospel, for which I am suffering, bound with chains as a criminal. But the word of God is not bound! Therefore I endure everything for the sake of the elect, that they also may obtain the salvation that is in Christ Jesus with eternal glory. The saying is trustworthy, for: If we have died with him, we will also live with him; if we endure, we will also reign with him; if we deny him, he also will deny*

237

*us; if we are faithless, he remains faithful—for he cannot deny himself..."*

*—2 TIM 2:8-13 ESV*

Stake your claim on *Jesus*, friend.

Suffering well comes down, entirely, to whether you *believe* the story about Jesus or not. Do you believe He is God? Do you believe He entered into actual space-time history as a man to suffer and die in your place for your sins –and you know you're a sinner; I know it too – and to rise again from death the third day for your salvation, defeating the power of Satan, sin, death, and hell forever? Do you believe He ascended to His Father's right hand after resurrecting to sit down in victory and begin interceding for you? Do you believe He'll come again in glory from that place to judge the living and the dead and to inaugurate His Kingdom, which will have no end, a Kingdom in which *you* have a place?

*Do you believe it, or not?*

The *extent* to which you believe it, is the extent to which you will find yourself *able* to deal with suffering.

*"If you are INSULTED for the name of Christ, you are blessed, because the Spirit of glory and of God rests upon you. But let none of you suffer as a murderer or a thief or an evildoer or as a meddler. Yet if anyone suffers as a Christian, let him not be ashamed, but let him glorify God in that name..."*

*—1 PETER 4:14-16 ESV*

If you are *reviled* for the Name of Christ, you are blessed because the Spirit of glory, and of God, rests *on* you. Now you know *why* people revile you.

*They can't stand you because you are God's Neighborhood.*

238

*"...the Spirit of glory and of God RESTS UPON you..."*

—1 PETER 4:14B ESV

Who was 1 Peter written by? Peter. Of what ethnicity was Peter? Jewish. What was the original language of the Jews? Aramaic, which eventually grew and modernized into Hebrew. What does *"rest on"* mean in Hebrew?

*"Lee-sh-kan"* from which we get the word *"Mee-sh-kan"* which means "Dwelling Place."

*"Behold, the DWELLING PLACE of God is with man..."*

—REV 21:3B ESV

"Hee-neh *Mee-sh-kan* Eloheem eem Anasheem..."

And, wouldn't you know it, from the root word *"Mee-sh-kan"* we get the modern Hebrew word *"Schoo-nah"* which means (you guessed it) *Neighborhood.*

People hate you because you are, literally, where God lives; you're His Neighborhood! You make them uncomfortable because the rip-roaring Presence of God Most High lives *in* you. He dwells *with* you; you're His Neighborhood. And you should be a good neighbor, which means a lot more than keeping your lawn mowed, your children under control, and your dog poop restricted to your property (although each of those things may help to bring God glory in the eyes of your neighbors once they find out you're a "Jesus-Person"):

*"But let none of you suffer as a murderer or a thief or an evildoer or as a meddler. Yet if anyone suffers as a Christian, let him not be ashamed, but let him glorify God in that name..."*

—1 PETER 4:15-16 ESV

Don't *trample* the pansies (shout-out to "Father of the Bride II") or kill people; Christian Ethics 101.

Let's be straight about this: a lot of people rightfully hate Christians because many of the Christians they've encountered are, or at least act, hateful. We picket when we should be giving hugs, we write angry letters when we should be writing checks, we stand on principle when we should be standing with the broken, and we focus on looking good when we should be *doing* good.

Christianity's bad reputation is often *my* fault, and it might be *yours* too.

> *"For it is time for judgment to begin at the HOUSEHOLD of God; and if it begins with us, what will be the outcome for those who do not obey the gospel of God? And 'If the righteous is scarcely saved, what will become of the ungodly and the sinner?'"*
>
> —1 PETER 4:17-18 ESV

There's that *neighborhood* idea again: judgment starting at the *household* of God. Here's the point; if you're close to Jesus, you're going to get *whupped*.

*"Why?"*

*Because Jesus did.*

God is Holy; He is Judge. Jesus is our only hope and He is *also* our example, and Jesus laid down His life so that *others* might live. He laid down His life so that *we* might live, so *we* are going to do the same, trusting Jesus to see us through.

> *"THEREFORE, let those who suffer according to God's will entrust their souls to a faithful Creator while doing good..."*
>
> —1 PETER 4:19 ESV

"Therefore" is your bottom line.

> *"Therefore, let those who suffer according to God's WILL..."*
>
> —1 PETER 4:19A ESV

Next time you suffer, remember that none of it is a surprise to God, none of it is happening outside the context of His will, or beyond the reach of the Mercy that He has shown towards you in Christ!

So, trust Him.

*Trust Him.*

Setting your souls aside for Jesus, which is what "entrust" means. Take your soul, and set it aside for Jesus. Devil can't have it; that's for Jesus. Your worries can't have it, your stress can't have it, your troubles can't have it *because you've already set it aside for Jesus*, your Faithful Creator.

You haven't forgotten that Jesus made you, right? Jesus, God-the-Son-made-flesh, who – in His preincarnation – was known as the "Logos" (or "Word") of God, is the *spoken* Word of God that brought everything that is into existence. Without Him nothing was made that was made (John 1:3).

> *"In Him was LIFE, and that life was the light of all People..."*
>
> —JOHN 1:4

Jesus, the One who gave you life, is your Faithful Creator, so you can stop worrying and just focus on doing *good*. So, get out there this week, and turn *your* neighborhood into someplace *good*.

# TWELVE

# Finding Freedom

What does freedom look like?

Maybe it looks like a beach. If I close my eyes and imagine what it would be like to be free, I usually end up seeing myself somewhere sandy, with trees swaying in an onshore breeze blowing in over the surface of crystalline waters where a sailboat sways at anchor waiting for me. That's freedom to me.

For many years, and I say this as someone who grew up overseas, the flag of the United States of America represented freedom. The bald eagle, another symbol associated with the U.S., also conjures images of freedom, soaring high above the Rockies or over and above the troubles of everyday life. That said, I never did get super excited by the idea of staring off into the middle distance, perched on a pine branch. *"Free as a bird,"* they say; not sure that's for me.

How about the freedom of the "open road"? Do you love hopping in your car and taking a long drive outside the city limits? I do. I've been driving for almost three decades now and a twisty stretch of road with the windows down still does it to me every time. The whole "freedom of the open road" thing is closely connected to the idea of being free to go where you want, when you want. Have you ever done that? Sit down with a map (I realize we're almost exclusively digital with our maps now) and randomly picked out a route you've never taken to somewhere you've never been. Those are the best kind of vacations (at least, if you ask me), the ones where you don't over-plan every minute but kind of take it as it comes. You let the adventure "find" you. That's freedom.

My dad loved living that way. We'd go on these epic family trips, driving across the country, and my parents wouldn't prebook a *single* hotel. If the thought of that kind of "fly by the seat of your pants-ness" gives you hives, you might want to do some soul-searching to see just how tightly wound you've allowed yourself to become over the slow creep of years.

Granted, once in a while, my Dad's way of doing vacation led to us staying in some pretty sketchy places, or showing up somewhere to find there was no room in the inn, and we'd have to keep driving to the next town, or the next, until we found a spot. But once we ended up in a loft usually reserved for VIPs, or the family of the owners, in a boutique hotel, literally a stone's throw from the Berlin Wall, in 1989's West Berlin. (We settled in, ordered takeout, and watched a movie overlooking the East German patrols across the river.) Or we'd find ourselves snuggling into the eighty-year-old feather mattresses of the servants' quarters, literally in the eaves of the East Glacier Park Lodge in the Rockies (a hotel that no longer exists, sadly) while the snow fell gently outside and I marveled, even at eleven years of age, at how my Dad always managed to find such awesome places to stay.

*He found them because he had faith.*

Choose your own adventure; it's freedom, baby.

Freedom.

> *"So I exhort the elders among you, as a fellow elder and a witness of the sufferings of Christ, as well as a partaker in the glory that is going to be revealed: shepherd the flock of God*

> *that is among you, exercising oversight, not under compulsion, but willingly, as God would have you; not for shameful gain, but eagerly; not domineering over those in your charge, but being examples to the flock. And when the chief Shepherd appears, you will receive the unfading crown of glory. Likewise, you who are younger, be subject to the elders.*
>
> *Clothe yourselves, all of you, with humility toward one another, for 'God opposes the proud but gives grace to the humble.' Humble yourselves, therefore, under the mighty hand of God so that at the proper time he may exalt you, casting all your anxieties on him, because he cares for you. Be sober-minded; be watchful. Your adversary the devil prowls around like a roaring lion, seeking someone to devour. Resist him, firm in your faith, knowing that the same kinds of suffering are being experienced by your brotherhood throughout the world..."*
>
> —1 PETER 5:1-9 ESV

Some very famous lines in that piece of text right there.

"Cast all your cares on Him, for He cares for you..." Or that one where the devil is famously portrayed as a roaring lion. But the first section (all about "Elders") is usually pretty boring for most people because it's written to "Elders," the leaders of God's Church. If you're not a leader of God's Church, you might be tempted to race through this section, unless we considered it with the question of freedom in our minds, asking what freedom *looks* like.

Freedom looks decisive, it looks urgent, and it looks "old."

> *"SO, I exhort the ELDERS..."*
>
> —1 PETER 5:1A ESV

In the original language here, the word "Elders" is "Seniors." I love that the word "so" is used here. "So" is a *transitional* word with some power to it. The last chapter's crescendo was a command to entrust our souls to Jesus: to give them over to Him, to commit the *core* of our lives to Jesus. Then, in Peter's thinking at least (and in ours, if we're following along correctly), we take a breath and move on to the next big moment; all facilitated by that one little word.

"So..."

There's always a "next moment" with God. What's *your* next step? I sometimes feel like walking with Jesus is kind of like a video game, with ascending levels of difficulty. Just when you think you've "got it," you don't got it. Just when you think *"I'm good,"* something happens to make you realize you're not. You have a great *moment* where you think you finally understand the way life works, then events transpire even just slightly differently than you imagined and it hits you: *"I don't understand anything!"*

When this moment hits you can do one of two things. You can "rage quit." Do you ever do that? Throw your controller (figuratively) across the room and storm out? Granted, I'm not much of a video-game person, but my sons are (yes, I often wonder where I failed as their father), and I see this happen from time to time with them. Video games weren't really my thing as a boy; I was too busy outside climbing trees, setting booby traps for people, picking fights, and doing generally illegal things. Come to think of it, my childhood *was* a video game. But I've seen my sons "rage quit." "Stupid game! I can't do it!" and "WHAM!" there goes the controller.

(I've been telling them for *years,* it's a stupid game...)

Life with Jesus can be similar; you're going to be tempted to rage-quit it a couple of times, at least, over the years. You've experienced this, I'm sure. Things are tracking along nicely, you're happy, no huge stresses or miseries are immediately making you hate your life; maybe you're sitting down to a nice family breakfast, and then it happens. Disruption, trouble, turmoil with your name written on it shows up and, just like that, exasperation, frustration, fear, stress, and the urge to quit show up also. In a moment like that, what's your next step? If you want to be free, avoid stasis, and take the next step with some *urgency*.

> *"So I EXHORT the elders among you..."*
>
> —1 PETER 5:1A ESV

To exhort means "to incite by argument or advice: to urge strongly" (Merriam-Webster). You want to be free? Learn to live with a sense of *urgency*. Take one thing you have to do this week, one task, and do it with *everything* you've got: with some urgency. Performers are coached to do this physically. They are taught to translate their inner sense of passion, or urgency, into actual physical energy by "sending" their energy (actual physical force, or tension) *into* their body as they perform. I do this when I preach; so much so, that I'm usually sore for a day-and-a-half after a typical Sunday, almost like I just played a football game, from preaching so hard.

Urgency: put a little of it in everything you do, and you'll find yourself living free. Also, embrace your "oldness."

> *"So I exhort the SENIORS among you..."*
>
> —1 PETER 5:1A FROM THE GREEK

Oldness is a good thing in God's economy.

> *"The glory of the young is in their strength, the grey hair of experience is the splendor of the OLD..."*
>
> —PROV 20:29 ESV

I can relate, sadly. My wife tells me my hair is essentially all grey now. I like to think of it as platinum blond.

> *"Grey hair is a crown of glory. It is obtained by following a righteous path..."*
>
> —PROV 16:31 ESV

You know the whole thing in culture about stress turning your hair grey? Turns out, if Proverbs 16:31 is true, that doing the *right* thing (righteousness) is difficult and, sometimes, grey-hair-inducing; but it'll be worth it in the end because:

> *"The righteous flourish like the palm tree and grow like a cedar in Lebanon. They are planted in the house of the Lord; they flourish in the courts of our God.*
>
> *They STILL bear fruit in old age; they are ever full of sap and green, to declare that the Lord is upright; he is my rock, and there is no unrighteousness in him..."*
>
> —PS 92:12-15 ESV

You want to be free? Live like there are no diminishing returns with God. You need to begin living like you *expect* things to get better and better and better until you die and go see Jesus – who's the *best*, so you win! But living that way is radically countercultural.

What happens in our world as people age? Many fall into despair, decrepitude, and, eventually, just give up. Do you have a bitter old man in your neighborhood? You know the one I'm talking about, right? Always yelling at kids to keep away from his lawn, to quiet down, to skateboard somewhere else. He's quick to point out parking or noise infractions. He drives twenty in a forty zone and shakes his fist (or worse) at you when you pass him. That guy (or gal) is so common in our world that he's become a cliché, a caricature.

The old man who loves Jesus, though? He's not like that Grumpy Old Man at all. Our guy (the one who loves Jesus) is busy inviting the kids to come play on his lawn because he just mowed it

yesterday and it's going to feel real nice on their little feet. He probably has a spare football lying around in case you need it. He'll help
you park in front of his house, suddenly materializing behind you
waving his arms like he's parking a passenger jet, and you'll make
his week if you invite him to your Summer Block Party, because his
wife was the social one and she went to see Jesus last year, so
he doesn't get around as much as he used to and misses it. He's
always got a candy (or two) in his pocket and a good word in his
soul because he's a friend of God and, though he certainly is a little
more tired than he used to be (you often catch him napping in a
sunbeam on his porch on Spring afternoons) and doesn't move as
fast as he once did, in no way is he tired of life, because his Jesus
is good. You want to be free? Grow up to be like that guy. Reject
the law of diminishing returns and start living *now*, like it's *then*.

> *"...as a PARTAKER in the glory that is going to BE revealed..."*
>
> —1 PETER 5:1B ESV

Peter sees himself as a participant, meaning he's participating *now*,
in a glory that is *going* to be revealed. Strange? No, very cool.
Peter is building his identity in the "now" on something that is "not
yet." That kind of approach to life is powerfully instructive for us.
You are God's friend; you are His child. These are realities. You are
God's heir; you are a co-creator with Him (as you fill the earth and
subdue it) of a whole new way of being human, because of Jesus.
God makes it happen; you walk it out. You are working, with Him,
towards the renewal of all things. Simply put, you're a *time-bender*.

> *"And you were dead in the trespasses and sins in which you
> once walked, following the course of this world, following the
> prince of the power of the air, the spirit that is now at work in
> the sons of disobedience— among whom we all once lived
> in the passions of our flesh, carrying out the desires of the
> body and the mind, and were by nature children of wrath, like*

> *the rest of mankind. But God, being rich in mercy, because of the great love with which he loved us, even when we were dead in our trespasses, made us alive together with Christ—by grace you have been saved— and raised us up with him and seated us with him in the heavenly places in Christ Jesus, so that in the coming ages he might show the immeasurable riches of his grace in kindness toward us in Christ Jesus. For by grace you have been saved through faith. And this is not your own doing; it is the gift of God, not a result of works, so that no one may boast. For we are His workmanship, created in Christ Jesus for good works, which God prepared beforehand, that we should walk in them..."*
>
> —EPH 2:1-10 ESV

Ephesians 2 still makes my head spin. "You did this, but He did that, and He's gonna do this, so you'll do that, and you're doing this, even though you used to do that, so He did this, which means *that*, which means *this*!" Past, present, future: God's got it all under control. You *used* to be lost, *now* you're seated in Heaven, in Christ, *while* being here (on Earth in space-time) to do good works that God prepared *beforehand* for you to do. If you want to be free, live like Marty McFly. (Shout-out to "Back to the Future," greatest movie of all time. If you haven't seen it, go watch it as soon as you finish this chapter.)

*Christians are time travelers.*

The Bible says it; I believe it. It says you're seated in Heaven, in Christ, right now while being here, in the middle of actual space-time, to do good things for God's glory, your joy, and through your transformed life, the good of the world. You're in two places at once.

*Case closed: you're Marty McFly.*

Since we're talking about Marty McFly, what's the biggest thing that changed for him in "Back to the Future"?

*His perspective.*

Being a time-traveler changes your perspective; when you have a different perspective, you *behave* differently. For Marty, the big payoff doesn't come 'til the very last scene in the third movie in the franchise where he turns Needles down. It's a great scene; you're going to love it when you see it because it's so true to life, and the tension between perspective and action that lives within each of us. As Jesus- People, our different perspective causes us to *live* different.

> *"...shepherd the flock of God that is among you, exercising oversight, not under compulsion, but WILLINGLY, as God would have you; not for shameful gain, but eagerly; not domineering over those in your charge, but being examples to the flock. And when the chief Shepherd appears, you will receive the unfading crown of glory..."*
>
> —1 PETER 5:2-4 ESV

Peter is speaking to the leaders of God's Church here, so it's not immediately applicable to everybody, but if you stretch it just a little, this can speak to anyone who has a position of power or authority. Now, you may not have all the power you want or all the authority you could use, or even as much as you will *one* day have, but you probably have *some*. So, what Peter's saying can be instructive to you, even if you're not an "Elder" in God's Church; it can help you develop a way of being that brings God much glory, brings you much joy and, through your transformed life, does much good to the world around you, one beautifully lived moment at a time. What Peter is saying to leaders here is deeply challenging because it cuts to the heart of us.

Supervise without compulsion; do it *willingly*.

How many people do you know who have a job to do and consistently do it *willingly*, not from compulsion? It's more rare than it should be. Will you go to work this week because you *want* to, not because you *have* to? How much would your life have to change if you decided to start living in such a way that, instead of trading away the hours of your life for money, you lived deeply connected to doing what God made you to do while trusting Him (in faith) to provide for you, because you believed that provision follows calling?

What would it look like for you to reject "avarice"? (That's what Peter means by "shameful gain.") Do you think you could stop doing things always with an eye primarily fixed on what *you* were going to get out of it? What if you didn't manipulate and organize things such that your profit was always maximized anymore? Would your life change? Would the world?

If you want to keep becoming the kind of "free agent" who changes the world, embrace eagerness, don't domineer, and be a good example. Granted, these suggestions are different from what most renowned leadership examples I can think of would suggest – where stock value is the highest good, where net worth is worth sacrificing your life for, where everything is wired to maximize your profit, your gain, your power, position, and prestige. But if you want to be free, you're going to need to learn to play the *opposite* game.

*"What about me?"*

What about *them*?

*"But I want..."*

(Let's be free.)

What do *they* want?

*"Not my will but Yours be done, O Lord."*

You want to be free? No more living a "Me first" kind of life.

*"But I'll lose if I live that way!"*

Not if you belong to Jesus.

> *"And when the chief Shepherd appears, you will receive the unfading CROWN of glory..."*
>
> —1 PETER 5:4 ESV

*The victory laurels.*

You are becoming Michael Phelps, in Jesus. Unfading victory is your destiny! You want to be free? Live like a *champion* today because that's what you're going to be forever. I mean, since we've already agreed that you're Marty McFly, how 'bout you *time-travel* your champion-ness back from the future to the present, put on that medal, then go out there and take ground for God's glory and your joy like the champion you are! If there is any residual "victim mentality" hanging around in your life, cast it aside, put on the crown and get going – because you're a champion!

And this isn't just for seniors; you don't have to be old to qualify for this goodness.

> *"Likewise, you who are YOUNGER, be subject to the elders. Clothe yourselves, all of you, with humility toward one another, for 'God opposes the proud but gives grace to the humble.' Humble yourselves, therefore, under the mighty hand of God so that at the proper time he may exalt you, casting all your anxieties on him, because he cares for you. Be sober-minded; be watchful. Your adversary the devil prowls around like a roaring lion, seeking someone to devour. Resist him, firm in your faith, knowing that the same kinds of suffering are being experienced by your brotherhood throughout the world..."*
>
> —1 PETER 5:5-9 ESV

Let's hit this.

Headstrong Young Bucks, headstrong Young Does, *submit* to your Elders.

We just *love* how difficult the Bible can be, don't we?

What's the one thing a Young Buck doesn't want to do? Submit. The younger you are the less you want to submit to *anyone*, let alone to some Old Guy with the beginnings of a pot belly and grey hair. Here's the real rub of it all (and I write this as someone who is guilty as charged): the more headstrong you are, the more you *need* humility (if any of my youth pastors or early ministry mentors are reading this, they're laughing out loud right now). The simple truth is, we all need humility so much, we should wear it like *clothes*.

> *"CLOTHE yourselves, all of you, with humility toward one another..."*
>
> —1 PETER 5:5B ESV

This is awesome in the original:

*"Wear ye the servile apron..."*

Try that one on for size, literally; the apron that only *servants* wear. It's a badge of *dis-honor* and Jesus, through His Apostle, is telling you to put it on. Let me bring it into our century for you right quick.

*Real men wear aprons.*

Humility: we need to wear it like clothes.

You want to be free? Know your place. That's what true humility is. Knowing your place.

*"So, what does that look like practically?"*

It looks like somebody who clearly says, *"This is what God made me to do, and not that..."* Everybody has a "thing" (sometimes a thing or two) that they've been specially built to do. Do you know what yours is? What did God *make* you to do? Knowing who God made you to be (and not to be) and what He made you to do (and not to do) is the most important step on the road to humility.

*"I'm made for this, not that."*

Once you can say and believe that with conviction, you'll be free.

It's hugely important for you to know what God made you to be so that you can take the crucial step towards realizing and accepting that you are not the Body of Christ. You're just one part, not the whole thing.

*"I'm just the mouth..."*

*"I'm just the hands..."*

*"I'm just the eyes..."*

*"I'm just the butt..."*

Wait a minute, the butt?

*Yes, the butt.*

The butt is a wonderful thing; it's where all the strength comes from to do heavy lifting. You need something hard done in your life or organization? Make sure you've got some "butts" around because their strength gets things done. If you're going to lift people up, you're going to need some butts.

*You only run into problems with butts when they start acting like heads.*

Know who you are. Know where you fit. Know what you're supposed to do. Stop striving to be everything else. Stop being jealous of the other parts and what they've been built to do. Be *only* who God made you to be.

*Be humble.*

> *"...for 'God OPPOSES the proud but GIVES grace to the humble'..."*
>
> —1 PETER 5:5C ESV

Would you like to be God's enemy, or His beneficiary?

*"Umm, His beneficiary, obviously. But how?"*

> *"Humble yourselves, therefore, under the mighty HAND of God so that at the proper time he may exalt you..."*
>
> —1 PETER 5:6 ESV

Finally, here, the whole "freedom" idea really comes home to roost. In the original language, what you've just read above is pure fireworks. Because, "Humble yourselves under the *mighty* hand of God..." means under His mighty *holding-hand* in the original language. The same mighty hand and outstretched arm with which He set His people *free* from slavery in Egypt. The same outstretched arms that were *pierced* to nail Jesus to a cross so that He could suffer and die in your place for your sins, to set you free from the power of Satan, sin, death, and hell once and for all! The same mighty hand of the Holy Ghost that *nudged* the Logos awake that very first Easter Sunday morning so that He might walk *free* from His tomb! The same mighty hand that will one day wield the last trumpet and sound it with the voice of an Archangel! The same mighty hand that will pick up the rod of iron to *rule* the nations, setting His people free from tyranny forever! The same hand that lifted you up out of Psalm 40's "miry clay" and "pit of destruction"!

You want to be free? Humble yourself under *that* mighty hand – God's mighty *holding-hand* that sets His people free!

*Start defining your place in the world by what Jesus has done for you.*

Are you lost and without hope, or did God the Son put on flesh? Are you left to your own devices or, in the fullness of time, did Jesus the God-Man (fully God and fully man) ascend the cross and allow Himself to be pinned there like a butterfly, so that God the Father could lay on Him the iniquities of us all? Are you a helpless and constant prisoner to your sin or, as Jesus hung on that cross, was your sin (and mine) and, in fact, the sin of the *world* laid on Him? Do you need to continue living with guilt like you're under God's wrath, or did God the Father pour out His wrath on God the Son at the cross? Are you lost and without hope, is this life all there is, and when you die, you're done – or, did Jesus Christ rise again the third day, defeating, in His body, the power of Satan, sin, death, and hell forever? Is this world all there is, or did He ascend, right in front of His disciples' eyes, to the Father's right hand where He sat down, in victory, a place where He sits even now, interceding for you; a place from whence He'll come again in Glory to judge the living and the dead and to inaugurate His Kingdom which will have no end, a Kingdom in which *you* have a place?

*Is the story about Jesus true, or isn't it?*

If this story is true, then nothing will ever be the same for you again. And, it's once you've *received* this new life we're talking about (and only then) that the next bit becomes *possible* for you.

> "CAST all your anxieties on him, because he cares for you. Be SOBER-MINDED; be watchful. Your adversary the devil prowls around like a roaring lion, seeking someone to devour. Resist him, firm in your faith, knowing that the same kinds of suffering are being experienced by your brotherhood throughout the world..."
>
> —1 PETER 5:7-9 ESV

*Toss* every worry on Jesus, because He cares for you. Toss, like you'd toss out a bag of garbage. Toss every worry on Jesus

257

because *He* cares for you! Toss your anxiety on Jesus. Are you looking for more sobriety? It's found in Jesus. Need to get your mind right? Jesus can help you with that.

It occurs to me (and I don't think I'm stretching the point past credibility here) that it might not be a coincidence that we have fewer Christians in North America today than at any other time in our history, while at the same time more North Americans than ever are trapped in anxiety, addiction, and despair. The connection seems pretty clear to me; it's just that no one's saying it. I also know *why* the connection is real.

*Because evil is real.*

I know it's not popular to say it, but it's true. The devil is out there in culture like a roaring lion seeking any old target he can find whom he may be *"down-drinking"* (that's what *devour* means here). The devil is getting drunk off the despair of the world, but you don't have to let him drink you like a shot anymore, because of Jesus. Instead of letting Eden's snake get high off your misery, *resist* him.

> *"...firm in your faith, knowing that the same kinds of suffering are being experienced by your BROTHERHOOD throughout the world..."*
>
> —1 PETER 5:9 ESV

You think your life is hard? Remember, lots of people out there in the wider world are suffering as badly, or worse, than you. You are not alone. This doesn't mean that what you're going through isn't hard; it certainly is and always feels that way from your perspective, but keep your mind right. You're not cursed, you're not in the worst situation there ever was. To borrow a line from a very famous redhead from the 1920s: *"The sun will come out tomorrow..."*

*You're not alone.*

You don't have to allow yourself to be some random target for misery anymore. You can take the next step; you can live with some urgency and like the best is yet to come. In fact, my friend, you can live like it's "then," now. If you want, you can live like you're Marty McFly, and even play the "opposite game" once in a while. You could live like a champion today because that's who you are going to be forever; I mean, you might as well get a head start.

*You're Michael Phelps, baby!*

You can wear humility like a uniform, knowing your place before God and His people; heck, you could even *celebrate* it, even if it ends up that you *are* the butt! Because butts are strong, like God's mighty hand and His outstretched arm that saved you and saved me – which is why I don't have to worry anymore, and neither do you. I mean, you and I both could just *toss* that care on Jesus: *the God who sets His people free.*

# THIRTEEN

# The Greatest Do-It-Yourself-Er of All Time

Some things you can do yourself; others, you're going to need a little *help* with.

Take my swimming pool, for example; it's mostly clean, most of the time. I figure, if you're going to have a feature at your house that invites people to disrobe and, basically, *bathe* together, you sort of owe it to them to keep the water they're dunking themselves in as clean as possible.

Like, Greek Islands clean.

My crazy parents took my brother, sister, and I on a two-month odyssey through Europe when I was fourteen, and I will never forget the waters of the Greek Islands (or the girls of the Greek Islands either, for that matter; but that's for a different book). I remember kayaking off the beaches of Mykonos and being just so completely blown away that I could see fish swimming forty feet beneath me, clear as day.

So, with my swimming pool, Mykonos is my literal high-water mark in terms of the clearness level I'm shooting for. If you have a pool, or have visited one frequently enough, you know there's a fine line between a pool being chlorinated *enough* to make it sparkle like the Islands, and too chlorinated, like a public pool, where no one would choose to swim for pleasure if they had an option. So, I'm always trying to find the "sweet spot" where my pool is pristine enough to make you want to take your clothes off and jump in, but still feels like there are no chemicals in it.

Like the Greek Islands.

Here's the point; I can handle my pool, myself.

My back hair, though? I'm going to need some help with that. Can't reach it, plain and simple. I'm going to need a little help with my back hair before summer comes around and the pool starts calling.

Keeping it in the backyard for a moment and still on the do-it-yourself theme, I can build a simple stone patio myself. I've done it four times now. Twice with large patio stones framed by 6×6 cedar posts, once a large interlocking stone one, and, just this past summer, my wife and I spent an entire week building a flagstone patio for my mother-in-law. (And we ended up profaning the Sabbath to get it done the Saturday before a large baptism party at our house.) Yes, my mother-in-law lives with us. That's *also* another book.

Every day after working hours, we'd toil in the sweltering summer heat until well past dark in a race against time to get it done by Sunday. Saturday morning came around, we were almost done, and had no choice but to get out there, in the pouring rain by this point, and push through. It was horrible. Why didn't we hire someone to do it? Well, because they quoted us fifteen thousand dollars, that's why, and (stupid me) I thought to myself, *"Surely we can figure this out ourselves for much less than that..."*

The second that kind of "do-it-yourself-er" thought pops into your head, slap yourself.

Nice thing though, the patio turned out pretty good, and – you know this from experience – life's not always like that. Sometimes you bust your butt, put in long hours, toil in the rain racing against the clock, give it everything you've got, and it *still* turns out less awesome than you'd hoped. That's the curse of Adam catching up to you right there. Nothing we'll ever do will ever go *perfectly* to plan. So, when it *does*? That's something to celebrate.

A simple backyard patio? We can handle that.

But don't ask me to install your dishwasher. I did that exactly *once,* back when we were so broke I that I literally had no choice but to do it myself. Do you remember that phase? Maybe you're still in it. If that's the case (you're broke), don't give up. Just keep going, doing what you've been made to do and, in fifteen years or so, you'll look back and realize you're not as broke as you used to be. You can afford all the Kraft Dinner you want now, and your *kids* will eat it.

Back then, life was hard. We saved and saved and saved just to buy the dishwasher, but by the time we got to purchasing it, we were so to the wire that we couldn't afford a professional to install it.

So, you do it yourself.

And break the fifty-year-old plumbing while you're at it which means you now have to completely replumb the sink (congrat-ulations – you're now a Preacher/Dishwasher Installer/Plumber), which means marrying PVC to the ancient copper stuff that was already there, so a task of three hours turns into one of ten-and-a-half, to be exact. That's right, it took me ten-and-a-half *hours* to install our new dishwasher. "I hate my life" doesn't even *begin* to describe how I felt.

Next time? *I'm going to need a little help with that.*

I can cook a simple meal. Over time I've developed a few go-to recipes that I can carry off without much stress. I sometimes find myself feeling pretty good about my chef skills until my brother-in-law comes over to cook or we're invited to the house of someone from our church, which happens to be unusually filled with former professional chefs, and I sit down to a meal so amazing it makes my best efforts in the kitchen seem absolutely juvenile and pedestrian by comparison. See, I can handle cooking for a night of casual entertaining, but if I really want to blow minds? I'm going to need a little help from @jared.n.irvine or @aarondavidfraser for that. Those two guys are so far above my pay grade (when it comes to the kitchen) that when they show up at my house, I just have to sit down and be humble.

*Sometimes you're going to need a little help.*

Fortunately, the greatest "do-it-yourself-er" of *all time* has got you by the scruff of your neck.

> *"And after you have suffered a little while, the God of all grace, who has called you to his eternal glory in Christ, will himself restore, confirm, strengthen, and establish you. To him be the dominion forever and ever. Amen. By Silvanus, a faithful brother as I regard him, I have written briefly to you, exhorting and declaring that this is the true grace of God. Stand firm in it. She who is at Babylon, who is likewise chosen, sends you greetings, and so does Mark, my son. Greet one another with the kiss of love. Peace to all of you who are in Christ..."*
>
> —1 PETER 5:10-14 ESV

We're going to attack this one in reverse, if you don't mind. We'll hit the back half first, then come back to the start. This is the kind of chapter my wife will like. If "needing a little help" describes you, then you're going to find this chapter to be one nonstop symphony of encouragement.

(Kind of a nice way to finish a book, come to think of it)

First note of positivity: you are not *alone*.

> *"By Silvanus, a faithful brother as I regard him, I have written briefly to you, exhorting and declaring that this is the true grace of God. Stand firm in it. She who is at Babylon, who is likewise chosen, sends you greetings, and so does Mark, my son. Greet ONE ANOTHER with the kiss of love. Peace to ALL of you who are in Christ..."*
>
> —1 PETER 5:12-14 ESV

Notice the many different *people* who show up here at the end of Peter's letter? We've got *Peter* who is writing by *Silvanus* (probably Peter's secretary), the Roman *Church* ("She who is in Babylon"), then Peter refers to *Mark*, "his son" (not biological, but in the Gospel), and then *everyone* to whom his letter was written is encouraged to kiss everyone *else*. Clearly, you are not alone; there are a whole bunch of *friends* at the party with you. If you want to start living like a Joyful Misfit, you're going to need to learn to reject Evil's persistent lie that you are the *only* one dealing with difficulty, and *nobody* understands.

*Remember, evil isolates.*

If you find yourself sort of spiraling into a season of aloneness and isolation, you should be very concerned and, once you notice what's happening, do whatever it takes to stop that spiral. That feeling you get like you're the most hard-done-by person who ever lived? Not true. You're not alone, and somebody *does* understand your pain. His name is Jesus, and He has a bunch of people just like you who have gone through valleys just like you're going through, and He's seen them through too.

*You are not alone.*

The story of Jesus and His people soundly declares that, ultimately, you have never been alone. We see this imaged in the

Person, and Personality, of God Himself: Father, Son, and Holy Spirit. Even *God* is not alone. Theologians refer to this perfect and constant togetherness that God experiences as *"Perichoresis"*: perfect, unbroken fellowship at all times. That's how God rolls. I'll never forget my Theology professor driving this point home to remind us that God didn't create everything that is, from loneliness. He did not create the Universe, and all its creatures, to fill in some "gap" in His existence. He is God from all time, perfect in and of Himself and in all He does. He's even perfect in relationship *with* Himself: Father, Son, and Holy Spirit.

God's not lonely.

And neither have you ever been alone, though you may have felt that way from time to time. Remember, when God made the humans, He created them male *and* female, and put them in the Garden of Eden *together*, so that they would not be alone. God Himself made Eve for, and from, Adam after noting:

> *"It is not good for the Man to be ALONE. Let us make Him a Helper comparable to Him..."*
>
> —GEN 2:18

Adam and Eve were *together* in the Garden. *Together* they fell into sin, curse, and banishment after disobeying God in the matter of the Tree of the Knowledge of Good and Evil. Together they were cast out of the Garden to begin eking out a life East of Eden. But even in their fallenness, even in their cursedness, they were not alone. God was still with His people. He still spoke to them, and guided them, even *in* their banishment.

*You have never been alone.*

Even when God saw fit to destroy everything that lived on the Earth in Noah's day with the Great Flood, He did not send Noah into the ark alone, but with his *family*. Even the animals He sent in, in *community:* two by two, so that, once the Earth was cleansed, they could do what couples do, and refill the Earth to God's glory. God *likes* togetherness; He thought it up. Aloneness was never part of His plan for you.

We are the *people* of God. Through from Noah's day, forward into the long history of Judaism, we see again and again that – like us – God's people are very prone to mistakes and evilness and constantly ruining everything they touch. Even then, God does not leave them alone.

Even through four hundred years of silence between the death of the last prophet in Israel and the coming of the Messiah, God did not forget His people. He was waiting for the perfect moment, the "fullness of time," to send His One-and-Only Begotten Son to become the God-Man, Jesus Christ, fully God and fully Man, one with the Father, walking around in the dust of the 1st Century: Emmanuel, *with-us-God*. Jesus, our Example and Substitute who would perfectly fulfill God's Law, never transgressing it once, while walking completely in His Father's will all His days. Jesus was a kind and powerful man who reached out to the downtrodden and the oppressed, to those who were outcast and alone, welcoming them into His embrace.

Jesus told anyone who would *hear* Him that His Kingdom was *full* of misfits, people who *used* to be alone but who were now the people of God, welcomed into *community* with God and each other.

The only "aloneness" I see in the Gospel is that moment when Jesus, hanging on the cross alone, atones *Himself* for your sins, bearing the penalty alone. He *alone* is suffering and dying in that moment in your place for your sins, and the weight of them, He bore *alone*. He is most *profoundly* alone in that moment when He cries out, in fullest anguish now, *"Eli! Eli! Lama Sabachtani?!"* "My God, My God, why hast Thou *forsaken* Me?" Because, in that moment, God the Father and God the Holy Spirit turn their back on the sinful filthiness imputed to God the Son and, in Their unrelenting Holiness, they *abandon* Him to death.

Jesus was buried alone, and He laid there over the weekend, alone. The King of Glory in His grave, all by Himself. Until Easter Sunday morning when, if we believe the story, the Holy Spirit shows up to wake Him up! The Holy Ghost wakes up His Friend, the Logos, because it was not good for the Last Adam to be *alone*!

It's worth noting that, as soon as He is raised, Jesus begins being *social* again. He appears to His friends in the garden where His tomb was. He walks with two of them on the road to Emmaus. He shows up in their living room at suppertime, by the beach for breakfast, and even in dreams and visions after His ascension. Next time you feel alone, remember that the God of the Universe is *with* you, even now, interceding for you, from the throne to which He ascended and from which He will come again in glory to judge the living and the dead and to inaugurate His Kingdom which will have no end: a Kingdom in which He has prepared a place for *you*, and for *everyone* who ever loved Him! You're on His heart, on His mind, and even being spoken on His lips.

*You are never alone.*

> *"...this is the true grace of God. STAND FIRM in it...."*
>
> —1 PETER 5:12C ESV

Think you could do that, now that you know you're not alone?

*Stand firm, in grace.*

Imagine the difference that would make in your life, if you could know, and believe, that you are no longer alone because of what Jesus has done for you. Secure in that knowledge, you could stand firm.

> *"...this is the true GRACE of God..."*
>
> —1 PETER 5:12C ESV

And "grace" comes from the word *"Charis"* which means *gift* so, properly understood, this means: "Stand firm in the *gift* that God has given you..."

Think for a minute about the most incredible gift you've ever been given. Would you ever just give it away? Not normally. Maybe if you met someone in direst need and God spoke to you and told you to give it away, well, then you'd obey, of course. But only then; that's how precious that gift is to you. Other than God speaking directly to you, when somebody gives you an extravagant, awesome gift, you hold onto that gift with *everything* you've got. Let it be so in your life with you and the *grace* that God gives you.

> *"Stand firm in it..."*
>
> —1 PETER 5:12D ESV

Don't give away the confidence you've been given in Jesus.

> *"For I am sure that neither death nor life, nor angels nor rulers, nor things present nor things to come, nor powers, nor height nor depth, nor anything else in all creation, will be able to SEPARATE us from the love of God in Christ Jesus our Lord..."*
>
> —ROM 8:38-39 ESV

Nothing can separate you from God's love.

*Nothing*.

Why? Because you've been chosen.

> *"She who is at Babylon, who is likewise CHOSEN..."*
>
> —1 PETER 5:13A ESV

Peter *loves* this idea of chosen-ness.

> *"But you are a CHOSEN race, a royal priesthood, a holy nation, a people for his own possession, that you may proclaim the excellencies of him who called you out of darkness into his marvelous light..."*
>
> —1 PETER 2:9 ESV

*You* are a *chosen* race. *You* are God's own *special* people. *You* are the ones He *called* out of darkness into His marvelous light!

Did you ever get picked *last* for a game in grade school? If you did, you know exactly how awesome this *choosing* of you that God has done is! You remember how it works, right? They're gonna play football or kissing tag (yes, "contact sports" of all kinds were still allowed when I was boy), so they line you all up to pick teams.

It's horrible.

*Because kids, like life, are ruthless.*

Always the same fast, athletic, popular kids get picked first; the slow, fat, nerdy kids that nobody likes get picked last. You can *see* the horror on their sad little faces as they realize that it's going to happen *again*. They're going to get picked last. Again. And what makes me really sick about it (even years later, writing this) is how they never seemed to get *used* to it. They've been getting picked last for *years*, ever since kindergarten, and, still, every time it happens again, it hurts as much as it did the first time.

*Even in little hearts, hope springs eternal.*

*"Maybe today's the day I won't get picked last!"*

Can you see the hope springing in their eyes at the start of the lineup?

*And then it happens again.*

Again and again, disappointment and rejection crush their little souls, until that recurring pain turns into shame and an expectation of failure. Then one day, many dark years later, they wake up as adults who feel like the world *hates* them, so they hate it back.

What's really horrible about this is that it's not their fault that they were born short, or with more fat cells than you. It's not their fault that they're good at math, not basketball. But, after enough years of being treated like dirt, they begin to think it is *their* fault.

I remember, once I figured this out, every time I got picked to choose a team (yes, I was one of the fast, popular ones), I would intentionally pick "Coke-bottle-glasses" first. I can still remember the first time I said I'd pick "Eugene" first; you should have seen his face light up! Eugene nearly jumped out of his twice-mended trousers and hand-me-down runners that day, because joy, unlooked-for, had come into his life at recess.

You see where this is going, right?

*You are Eugene to Jesus.*

He'd pick you every time!

Next time you feel weak, broken, cast aside, or second-best, remember "Eugene" and know that Jesus loves misfits! He loves them! Tax collectors, sinners, whores, morons like me – Jesus looks at this mess and says: *"I'll take that guy..."* Every time, He singles you out of the crowd and says (with quite the smile on His face), *"Yeah, I'll take that girl..."*

*He'd pick you every time, Eugenie.*

This is why Christians have joy. This is why we're kissing on each other and smiling and singing all the time: because Jesus *chose* us!

> *"Greet one another with the KISS of love..."*
>
> —1 PETER 5:14A ESV

It was the best day of my life (at 16) when I discovered that verse and its implications. That's every young Christian man's life verse at Youth Camp.

*"Sister, haven't you read that the good Word says to greet one another with the kiss of love?"*

Awesome.

What's great is that "kiss" here means *"fond-effect,"* which is much better than a mere kiss, isn't it?

*Jesus' fondness for us is making us fond of each other.*

And notice how *difficult* the Scripture is; it pulls no punches. Notice how, *without* the grace of God shown towards us in Jesus, *none* of this would be possible. It doesn't say: *"You know, you really ought to learn to tolerate one another..."* You never hear Jesus say: *"What I'm really looking for is for My people to put up with each other admirably well..."*

*He wants kissing.*

Kissing is much harder than tolerance.

You kiss someone because you're *so* happy to see them that you can't help yourself. I've experienced this. I mean, I get so happy – in Jesus – that sometimes I find myself kissing other *men!* That's when you know the Holy Ghost is *moving*, when you're kissing Chris Jones' or Reuben Beitz's stubbly cheek. Once in a while a dude will look at me strange when I kiss 'em (it doesn't happen *that* much, keep your hair on) but I just smile at 'em and say: *"Don't worry baby, it's Biblical!"*

I'm so happy about the fact that Jesus chose me, in my unimpressive-ness, that it makes me so happy to see you, another one of Jesus' chosen people, that I forget myself, and greet you unselfconsciously with the kiss of love, because God's fondness for me is having an *effect* on me.

So, look, if there's someone in the context of your Christian community (or even just your circle of friends) whom, if you're honest, you'd have a hard time kissing right now, you need to look deeply into the Gospel until your heart (and attitude) changes. Learning, and then accepting, the fact that you've been extravagantly loved by God, in God, is the only way for you to love extravagantly yourself. So, if you have relational problems, or love problems, what you *really* have is a Gospel problem. Have you got angry people, grumpy people, people who are just tolerating one another (heck, maybe you *are* those people) and there's not anywhere near enough kissing in your social network?

*You've got a Gospel problem.*

Knowing you've been loved by God, in God, helps you to love. Same way as knowing that you have peace with God is the only way to *live* in peace.

> *"Peace to all of you who are IN Christ..."*
>
> —1 PETER 5:14B ESV

Peace comes from being *in* Christ.

*"So, how does that work, exactly?"*

We'll have to go back to the beginning for that.

> *"And after you have suffered a little while, the God of all grace, who has called you to his eternal glory in Christ, will HIMSELF restore, confirm, strengthen, and establish you. To him be the dominion forever and ever. Amen..."*
>
> —1 PETER 5:10-11 ESV

Peace works because *you* don't have to do the work.

But first, let's all acknowledge that there's some work to be done, right?

> *"And after you have SUFFERED a little while..."*
>
> —1 PETER 5:10A ESV

You're going to suffer. Life isn't perfect; it needs work. Life is like my jiggly-ness. Do you have any? I was washing the car in the driveway this past summer, having a good old time, until I realized (while scrubbing vigorously) that other bits of my body, besides my arms, were *moving*. Right then and there the Fall of Man was proved true.

*I am no Adonis. I jiggle. I need work.*

Nothing is perfect. Everything needs work.

> *"And after YOU have suffered a LITTLE while..."*
>
> —1 PETER 5:10A ESV

You and I live in a world that needs work, a world that brings and causes suffering. The funny thing about suffering is that we all want to avoid it altogether, despite the fact that the Bible is full of words about suffering, assurances that we *will* suffer, and examples of it happening to people like us, over and over again. But we prefer to pretend that suffering isn't really real, like nothing that bleak could ever happen to us. The problem with this kind of worldview is that we end up shocked (and dismayed) whenever something awful *does* happen to us. We've lived in denial for so long that we've forgotten the way things really are.

Let me set you straight. We are promised that we *will* suffer, but only for a *little* while. God's not going to push you over the edge. Even at the end of all things, He shows mercy.

> *"But when you see the abomination of desolation standing where he ought not to be (let the reader understand), then let those who are in Judea flee to the mountains. Let the one*

*who is on the housetop not go down, nor enter his house, to take anything out, and let the one who is in the field not turn back to take his cloak. And alas for women who are pregnant and for those who are nursing infants in those days! Pray that it may not happen in winter. For in those days there will be such tribulation as has not been from the beginning of the creation that God created until now, and never will be. And if the Lord had not cut short the days, no human being would be saved. But for the sake of the elect, whom he chose, he shortened the days..."*

—MARK 13:14-20 ESV

That's Jesus speaking about the End of All Things right there. Some scholars think that he's speaking exclusively about AD 70 when the Romans would sack Jerusalem, destroying the Temple and leading God's people into their great and final Diaspora in what would become Continental Europe, home of the Crusades, the Pogroms, and the Holocaust. Others think that Jesus is here looking forward to the "End Times," the "End of the Age," the "Great Tribulation" that will precede His return.

What I find interesting about this is that God's people survived AD 70 and God's people survived the combined terrors of Continental Europe with its race-inspired hatred and horrific Holocaust and, though I'm not (strictly speaking) a "nationalist" of any kind, I do find it amazing that *"Am Yisrael Chai"* (The People of Israel Live). Israel stands to this day as God's people and there is an actual modern state in existence today where Jews sit in government, where worship has been restored in Jerusalem, and where the desert is in bloom.

So, when I think about Jesus' words in Mark about the "End of the Age," I take comfort in a couple of things. 1) Rome tried to wipe out God's people. Rome is gone, but *"Am Yisrel Chai"*; The People of Israel Live. 2) Hitler tried to wipe out God's People. Hitler is gone, his

275

name and work living on in infamy, *but Israel lives*. I take great comfort in those nearly incomprehensible *facts* of history and I find great hope in the promise that God has, and will, *"Shorten the days..."*

In light of these great facts, from history and from God's Word, I'm pretty sure that *you* and I are going to be able to survive whatever it is that ails us, ultimately, because God's got us by the scruff of our necks.

> *"...the God of ALL grace, who has called you to his eternal glory in Christ..."*
>
> —1 PETER 5:10B ESV

The God of *all* grace, which is – in the original – the God of *every* grace.

Every good thing comes *from* Him; every gift comes *from* Him (James 1:17). The God of every good thing has called you!

> *"And we know that for those who love God all things work together for good, for those who are called according to HIS purpose. For those whom he foreknew he also predestined to be conformed to the image of his Son, in order that he might be the firstborn among many brothers. And those whom he predestined he also called, and those whom he called he also justified, and those whom he justified he also glorified..."*
>
> —ROM 8:28-30 ESV

I want you to notice there how God is doing *all* the work. He called. He foreknew. He justified. He glorified.

*God is the "Active Agent" here.*

> *"(He) will himself RESTORE, CONFIRM, STRENGTHEN, and ESTABLISH you..."*
>
> —1 PETER 5:10C ESV

God Himself will *restore*, which means *"to be adjusting."* Next time you get that sinking feeling like you need a little adjustment? Know that God is in that business too. He will adjust you when you need adjusting and He will *confirm* you. To "confirm" means to *"be making steadfast."* So that means that, even when you feel like you're losing traction in your life, losing your grip on things, God Himself is making you steadfast.

*He's doing it.*

He Himself will strengthen you. To "strengthen" means to *"make firm."* So if, when I was writing earlier about you learning to "stand firm" in your faith, even as you read it, in your heart you didn't think you have what it takes to do it? Know that God *Himself* is the One who is *doing* the work *in* you.

*He is at work.*

He Himself will establish you. To establish means *"found-ing,"* meaning you haven't only been found once, but He is *"found-ing"* you. You are *continuously* being found in Christ! So next time you feel lost, remember that God Himself "establishes" you; He never gets tired of playing Hide and Seek.

> *"To HIM be the dominion forever and ever. Amen..."*
>
> —1 PETER 5:11 ESV

He's got it. He's doing it. The dominion is His! The power is His! The might is His! The glory is His, forever and ever and ever and ever and *ever*! From eon into eon, *He's got it under control.*

God is in the restoration business and *you* are His favorite project.

So, the next time you feel like you need a little help, you know Who to call.

*1.800.thegreatestdoityourselferofalltime.*

# AFTERWORD

I hope this book helped you. I hope it gave you a new picture of who Jesus is and what that means for you. I hope you've found in these pages some courage and inspiration to keep living a *misfit* kind of life: the kind of life that would make the World a better place, make you a happier person, and make Jesus smile.

If there are things you're wondering about after reading this, I'd love to hear from you. Drop me a line sometime: *toddcantelon@gmail.com.*

If you're ever in the Guelph area on a Sunday morning, come see me at Grace.
(gracecommunity.ca/visit)

*I'll be the misfit up front shouting about Jesus.*

☺

Much love,

T

# ABOUT THE AUTHOR

**Todd Cantelon** serves as Lead Pastor at Grace Community Church in Guelph, Ontario. Previously, Todd was Co-Founding and Lead Pastor at FreeChurch Toronto, a progressive multi-site church in the heart of Canada's largest city. Todd has also planted a youth church (back in the mid-90's when they were still cool) and was a Writer and Producer in television and film for twenty years. Todd spoke extensively at conferences and festivals through the early 2000's before settling down to Preach and Pastor locally while enjoying the wife of his youth, his four teenaged kids, and his sailboat. Follow Todd on social *@toddcantelon*.

www.ingramcontent.com/pod-product-compliance
Lightning Source LLC
Chambersburg PA
CBHW030820090426
42737CB00009B/799